# LET IN THE LIGHT

# LET IN THE LIGHT

## LEARNING TO READ ST. AUGUSTINE'S *CONFESSIONS*

*With Attention to the Latin Text*

## JAMES BOYD WHITE

Columbia University Press   *New York*

Columbia University Press
*Publishers Since 1893*
New York   Chichester, West Sussex
cup.columbia.edu

Copyright © 2022 Columbia University Press
All rights reserved

Library of Congress Cataloging-in-Publication Data
Names: White, James Boyd, 1938- author.
Title: Let in the light: learning to read St. Augustine's Confessions,
with attention to the Latin text / James Boyd White.
Description: New York: Columbia University Press, [2022] |
Includes index.
Identifiers: LCCN 2021035502 (print) | LCCN 2021035503 (ebook) |
ISBN 9780231205009 (hardback) | ISBN 9780231205016 (trade
paperback) | ISBN 9780231555791 (ebook)
Subjects: LCSH: Augustine, of Hippo, Saint, 354–430. Confessiones.
Classification: LCC BR65.A62 W45 2022 (print) | LCC BR65.A62
(ebook) | DDC 270.2092—dc23
LC record available at https://lccn.loc.gov/2021035502
LC ebook record available at https://lccn.loc.gov/2021035503

Cover design: Milenda Nan Ok Lee
Cover photo: Charles Crust / Alamy

*To my Latin teachers with deep gratitude*

# CONTENTS

# PREFACE

I can best explain what kind of book you have in your hand if I tell you first how it was that I became engaged with the *Confessions* of Augustine. It is a simple story. I had heard over and over again that this was one of the most important and valuable books in the Western tradition: the first full expression of human inwardness, the deepest actualization of the human self as we have come to know it since, full of depth and mystery. It was fascinating, enlightening, and a true shaper of our culture.

I started to read the *Confessions*, many times in many translations, but I found it impossible. I felt that I was drowning in an ill-shapen mass of pious platitudes taken from second-rate nineteenth-century theologians, who seemed to speak as if their language was not problematic in any way, but simply said what needed to be said clearly and with the authority of the ages. I could not grasp either the outline or the details of the story. I could not imagine building on what I read.

In these English versions,[1] Augustine seemed to use theological terms in what lawyers call a conclusory way, that is, as though they did not need further elaboration or definition. His psychology likewise seemed elementary and unsophisticated, again as though his words explained themselves. As for the narrative, that seemed pointlessly complex and substantively trivial. What, for example, is this big deal about stealing pears? It was an adolescent prank, not a serious sin. And why was the story more generally so hard to follow? Why does he so often fail to tell us where he is and who he is with? And so on. If you have tried to read the *Confessions*, maybe you have had such a response yourself.

None of this helped me discover what his religious experience was, or how the language he used might be connected with the events of ordinary life, in his era or our own. The whole experience was deeply unsatisfactory. I know other people have had different responses to the translated Augustine, but this was mine, and I saw no way to change it.

Then—now many years ago—I read the first page of the *Confessions* in Latin. I was, in the modern idiom, blown away. All the impressions I had of this text were exploded. It was full of life and immediacy and urgency. In the Latin text Augustine seemed to use his terms of theology and psychology, indeed all of his languages, with a constant sense of what they could and could not do, of what they left out or distorted. His sense of God was not reducible to theological cliché, but was deep, vital, and original. I felt that I was directly hearing his actual voice, not listening to a voice muffled and distorted by being forced to speak English.[2]

In recent years my retirement has made it possible for me to read the whole work through in Latin, and for me it has become one of the most important books of all.

The present book is meant as a reading of the *Confessions* that recognizes it as a Latin text, as it was written by Augustine himself. I want to help you see how it is that this book can take on meaning of a different and deeper kind when it is read in its original language—and read closely. Thus in early chapters I shall try to explain in detail how Augustine is at work in the Latin in a small number of sentences, so even if you know no

Latin at all you may get a sense of the way it works here and to what end Augustine directs it. As we proceed, we will do less of that, but I will always try to give you, in English, a sense of the Latin text at hand.

If you do not have any Latin, I want to help you learn just a tiny bit, enough to enable you to get some feel for what this text is actually like as it was written. My hope is that the experience of being exposed to the mind of Augustine speaking the language in which he lived and thought will bring you to want to learn at least a little more.

Working with the Latin as well as the English will, I hope, be a rewarding process, but it will necessarily and properly be a very slow one. It is an extreme form of close reading, which is in my view all to the good. The result is that in Part I of this book I will treat in detail only the first book of the *Confessions*. In Part II and Part III I will give less comprehensive attention to the other books.

The question I ask throughout is: What is it like to read the *Confessions* of St. Augustine? In addressing this question, why is it important to read the *Confessions*, at least in part, in Latin? Why exactly can it not be fully and properly translated?

\* \* \*

I will speak to these questions repeatedly throughout the book. But I can say now that one important reason for reading at least some of it in Latin is that Augustine's mind is present in the original text in a way it cannot be in a translation, even a very good one. Of course there are good translations of books from one language to another, and we should be thankful for them. But there are always what the Spanish scholar Ortega y Gasset called "exuberances and deficiencies" of meaning, that is, ways in which the translation both fails to express what is said and done in the original and adds meanings that are not there.[3]

This is true not only of translations across languages but translations within a language. Think of a poem, for example, and how much its life and meaning are particular to its form. If you want to engage with the mind of Shakespeare, you will insist upon reading his own words, not a version found in student aids like CliffsNotes. Or, if like me you are a lawyer, think how hard it is to explain what is meant by terms like "jurisdiction" or "equity" or "common law" to those who do not have a legal training. To understand these words you need to learn the language. That is in fact what happens, or ought to happen, in law school.

If we hope to engage in a full way with the movements of Augustine's mind and imagination, then, it is important to read him at least in part in Latin. Another way to put it is to say that his voice can fully be heard only in that language, and as I will try to show, his voice is crucial to the meaning of the whole. Or, putting it another way, in the Latin he is present, in mind and soul, in a way he cannot be present in English.

Another reason to read the Latin is that the Latin language that Augustine learned as a child and worked with as an adult was a carrier of his culture, a culture in which he was caught up when he was young—as we are all caught up in the cultures in which we are raised—and of which, when he was older, he came to be in some ways critical, in others accepting, in still others transforming. To put it slightly differently, a central part of the drama of the *Confessions* lies in his struggles with his culture and the language that embodied it. In this sense the Latin language he knew is one of his most important subjects. We can have access to what he does with this language, and why, only as we come to share it.

In addition, as I hope to show, Augustine not only uses the Latin he has inherited; he remakes it in important ways as he uses it. In doing so he is teaching us how to remake our own languages, our own ways of imagining and talking. All this requires us to pay attention to what he has done in the Latin.

This point is all the stronger, for me at least, when I recognize how little of what Augustine says can be reduced to a set of propositions. Sometimes scholars seem to see him as promulgating a philosophic or theological system. But in my experience this is just what he is *not* doing, at least in the *Confessions*. The life and meaning of what he does lies rather in the way he confronts and uses his language and the expectations it generates; in the way he establishes and builds relations with his two audiences, his reader and his God; and in the way he stimulates perception, feeling, thought, and imagination in us. This book is not reducible to a narrative, nor it is it propositional in character. Rather, I think it can best be understood as offering us as we read it a set of experiences, in our minds and our inner beings. It is in these experiences that its meaning lies.

\* \* \*

A third benefit of reading some of it in Latin is that its very foreignness and difficulty forces us to slow down as readers—to admit uncertainty, to look for meanings that are not obvious on the surface, and to regard our initial understandings as incomplete, all in a good way.

Think of what it is like to skim through a newspaper column or detective story in English. It can go so easily that it is hardly happening at all. In a way it would not necessarily be a huge advantage to us as readers of the *Confessions* if we were as fluent in Latin as we are in English, for then we might just skim through it. This book should not be read in such a way, nor should it be swallowed whole. Rather, like Shakespeare's plays or the poetry of Donne or Eliot, it requires sustained attention and thought, an active and imaginative engagement, if we are to read it well. One of the advantages of the Latin is that it makes skimming impossible, at least for us. We are forced to slow down, and that is a good thing.

Also, in reading the *Confessions* we are reading a book that has an original form. It is a new genre, and to read it well we need to see how that genre is given shape and meaning as the book is written. This requires us to look with special care at what Augustine says, and how he says it. To do this we need to pay attention to its language and how he uses it.

Despite all I have said, I know that good translations obviously have their own importance and value. In what follows I myself translate almost every Latin passage into English. If I have done my job well, there and in the commentary, I think that even if you were to read only these translations, skipping the Latin entirely, you would acquire a real, though incomplete, sense of who Augustine is and a deeper connection with him and his life.

As for the Latin, I hope that even if you cannot read it, the presence of this language is a constant reminder that you are not reading the real thing. I hope you will be aware that the English you do read in the translations, including my own, has something unexpressed behind it, something you can see and in a sense touch, or let touch you. I hope that the Latin in this book can in this way have real value even for someone who reads little or none of it.

\* \* \*

The first chapter of this book is a kind of summary of the whole of the *Confessions*, offered not as a scientific statement of some kind but simply as one reader's effort to sum the work up. My hope is that this will help you start to tune yourself to the actual text when we turn to it. The next chapter will focus on the opening sentences, which are reproduced in Latin with notes and comments. Subsequent chapters will build on these two. From time to time throughout the book I will ask you to think about the way a particular Latin sentence actually works, giving you what help I can.

It is important to understand that while we shall work with passages taken from each of its books, we shall in total read only a rather small portion of the *Confessions*. My choice of passages is of course not beyond criticism, but it is perhaps comforting to think that our selection of passages will leave lots of the *Confessions* for you to turn to when our work together is over.

* * *

I should add, loudly and clearly, that I am not a professional Latinist, nor an Augustinian scholar, but just one mind engaging as well as I can with what Augustine has written. This is not a work of scholarship in the usual sense, but an exploration of the experience this wonderful book offers its readers. You might perhaps think of me as a friend with whom you happen to be reading this text closely, asking questions, making suggestions, and in general carrying on a conversation, without making any claims to perfection.

In this connection I imagine you, the reader, as someone who wants to come to terms with the experience of reading this text, even to the extent of learning to use at least a little Latin, and who is willing to give the conversation that it wants to establish with you a try. I think that if you ever studied Latin, in high school say, you should be able to follow a good bit of the Latin you will be presented with. If you have no exposure to Latin, you may want to look also at the resources in the note appended to this paragraph, or even better, to ask a Latinate friend to help you. Everything I do here is meant as an invitation or introduction, a first step in coming to terms with this remarkable work.[4]

Finally, I might add that in having these hopes for the use of Latin I am moved by my own experience, not of Latin this time, but of Dante's Italian. With a couple of friends, one of whom knew Italian well, I read through the *Commedia*, one canto every week for three years. I used a text with Italian on one side, English on the other. I was never able simply to read the Italian, but I could often reconstruct much of its meaning with the help of the translation, then read it in Italian. This gave me an experience of reading Dante in Italian, which changed my whole sense of what he was doing and how.[5]

What happens in such a case is that the language is brought to life as a language, even though not fully understood, and this connects the reader with the mind of the writer in a new way. In the case of Augustine you will find that what is written in Latin, when it is understood even a little, will have a kind of firmness or solidity, as well as a life, that a translation cannot have. These are the words he wrote; there is nothing behind them but his mind. With a translation, by contrast, there is always something behind the language you read, something hidden, uncertain, obscure.[6]

As you will see, I am present throughout the book as an interlocutor with you, the reader, continually making comments and asking questions. I hope you will look at these critically. I do mean what I say, but I do not propound it with any external authority. As you read, ask what you think of my comments and questions, and the way, or ways, of thinking they express. How would you do it differently?

On another note. It has been suggested to me that you may already, and understandably, have an unappealing image of Augustine as an authoritarian, rigid, misogynistic, self-certain figure constantly engaged in doctrinal battles that have no real meaning today. While I cannot speak of all of his writings, I hope that you will discover that the Augustine at work in the *Confessions* is not like this at all. As you will see, his central term is *caritas*, another word for "love."

If you do need a quick antidote to the image I have presented above, I suggest you read his Sermon 9.[7] Here he treats the sin of adultery, which men in his culture felt privileged to commit, while women were meant to be completely faithful. The women, who are present with their husbands in the congregation, are understandably afraid to speak to them about this difficult subject. Augustine speaks for them, in the presence of their husbands, giving them a voice they otherwise would not have had and claiming for them in no uncertain terms a fundamental equality in the face of a culture that denies it. While doing this he explicitly creates a sense of the Scriptures not as demanding grim obedience to a set of severe commands but as offering a life of song and joy.

\* \* \*

There is one more aspect of this work I want to mention now, namely, its connection to the world in which I write—a world in which we face a serious pandemic, the possible loss of our democracy, and the consequences of global warming. In this world it is not possible to rely unthinkingly on existing institutions or traditions or established practices and attitudes. We do not know where we are going but we know it is not into a version of our own past. In 2019 I published a book, *Keep Law Alive*,[8] which was about contemporary threats to our way of doing law, indeed to law itself, in which I tried to show how we might keep alive this crucial element of our culture. I had to consider as well how we might respond if we lost the law as we know and admire it; my response was to turn to Augustine who lived in a worse world than our own—one in which the Roman Empire was collapsing and invaders were taking its place—yet in my view found a way to maintain his psychic and intellectual integrity, his integrity as a person. The chapter in which I tried to explain this reappears with little change in this book as its first chapter. The rest of this book could be read as an elaboration of what I saw to be so remarkable in Augustine's *Confessions* and what it might mean for us, living as we do in a culture that is collapsing, perhaps to be reborn, perhaps not.

# ACKNOWLEDGMENTS

I want to thank as warmly as I can my friends who have read and commented on my manuscript: Walter Brueggemann, Sherman Clark, Wendy Doniger, Sarah Higinbotham, David Jasper, Cathleen Kaveny, John and Anne McCausland, A. E. T. McGloughlin, Julian Davis Mortensen, Leonard Niehoff, Jefferson Powell, Jack Sammons, Dean Strang, Winnifred Sullivan, Sanjaya Thakur, and Mary White. The book is much better for their ideas and corrections. Special thanks go to Winnifred Sullivan, without whom this book would never have been published and to Sanjaya Thakur, without whom it would never have been written.

I also want to thank the teachers who brought me into Latin and Greek to begin with. In chronological order: James McCarthy, Melvin Mansur, Norris Getty, Wendell Clausen, John Moore, Arthur Adkins, James Redfield, and especially my beloved friend, Gerda Seligson.

I have consulted with great profit the extraordinary work of James J. O'Donnell in editing and commenting on the text of the *Confessions*. It is his text that I use throughout, with his kind permission.[1] This is one of the major works of recent classical scholarship, and I thank him for it. I also want to thank Carolyn

J.-B. Hammond, whose excellent bilingual edition in the Loeb series I used on a daily basis. I have tried to make my translations fresh as well as accurate, but I am sure that some of her words crept into my mind and into this book. I hope she will forgive me.[2]

# AN OUTLINE OF AUGUSTINE'S
# LIFE UP TO THE COMPOSITION
# OF THE *CONFESSIONS*

354 CE: Augustine was born into a family with a small landhold-
ing in Thagaste, about 60 miles south of the Mediterranean
coast, in what is now Algeria. His mother, Monnica, was a
devout Christian and an immense influence in his life. His
father, Patrick, was a pagan.

366–369: He was schooled first in Thagaste and then in a nearby
town, Madauros, largely in "grammar," that is, the reading of
Latin and its literature.

369: He returned to Thagaste for a year while his father saved up
money for the next stage of his education. This is the year in
which he committed the famous sin of stealing pears.

370: With the help of Romanianus, a wealthy family friend in
Thagaste, he was sent to Carthage to study "rhetoric," that is,
the art of persuasion as established by Cicero and other ora-
tors and students of rhetoric.

372: The woman with whom he was to live faithfully for many
years bore him a son, Adeodatus—"given by God." In this
year his father, Patrick died.

373: He read the (now lost) *Hortensius* of Cicero, which converted him to the value of philosophy. He formally became

a Manichee, that is, a follower of the Persian quasi-Christian mystic, Mani. His status was that of Hearer, not Elect.

375: He returned to Thagaste to teach "grammar," which he found unrewarding.

376: Grieving the death of a close but unnamed friend, he returned to Carthage, with his two life-long friends, Alypius and Nebridius. He set himself up as a teacher of rhetoric.

383: Dissatisfied with the unruly behavior of his students, he accepted an appointment as a teacher in Rome, obtained for him by Romanianus.

384: Finding that the Roman students refused to pay their fees, Augustine leapt at a chance offered him by Symmachus, another powerful connection, to become a rhetorician at the Imperial court in Milan. In Milan he was exposed to Ambrose, the powerful bishop in that city, and under his influence began to be able to imagine God not as a material presence or force, as the Manichees did, but as a spiritual being. He was also exposed to and influenced by the Neoplatonists, for whom there was only one God, immaterial but present everywhere in the world. Monnica followed him to Milan and arranged a marriage for him to a girl of wealth and standing. He sent away his lover of many years.

386: In a dramatic scene in a garden in Milan he was converted to Christianity. He resigned his position as rhetorician, which he characterized as the teaching and practice of lies, and withdrew with some friends to a villa in Cassiciacum, where he and they hoped to establish a life of philosophic and religious retirement.

387: He was baptized by Ambrose.[1] He and his friends, all Africans, returned to Thagaste where they established their religious community. Monnica and he had a mystical vision in Ostia on the way home, after which she died.

390: His son Adeodatus died.

391: While on a visit to the coastal city of Hippo, Augustine was physically forced by a congregation to become a priest.

396: He was made an assistant bishop, then the Bishop of Hippo.

397: He looked back over his life and began to write the *Confessions*.

# PART I

# 1

## THE SHAPE OF THE
### *CONFESSIONS*

THIS CHAPTER OFFERS an account of the *Confessions* as a whole, meant as an introduction to the more specific discussions that follow.

## THE NARRATIVE

To start with the narrative: the story is that of a very bright provincial boy making his way upward in the world through the power of his mind and tongue. He started in the obscure town of Thagaste in North Africa, near the Atlas Mountains on the south side. This is where his education began, but it quickly took him to Carthage, the second city of the Western empire, where he studied rhetoric, the queen of disciplines of the time, uniting intellectual skill and practical power.

He was an academic superstar, and became a teacher of rhetoric, first in Carthage, then Rome; then in Milan, the seat of the Empire, he became a practitioner of the art on the staff of the emperor, for whom he personally performed a public panegyric. He had made it to a position of power and almost certain wealth. The next step would have been marriage into a wealthy and powerful family, and perhaps the governorship of a province, with all that implies.

But in Milan, just when an appropriate marriage had been arranged, he experienced a conversion to Christianity, the religion of his mother. He decided to resign his position, and to withdraw with some friends to lead a life of philosophical and theological reflection, first in a borrowed villa near Milan, then back in Africa, where they had all originally come from. On their way home his mother died in Ostia.

At this point the narrative portion of the *Confessions* comes to an end. As I tell it, it may sound like the story of a man who "discovered God" and simply turned his back on the world.

But hold on.

## AUGUSTINE THE WRITER

By the time he wrote the *Confessions*, ten years after the date of his return to Africa, it was apparent that Augustine's life had not proceeded according to his original plan of religious and philosophical retreat. After three years in Thagaste, his hometown, he visited Hippo, a city on the coast, where he was physically forced by a congregation to become a priest—they simply would not let him leave the building until he agreed. About five years later he was made a bishop.

From this point on he was to continue the rest of his life in the active role of priest and bishop: running religious services, giving hundreds of sermons, adjudicating disputes among his flock, carrying on theological wars with those he regarded as heretical—and doing so in a context in which religious difference often led to serious violence.[1] After the fall of Rome, in

410, he was to spend many years writing his magnum opus, *The City of God*, simultaneously a comprehensive critique of Roman culture and an equally comprehensive defense of Christianity, made in response to the astonishing and frightening destruction of Roman power. When he died in 430 the Vandals were besieging Hippo, the town where he had lived and worked for decades.

By the time he began to write the *Confessions*, in about 397, he could already see that he was not leading a life of philosophic and religious retreat after all, but was deeply and actively engaged in the world, with all its difficulties, disappointments, and dangers. It is true that he was in the church, not the state, but his life was deeply of the world, and in its own way immensely successful.

Although as I say this life was of the world, it was deeply different in quality from that other life on which he had first embarked, his life as a teacher of rhetoric. What had changed? This is perhaps the true subject of the *Confessions*, written about ten years after the end of the story it tells.

## THE MOVEMENT OF THE *CONFESSIONS*

Here I will sketch out my sense of what had changed, and how and why. In later chapters we shall come back to different elements in the story in greater detail.

Usually autobiographies are stories of success, but the *Confessions* seems to involve failure after failure, collapse after collapse, not only in Augustine's life but in the very structure of the text.

While the narrative is in one sense positive, that is, leading to Augustine's conversion, in another it is the story of loss of confidence and competence, a kind of dismantling of the self. He starts out with immense confidence in his intelligence, in his ability to understand the world and himself, and in his powers of persuasion, but near the end of the work says, in effect, that the only thing he really knows in the world is that God exists, and exists within him.[2] The life that brings him to that point, the life of which he has been telling the story, is in a sense now an unreality, without meaning except for the fact that it led to a new life.

Let me elaborate. Before he was converted to Christianity, Augustine was a rhetorician with the interests and hopes of a philosopher. First, under the influence of Cicero's *Hortensius*, he discovered philosophy. Then he joined the Manichean religious sect, really on philosophic grounds: he thought they succeeded in explaining the presence of evil in the world by positing not one good and omnipotent God, but two opposed forces, one good, one bad, one light, one dark. But what he was assenting to was for him more a theory than a way of life. His next conversion was to Neoplatonism, again primarily a philosophic system, though one with strong religious overtones.

In Milan, as he tells it, he had experiences of a different kind, deep in his soul, that led him to convert to Christianity, and in so doing moved him to abandon the philosophic way of understanding the world. In his experience the whole structure of life based on philosophy just breaks down.

Theology breaks down too, at least if theology is thought to be a way of "talking about God." In fact, in the *Confessions* theology never gets going at all, for in it Augustine never talks *about* God; instead, from the first lines to the last, he is talking *to* God, the audience addressed in every sentence. The *Confessions* is not a work of theology in the usual sense, then, but a sort of invented genre, a book-length prayer or psalm, which undercuts every other form of thought and imagination in which Augustine or his reader are tempted to engage. At the end, for him there is only Augustine, God, the Scriptures, and the reader.[3]

The *Confessions* thus look both backward, seeking to explain how Augustine could become the person who could speak to God as he does here, and forward, tracing at least in outline the kind of life that this transformation has made possible.


## MEMORY

The first nine books of the *Confessions*, briefly summarized above, are offered by Augustine as the core narrative of his life; the tenth book, where he gives up the narrative mode entirely, is a reflection on memory; the eleventh is a study of time; and the last two are extensive and imaginative readings of the first few verses of Genesis.

Why does Augustine not simply stop at the end of Book 9, when the narrative comes to an end? Does the other material have an important function, and if so, what is it?

I think that this material is crucial. One way to put it is to say that in Books 1–9 Augustine tells the story of his early life; in Books 10–13 he shows how life can be lived, now—by him as he now is and by the reader as they now are. To put it slightly differently, he is not only telling us, he is showing us how life can be lived on these terms, especially as it is built upon Scripture and the church; and he is not only showing us something, he is inviting us to participate in that way of living.

Some understanding of what he achieves in the last few books will I think help us in our work on the early ones, so let me sketch out what I mean in a little more detail.

In Book 10 Augustine focuses on memory, the central human capacity he has himself been exercising in the first nine books. Thus far he has been telling us what he remembers about his life; in Book 10 he makes a memory itself a problem.

As he presents it, we start out with the inexplicable and incomprehensible gift of life. Thereafter we use memory constantly, not only when we write the story of our lives as he has been doing, but in leading our lives from day to day. Memory is the embedded experience upon which we rely for everything, from the use of language to the formation of desires to the management of social relations. But, as he makes us see in our own forgetfulness of what he himself has told us, memory is profoundly unreliable. In a sense this book is the beginning of his real confession: the confession not of bad things he did as a boy, but of what he has come to know that he does *not* know, even about himself.

What we remember, after all, is not sense data, but sense data processed by thought and imagination. It is a way of locating ourselves in a process of which we know neither the beginning nor the end; a process that is in its essential nature internal, and in a deep way unverifiable. The "narrative" he has just told is really just the memory of memories, not a story of facts.

As Augustine comes to realize that all he knows of the world depends upon his memory, which is mysterious and misleading and incomplete, he also comes to see what is for him the ultimate fact about his knowledge: that virtually all he can be certain of is that God exists and is within him. This is a long way from the bright young man proud of what he knew and could do with his knowledge. Everything except this new knowledge, everything from narrative to autobiography to philosophy to theology, is buried in the mystery of memory.

## TIME

In Book 11 Augustine continues this line of thought by reflecting on the mystery of time. His main idea is that all that is past is no longer real, all that is future is not yet real; so all we have is the present, which is itself not stable but a tiny, infinitesimal razor edge of awareness, disappearing as fast as it emerges. By the time you get the end even of a single word, its beginning is in the past.

The razor edge can be extended slightly by memory and imagination, but it is where we live, in a constantly disappearing present.

To the God to whom he is speaking he says something like this. By an act of inexplicable grace you call upon me, in this edge of time in which I live. That is my only true reality: my presence, your presence, my voice, your voice. On these conditions, nothing else can truly be known. This is I think the position out of which the *Confessions* is written, and where it ends.

In all of this Augustine is bringing his consciousness to face both the essential mystery of his own existence and the essential quality of that existence, which is that except for the presence of God within him everything passes away. Nothing can be held on to and apprehended.

Thus it is that in these closing books we find Augustine, who once knew so much, saying again and again, I do not know, I cannot know, this is beyond me.

## BENIGN HUMILIATION

As one who has been by career a teacher of law, in all of this I cannot help thinking of the bright young lawyer who structures their life by certain objects of ambition: high grades, a law review position, a Supreme Court clerkship, a job with a famous and rich firm, early partnership, argument before the Supreme Court, etc. This was Augustine, who was fulfilling his, and his mother's, dream of success. But it all collapsed: philosophy, theology, prestige, power, wealth, even his memory—even his capacity to tell a story.

But Augustine's sense of loss has a paradoxical effect, namely, that it gives what he says and thinks an extraordinary immediacy and life, an authenticity and truth, both for himself and for us, more than 1,500 years later. He is wholly in the present, in the present created by this text, and we are too, together with him in that present.

Augustine's story is one of benign humiliation, the destruction of his own pretenses and claims, often against his will and without his knowledge, until he is at the end stripped naked and vulnerable and ignorant; but in that condition able to live in a new and deeper way.

Such are the conditions of life, for him then and for us now. The moment passes: are we alive in it, alive to it? Can we speak out of the center of ourselves, aware of what we do not know, cannot be? The *Confessions* is written to bring us to the point where such questions are real for us.

Augustine found a way to work out of his awareness that all learning, all expectations, were provisional only. He knew the world could change and that he could change. He not only worked on these terms, but worked brilliantly, far better than he would have done had he remained the expert rhetorician he started out to be. The very ephemeral quality of things made it possible for him to be present as mind and imagination in a new and much more complete way to what he was doing. The freshness and newness of life this entailed gave him immense power, in part because it seems to have erased his earlier susceptibility to embarrassment and his need to impress others.

## READING GENESIS

Finally, a very brief word about the last two books, which offer a deep and highly imaginative reading of the opening of

Genesis. In Books 12 and 13 the world Augustine has been creating expands. It now includes not only himself and his God,
in the razor edge of the present, but also God's Scriptures, his
holy word, the reading of which is not simply a matter of seeing
what it says, but requires an art of interpretation—an art all the
more complex when Augustine recognizes that other readings
than his own can be equally true, a fact at which he perhaps surprisingly says we should rejoice. He formalizes this principle by
saying that interpretation should always proceed on the basis of
charity, that is, on the basis of love of God and love of neighbor.

His reading is thus driven in part by truth, in part by an ethic
of generosity and charity. This also means that his world has
expanded to include other people, especially his readers. But not
just readers as we might imagine them: for the community of
people that is engaged on these terms, in this life of the present,
is for him the church, the presence of Christ in the world.

For me all this meant that the *Confessions* was no longer
abstract, confused, unconnected to life, but deeply illuminating
of our experience. Starting with Book 10 he locates us in a world
without time, without memory even, a world of sheer presence:
Augustine present to God, to Scripture, to his reader, as we too
are present to him. The reading of these chapters is itself not firm
or certain but must always be done again. Augustine ends up
wholly alive, and present to us, not just in mind or body, but in
his soul.

# 2

## THE FIRST THREE SENTENCES (BOOK 1)

WHAT IS IT LIKE TO READ the *Confessions* in real time, slowly, word by word, in the language in which it was composed? In this chapter I shall ask that question about the first few sentences of Book 1, with a lot of attention to the Latin language. In the next chapter I shall focus on the next brief section of Book 1, which constitutes an invocation of the God to whom he will be speaking through the whole work. The third chapter will consider the rest of Book 1. I hope by then you will have a feeling for the kinds of experience Augustine's text offers its reader, including the questions it stimulates. In what then follows I will of necessity discuss the later books of Augustine's text much more briefly, but I hope always with attention to the language in which it was written.

In this chapter I am turning from the general design of the *Confessions*, described above, to the way it works in its particulars, for it is here, in the life of its sentences, in its tones of voice, its conception of its audience, that the power and originality of the book most fully reveal themselves. This is what I discovered when I turned from what seemed to me impossible English translations to the vividness and life of the opening sentences in Latin.

I want to look at these sentences not with the idea of restating them, as if in that way we could "get" what Augustine is "saying," but in an effort to see them as performances both with his language and with us as readers. What are the resources and limits of his language, and of the culture it carries? How does Augustine use them, and to what effect? In doing so, what kind of relation does he establish with us, his human readers, and with the God to whom he is speaking throughout? How do these relations change in the course of the book? Through what motions does his mind run? Can we compare them with the motions of our own minds? Questions of this sort are not resolvable at this stage in the reading—in fact none of them may be resolvable ever—but should rather be seen as invitations and guides to the experience that lies ahead.[1]

In our reading of the *Confessions* I want you to feel that our goal is not to grasp its message or messages, but to learn to engage in a living way with the experience it offers. It is in that engagement that its meaning lies.

## A NOTE ON READING THE LATIN

As I have said, every passage is given both in Latin and in an English translation. My hope is that each reader will come to see the Latin text as the one Augustine actually wrote and seek to understand it as well as they can.

If you already know Latin well, this should present no difficulties. If you have had some training in Latin, maybe in high school, I think this should be manageable. The words may be difficult to interpret, the sentences hard to parse, but you will already have the awareness, deep within, that this is a language, not a set of unintelligible marks or signs.

I would encourage you to begin by reading the Latin aloud, which might revive some of what you think you have forgotten. You might find it helpful also to engage in "reverse engineering," that is by going from the translation in the English that you know well to the Latin, and read it in light of the English version, as well as you can. If you do read aloud from the beginning, and pay what attention you can to the Latin, I think you will find yourself gradually learning it as you read it—not perfectly of course but enough to have the sense that you are exposed directly to the mind, and I hope to the soul, of Augustine.

As I said in the preface, in my translations I try to follow as well as I can the structure of the Latin sentence, generally placing a line of English just below the Latin equivalent, and thus putting the words close to their mates in the other language. This is of course not always possible, but when it is you may find it easier to get some sense of the shape of the Latin sentences and in this way to begin to come to terms with that language.

My translations have all the limits of other translations: the most they can do is give a rough and provisional idea of what is being said and done in the Latin, so do not make the mistake of thinking they are somehow what Augustine really said. English can never fully capture the Latin. But to put the Latin and the translation beside each other, as I do, may bring to your attention the parallels between it and the original. This in turn may help you move from the English to the Latin. I hope so.

If you have no experience of Latin at all, one obvious option is just to read the English translations. If you do this thoughtfully, I think you will still get some sense of what Augustine is doing. The presence of Latin will constantly remind you that what you are reading is not the original text, which appears in all its mystery on nearly every page. This itself would be a good thing. But I think you can do more, particularly if you use any of the materials recommended in the note in the Preface above.[2] You may find yourself beginning to learn a new language, one in which important things are said and done. As I said, I would recommend that you begin by reading the Latin aloud, as a way of reminding yourself that it is a language after all.[3]

I would enourage all readers to try to connect in some way with the Latin. You might for example write down your own translation of a sentence you have been studying and then ask yourself what the differences are between your translation and the Latin original. If you do, you should have the experience, more and more frequently, of seeing something that seemed at first obscure or impenetrable become clear on the page and in your mind. That is a great pleasure in itself, and when it happens you will have brought the Latin to life as a language, the language used by Augustine.

## A NEW GENRE

The opening of the *Confessions* has I think no parallel in earlier Latin or Greek literature. It defines a new genre, a new kind of book, and a new way of writing it.[4] For relevant comparisons one might think of the Gospel of Mark, which also seems to have invented its genre, or the dialogues of Plato, of which much the same could be said.

This newness is apparent in its first sentence: *Magnus es, Domine, et laudabilis valde*, or roughly: "Great are you, Lord, and highly worthy of praise."[5]

This may seem the opposite of something new, a tired old sentence, something we have heard a thousand times. Praise God? This sounds like theological cliché.

But think of the questions the sentence presents.

To whom is Augustine speaking? *Domine*, "Lord," is a version of the "God" of anglophone Christians. But why does Augustine speak to God at all? If this God has the usual divine attributes, he knows everything already, and does not need to be told anything. So we can ask of Augustine: Why do you speak to God? What are you doing when you try? Is there any point at all in doing it? Do you think God will speak back to you, and if so, what kind of conversation will this be, and if not, what are you doing?

These questions, though often unnoticed, are central to the life of the Christian believer: Why do you speak to God? What can you hope to say or be in the words you use? What do you hope to result from your speaking?

We can also ask of Augustine: Why do you *write* to God? He knows what you think and feel before you say it, certainly before you write it, so why write it at all?

Augustine is going to publish this work in the manner of his day, namely, in the form of painstakingly prepared handwritten books or scrolls that are sent around to other people to read. So are those people the real audience? If so, why does he not address them? Or if he does address them, and us, how does he do so?

It looks as though we are being invited to listen in on a one-way conversation he is having with God; but Augustine is certainly aware that we are listening, indeed he invites us to listen—so is he really talking to us? If so, why does he talk this way, instead of directly? Does the fact that we are present as an audience reduce or impair or otherwise affect the authenticity of what he is saying to God? Indeed, is his authenticity only apparent, a kind of artifice, and if so, why does he use it?

More particularly, why does he call God *Dominus*? He could have called him *Deus*, which means "God." *Dominus* is an originally nontheological term that in Latin means "master," as in "master" of slaves or a household. In the Latin Bible it is a translation of the Greek word, *kurios*, which has much the same meaning. Why does the Christian tradition call "God," the ineffable and unknowable one, by the names *Kurios, Dominus,* Lord?[6]

Why does Augustine say that God is *worthy of praise*? Who is Augustine, a mere human, to say that the Creator of all things, of all life, is *worthy of praise*? Is he the judge of these matters? And why does he praise God in the first place? James J. O'Donnell, the great editor of the *Confessions*, suggests that the whole work is driven by this question.[7] One of the aims of the *Confessions*, on this view, is to show what kind of education, what kind of experience, leads a person to see that "praise" is the most complete and natural response to the God who created us.

This sentence is in this way an invitation for us to read the *Confessions* and to make it our own, and thus to join Augustine in this perpetually repeated gesture of praise—and that means to join the life of the church as he defines it, where praising and thanking are fundamental practices. This is a way of saying that the community he seeks to reconstitute in this text is the church—not in the sense of an institution, like the Roman Catholic Church or the Eastern Orthodox Church, but as the whole community of believers; or at a different level of magnitude, at the relations between one believer and another, for that relation too is the "church." I think it is Augustine's idea that when you come to the end of the *Confessions*, you will already be a member of his version of the church, whether you know it or not.

Here is another crucial element in the composition. An alert contemporary reader might have noticed what most of us would not, namely, that his sentence is not a fresh composition by Augustine, but taken almost verbatim from several of the Psalms.[8] In undertaking the bold feat of actually addressing the creator of the universe, as O'Donnell says, Augustine begins by using what he regards as the language of God himself.

In doing so is he impliedly saying that Scripture affords the only language in which we can adequately talk to or about God? The idea might be that our own language is inherently inadequate, or fallen, the language of Scripture uncorrupted and true. But what of the fact that the rest of this book is not just a series of quotations from the Scriptures, but mainly written in Augustine's own language and composed by him?

What does it mean, then, that this particular sentence is not in Augustine's own language, but in what he seems to believe is God's language, a quotation from the Scriptures? What does it mean that the quotation is from the Psalms? Is Augustine implicitly saying to his reader, the book you have in your hands is in structure and meaning like a psalm? Or is it in fact a new and modern psalm, with the same audience, the same themes?[9]

These questions will get new life in the last two books, which consist of the reading of the first two verses of Genesis. By this time Augustine has largely stripped himself of confidence in his high intelligence, in his ambitions, in his belief in the reliability of memory, and is impliedly saying that the only thing one can really do, on the conditions of life as he has made them real for us, is to read the Scriptures and try to live them out.

But, as we notice when we check the originals, Augustine changes the language of Scripture as he uses it, even in this first sentence. For the Psalms from which this sentence is taken all speak of "the Lord" in the third person: in the Psalms it is "he" who is *magnus et laudabilis valde*; but Augustine uses these terms not to *describe* God, but to *speak to* him (using the second person singular of the verb "to be," namely, *es*). So it is "you," not "he," who is worthy of praise. What is the significance of this change? Who is Augustine to change the Scriptures as he uses them?[10]

Is the whole of the *Confessions* then to be read as an astonishingly long psalm, or perhaps a prayer? Why would Augustine write out such long prayer? Is it to get God to do something for him? Or, more promisingly, is it because the act of writing it may change him, Augustine, in ways he cannot predict at the outset but hope will be good? Or does he write in the hope that he will produce a text that has a meaning, when he reads it as a whole, of which he himself was not aware as he wrote it? If so, is he really his own audience?

Are we to see this, as I suggest above, as a kind of constitution, or reconstitution, of the church, whether by that term is meant the institutional church or the church every Christian should be creating every day in the relations he or she establishes with others? If so, how does that fact affect our experience of reading?

All of this is complicated by what we already know about the book before we pick it up, namely, that it is some sort of autobiography. This means that as the story is told there are at least three Augustines present, not just one: Augustine, the person whose past life is being told, more or less chronologically; Augustine, the narrator who is telling it, stage by stage, as things happen, capturing as well as he can his own earlier stage of life, but nonetheless knowing now what he did not know then; and Augustine, the composer of the text—including both the narrative and the voice or voices in which it is told. This Augustine, who in this text is the creator of the other two, can look back on the whole, both on his actual life as he lived it and on its representation in the writing before us, to see what it all means at the end of the story.

Let me explain a little. Of course I don't mean that there are three different human beings at work in the composition of the *Confessions.* Every word is written by Augustine the flesh and blood human being. But I find the idea of three Augustines useful as a way of thinking about and reflecting on the different ways he is present to us in this text: as the one whose life is its subject; as the narrator who tells the story (almost always in the first person); and as the one who gives structure and meaning to the whole. Thus we can ask of any particular event—say the theft of the pears, or the conversion in the garden—three questions: What is this event like, and what does it mean, for Augustine the pilgrim as he experiences it? What is it like and what does it mean for Augustine the narrator when he writes the story? What is it like, and what does it mean, as it is placed in the larger composition of the text as a whole by Augustine the composer? Each of these questions can be pursued by a close reading of the text as we have it.

\* \* \*

Another way to put this is to say that when the actual events of Augustine's early life, described in chapter 1, came to an end with his return to Africa, another process began for him, that of thinking about his experience and writing it out. That process naturally produced changes in his understanding, in his deeper self, and in his voice. These changes are partly captured in shifts and changes we see in the narrator, partly to be found in the fact that Augustine the composer constructs the whole in such a way as to invite us at the end to look back with new eyes upon the whole text, the whole life, in contemplation and understanding. In the end it is not simply "his life" that he reflects upon, and asks us to do likewise, but his life as composed and written here. It is significant in this context that the very last words of the *Confessions* are not a kind of backward-looking summary of what has been said, but a forward-looking invitation to life on new terms, with a reference to the passage in which Jesus says, "Knock, and it shall be opened unto you" (Matt. 7:7–8).[11]

For us this suggests a series of questions. What will be the relations among these processes, among these three Augustines—each of whom may change in the course of the book? Between each of them and God? Between each of them and the reader? How do these relations themselves change over time and with what significance?

A similar problem arises in the reading of Dante's *Commedia*, which tells the story of the journey of "Dante" through the *Inferno*, *Purgatorio*, and *Paradiso*. In talking about any passage it becomes important to make it clear whether we are talking about Dante the poet, who is writing the text, or Dante the character in the text, who takes this journey. The latter is often called "Dante, the pilgrim"—a usage, perhaps anachronistic, but in my view helpfully suggestive, which I often use in this book to talk about the character of the Augustine whose life is the subject of the *Confessions*, calling him "Augustine the pilgrim."

To sum up what I have been saying, we can see that the book is partly about itself: about its own premises, its own activities, its own problems. Can we make sense of these things? What happens when we do, or when we try?

These are some of the questions presented by the first sentence of this book, which in this way invites or entices the reader to keep going, to engage with what follows. How will Augustine answer or at least address them? Here I will only add that I will try to keep these questions alive right to the end of the *Confessions*.


## LATIN

As I said in the Preface, there is another immense and complex question for us here, which is what it means that the *Confessions* is written in Latin, not English. I will be talking about this issue throughout the book. Here follows a very short and incomplete introduction to the structure and nature of Latin itself.

The first thing to understand about Latin is that it is an inflected language, that is, one in which most words, both nouns and verbs, have endings, or other transformations, that indicate their role in the sentence. We have some of this in English in our verbs, which are marked for past tense by an "–ed" at the end, or by a transformation of a vowel, as in "sing"/"sang," or by a larger transformation, as in "catch"/"caught." (For the future and perfect and past-perfect we normally use auxiliaries: We "shall walk," "have walked," "had walked," and even "shall have walked.") With respect to nouns we have almost none of this, except markings for plural, often in the form of a final "s" or "–en" (as in "oxen"). With certain pronouns we have more: the words "I" or "we" for example are in what is called the nominative case, which means that they can be the subject of verbs. "Me" and "us" have the same referential meaning—the person speaking on his own behalf or that of the group he belongs to—but these words are in the accusative case and cannot be subjects of finite verbs, but only their objects. When we hear or read the word "she" we expect a verb of which "she" will be the subject; when we read or hear the word "him" we expect a verb of which "he" will be the object. For another example of inflection in English, consider something suggested by a friend: the triad, "who," "whose," "whom."

So few of our words have these grammar-referencing endings that for us word order takes their place. When we read, "The dog caught the cat," or "John hit the ball," we know by the position of the words in the sentence who (or what) did the hitting or catching, who (or what) was hit or caught. In Latin, by contrast, we would know these things from the forms of the words. Word order is significant in Latin, but it has nothing like the force it has in English.

Another way to put this point is to say that in an inflected language you cannot present a word without marking its grammatical function. There is no such thing as a simple word that just means "horse" in Latin, as there is in English. It will have markers that tell you, this is "horse as actor" or "horse as possessor" or "horse as donee" or "horse as acted upon" or "horse as agent," that is, one by which something else is done, or "horse spoken to" ("Oh horse . . .")—*equus, equi, equo, equum, equo, eque.*

What is true of nouns is true of the adjectives that modify or characterize them, which take a form that to some extent mirrors the form of the noun. What this means, among other things, is that in Latin words that belong together may be separated without losing their connection. Thus if a sentence begins with the word *bonus* (singular masculine nominative adjective, meaning "good"), we expect to find the word it modifies, which will likewise be masculine and nominative and singular, but it may come much later in the sentence—*animus*, for example, meaning "spirit," or, in another declension, *ignis*, meaning "fire." The experience of reading a Latin sentence is often one of a complex series of expectations first created, then, later on, resolved in whole or in part.

Words in Latin have forms that fit with other forms; they look at form to identify their role and their mate. I think for someone raised in this language perhaps the first thing noticed about a word was its grammatical form, not what we would call its content.[12]

In approaching the first three sentences of the *Confessions* I shall proceed word by word, very slowly, with the hope that by the end every reader can read these Latin sentences with ease and understanding. In what follows this section I will obviously have to vary the pace dramatically, sometimes simply summarizing a passage in English, sometimes making it available for the reader who knows a little Latin, trying to make sure that every reader has the experience of reading some sentences, or passages, in the language in which they were composed.

## THE FIRST SENTENCE

So now, at last, to our opening sentence, seen as a Latin sentence:

*Magnus es, Domine, et laudabilis valde.*

The first word is *magnus*, an adjective meaning something like "great," in size, in importance, or in worth. It creates just the sort of expectation that *bonus* would do, looking for a masculine singular noun, but as it turns out, that expectation seems to be disappointed: the next word is *es*, which means "you are." But the noun we have been looking for as the mate to *magnus* is actually there, buried in the verb, which, as often in Latin, has no explicit subject.[13]

*Magnus* has told us something else, which the verb alone would not tell us, namely that the addressee defined by the *es* is masculine and singular. *Magnus* is nominative because the verb "to be," here represented by *es*, typically connects or links two terms, an adjective and a noun, without either one acting on the other.

*Domine* is a form of *Dominus* in what is called the vocative case, that is, the form that is used to address another person. We achieve something of this form when we say, today, "O Lord . . ."

*Laudabilis* is an adjective that parallels *magnus*, that is, it is singular masculine nominative, but in a different declension, hence different in form. It is preceded by *et* (that is, "and"), which connects it explicitly with *magnus*. In form it comes from a word for "praise," (*laus*) with the suffix—*ible*, which means, in English as in Latin (which is where we get it from), something like "capable of" or "susceptible to" or "worthy of."

The last word is *valde*, meaning "very much indeed."

\*\*\*

The experience of the sentence is something like this:

—*Magnus*: here we are told that something or someone, masculine and singular, is "great."
—*es*: it is you who are great! But who are you?
—*Domine*: you are the Lord to whom I am speaking.

It could stop here, but the next word carries us on:

—*et*: "and" something, but we do not know what.

The function of *et* is to connect to things that are alike in grammar or function—it could be, for example, that it connected a whole second clause, e.g., "and always will be." Here what is connected is *laudabilis*, an adjective coupled with *magnus*.

Then: *valde*: "very much indeed."

* * *

Here is the sentence itself: *Magnus es, Domine, et laudabilis valde.* Can you read that aloud as a sentence you understand?

* * *

Let us do the next sentence as well—*Magna virtus tua et sapientiae tuae non est numerus*, or: "Great is your virtue and your wisdom knows no number" (i.e., there is no quantitative limit on your wisdom). Let us see how it works.

—*Magna* is of course related to *magnus*, an adjective meaning "great." But the ending promises a connection with a different kind of noun: one that is feminine singular (either nominative or ablative) or neuter plural. So which is it to be?

—*virtus* tells us, for it is feminine singular (despite the fact that *-us* nouns are often masculine and equally despite the fact

translated liberty w/ knows? How to explain "est" as "knows" when it is "is" before?

maybe better to "your wisdom is boundless"? → don't need to argue for the licensing of a new verb (i.e., "knows") that it is built on the word *vir* which means "man"). *Virtus* really means those qualities that in this culture are excellent for a man to have, which include such competitive qualities as power and prestige and status, but also moral qualities, such as courage and honesty. Which is it here? Some of both, so: "your qualities are the summit of excellence, both in power and morality"— something like that?

—*tua* tells us that it is "your" *virtus* we are talking about, and this pronoun is in the form appropriate to a feminine singular noun. Those two words are locked together.

—*et*: what two things that are alike will be connected by this word? We cannot know now, but we will soon see that it is two clauses: *Magna virtus tua* [*est*] *et sapientiae tuae non est numerus.*

The verb *est* is missing from the first clause, but when we read the second we find it, so it becomes, as Latin teachers like to say, "understood," in the first clause.

—*sapientiae tuae*: we might guess that *tuae* is another form of the word we just saw as *tua*, and that it goes with, or modifies or connects to, *sapientiae*. This is correct. But why the *-ae* endings? In the first declension they mark a feminine singular noun (or adjective) in the genitive singular, dative singular, or nominative plural forms. This could mean "Your wisdoms" or "of your wisdom" or "to your wisdom." Which shall it be? This question carries us to the rest of the sentence:

—*non est numerus*, which means "not is number" (*numerus* being a singular masculine noun), i.e., "there is no number" (or measure or, here perhaps, way of measuring).

But does this tell us how to read *sapientiae tuae?* Yes: it is genitive, or what in English would be an "of" word: "There is no number of your wisdom," or more idiomatically, "There is no way of measuring your wisdom."[14]

\* \* \*

Now we are here:

*Magnus es, Domine, et laudabilis valde. Magna virtus tua et sapientiae tuae non est numerus.* Again: Can you read these sentences aloud with the sense that you understand them?

## SOMEWHERE NEW

The next sentence takes us somewhere new: *Et laudare te vult homo, aliqua portio creaturae tuae, et homo circumferens mortalitatem suam, circumferens testimonium peccati sui et testimonium quia superbis resistis; et tamen laudare te vult homo, aliqua portio creaturae tuae.* Or: "And a person wishes to praise you, a person who is a part of your creation, carrying about with them their mortality, carrying about the testimony of their own sin and the testimony that you (God) resist the proud; nonetheless they, this part of your creation, wish to praise you."

Here is the way it is put together:

1.  —*Et laudare te vult homo*, or: "and a person wishes to praise you."

—Here *et* is "and," or perhaps here "also."

—*laudare* is the verb "to praise" in the infinitive. As in English, an infinitive normally requires a finite verb upon which it depends, here *vult*, which means "wishes" or "wills" or "wants."

—*te* is "you" in the accusative, and thus the object of the verb *laudare.*

—*homo*, nominative singular and hence the subject of the verb *vult*. It has a general meaning of "person," or "human being."[15] Thus: "a person," or even more strongly, "every person"?[16]

So far: "and a person wishes to praise you."

2.   —*aliqua portio creaturae tuae*, or "a person who is some part of your creation."

—*portio* (referring to the person) is a feminine singular noun meaning something like "portion" or "part"; *aliqua*, "some," is marked as its modifier by its feminine singular ending. Both words are in the nominative, in apposition with *homo*.

—*creaturae* is "creation," again a feminine noun, but this time genitive, with the matching *tuae*: "of your creation."

So: "a person who is some part of your creation."

3.   —*et homo circumferens mortalitatem suam*: "and carrying around with them their mortality."[17]

The first thing the person is carrying is their *mortalitatem*, i.e., "mortality" (a feminine noun properly in the accusative case, since it is the object of the action of "carrying").

But also:—*circumferens testimonium peccati sui*: "carrying around the testimony of their sin.[18]

And:—*et testimonium quia superbis resistis:* "and (carrying about the testimony) that you (God) resist the proud." This "testimony," in the accusative, is also the object of *circumferens*, and obliquely the subject of the clause, *et testimonium quia superbis resistis*, "testimony that you resist the proud."

4.   —Here *quia* here means "*that*," marking what is coming as a clause; *resistis* is the present tense of the verb from which we get our own "resist." The ending, "—*is*," marks it as second person singular. So this is "testimony that you [i.e., "God"] resist" something. What or whom do you resist? "The proud," *superbis*, appropriately plural and dative, because this verb takes, as some do, a dative object.

So far our sentence reads:

*Et laudare te vult homo, aliqua portio creaturae tuae, et homo circumferens mortalitatem suam, circumferens testimonium peccati sui et testimonium quia superbis resistis;*

"And a person wishes to praise you, a person who is a part of your creation, carrying about with them their mortality, carrying about the testimony of their own sin and the testimony that you (God) resist the proud."

5.   —The rest of the sentence is almost all a repetition of what we just read: *et tamen laudare te vult homo, aliqua portio creaturae tuae.* We know that *et* means "and" or "also"; *tamen* is an adverb meaning, roughly, "however"; *laudare* we know is an infinitive meaning "to praise"; *te* we know means "you," in the accusative, here the object of *laudare; vult* we knows means "wishes," and *homo* is its subject; *aliqua* we know means "some," *portio* means "portion" or "piece," and *creaturae tuae,* being genitive, means "of your creation."

Here again is the whole sentence: *Et laudare te vult homo, aliqua portio creaturae tuae, et homo circumferens mortalitatem suam, circumferens testimonium peccati sui et testimonium quia superbis resistis; et tamen laudare te vult homo, aliqua portio creaturae tuae.* Or: "And a person wishes to praise you, a person who is a part of your creation, carrying about with them their mortality, carrying about the testimony of their own sin and testimony that you (God) resist the proud; nonetheless they, this part of your creation, wish to praise you."

Notice that the last clause marks the whole sentence as a ring composition, repeating at the end the clause with which it

began: "And every person wishes to praise you, being some portion of your creation."[19]

Does this clause mean exactly the same thing when it is
repeated? Or has the intervening material changed your sense of
what it means, and how it means?


## THE SENTENCES TOGETHER

Now here are the first three sentences:

> *Magnus es, Domine, et laudabilis valde. Magna virtus tua
> et sapientiae tuae non est numerus. Et laudare te vult homo,
> aliqua portio creaturae tuae, et homo circumferens mortalita-
> tem suam, circumferens testimonium peccati sui et testimonium
> quia superbis resistis; et tamen laudare te vult homo, aliqua
> portio creaturae tuae.*

Can you read these sentences aloud in Latin with the feeling
that you understand them? Can you write out a translation into
English? If so, what are the differences between what Augustine wrote and your translation? What is missing, what is added?
I would encourage you to think hard about this question, and
maybe draft notes of a possible response.

What *is* different in the Latin? Part of it, as I have been suggesting, has to do with the way the words are connected with
each other, across space on a page, across time if they are said
aloud. Another part has to do with the words themselves, which
acquire their meaning not only from the way they are connected
with others in the sentence, but from their earlier use in other
sentences, with other words. Their fullest meaning can be perceived only by someone with deep experience of the language.

There is also the matter of sound, for they sound very different: is the sound part of the meaning? As you read these sentences, do you have a sense that you are connecting with the mind of Augustine himself? If so, how? If not, why not?

Let us take another look at the last sentence. Can you see how beautiful and firm this passage is, in its structure and in its details?

*Et laudare te vult homo,*
And a person wishes to praise you

*aliqua portio creaturae tuae,*
a person who is a part of your creation

*et homo circumferens mortalitatem suam,*
and carrying about with them their mortality,

*circumferens testimonium peccati sui*
carrying about with them the testimony of their own sin

*et testimonium quia superbis resistis;*
and [carrying about] the testimony that you [God] resist the proud;

*et tamen laudare te vult homo, aliqua portio creaturae tuae.*
yet nonetheless they, this part of your creation, wish to praise you.

OR:—a person wishes to praise you
    —a person who is part of your creation
        who carries about their mortality
        who carries about testimony of their sin
           and (who carries about) testimony
           that you resist the proud
a portion of your creation
wishes to praise you.

This is a structure made tight and firm by the way in which the words fit with each other. Look at your own written translation, or mine given above, and ask yourself what is achieved in the original that is not achieved in the translation. Is the beauty an important part of it? Do you hear different voices in the two versions? To what effect?

Among other things, as we shall soon see, this structure suggests questions to be asked, and in that way moves us to what comes next.

## MOVEMENT

Now let us look at what is happening in these three sentences taken as a composition of its own.

We can begin with the fact that there is a movement from the act of praise itself, as performed in the first two sentences, to reflection on the practice of praise, particularly as Augustine himself engages in it. In these three sentences, then, we see Augustine do something, then pause to look at it, then question what he has done.

The question he is implicitly raising is this: Where does this praise I have just offered up actually come from? My will? My reasoned choice? Augustine presents the question but cannot really answer it; rather, he sees the disposition to praise as just a fact, an unexplained fact, in the human being. It is a kind of primary datum about human beings, the raw material of our nature.

But can that be true? Do all people in fact wish to praise God? Augustine is mainly speaking about himself, of course, and of him it does seem to be true. His observation is in part a way of saying that he feels within him, without knowing why or how, the desire to praise the God to whom he is speaking. In this way he shifts his attention, and ours, from the gesture of praise itself to the wish or desire that gives rise to it within him, which he can name but not explain.

He is already marking out for us the limits of his mind and imagination by identifying parts of reality that he cannot understand or explain, a movement that, as I said in chapter 1, will become stronger and stronger as he proceeds. It will become in fact one of his central themes.

It is not clear whether Augustine is saying that he always feels the desire to praise, and always has—the way he desires food and water, and air to breathe—or whether this particular desire comes to life in him only on certain occasions. In particular, we may want to know, does it come to him just as he begins to write this book—as he begins, that is, the activity of writing that comes at the end of the activity of living of which the book will tell the story? We do not know. The important thing is that it seems an indelible, unchosen, inexplicable part of himself.

There is also an unstated question, which is to me at least unavoidable. He praises God; then he recognizes that he wants or desires to praise God, which is why he does it. Why is this not enough, for him or for the book? What more is expected of him than praise? Why not stop here after three sentences?

There may be a clue in the assertion that "mortality" is "testimony" or evidence of "sin." This is of course a reference to Genesis, where it is said that the consequence of the sin of Adam and Eve is death.

But what does the fact of sin have to do with praise? And exactly who are the proud whom he says (quoting from 1 Pet. 5:5) that God resists? In fact, as we proceed it will become clear that the proud include Augustine himself, whose pride in his intellect is one of his central subjects.

What I think makes simple praise not enough, or not enough for him, is the fact of sin as an inherent element of human experience, in particular the sin—perhaps Augustine's central sin—of pride. Augustine is saying that his relation with God, like all humanity's relation with God, is broken or incomplete. More is required of him and of his book than a single gesture of praise.

Another way to put this is to say that in this passage, where he says that the impulse or desire to praise God is an inherent, hence natural, part of a human being, he also suggests that we have impulses not to praise: we are doomed to die, after all, doomed by sin, both Adam's and our own, and we know that God resists the proud, which includes us. Why should we praise such a God? A real question. Augustine says—without explaining how this is true—that we do wish to praise you, for we are a piece of your creation.

This is a way of saying that in the human being, who is by nature the bearer of sin, there is another impulse, a redemptive spring of life, the impulse to praise the Creator and the Creation, arising out of a kind of fundamental gratitude for the fact that we exist at all. It is with this impulse that Augustine begins the *Confessions*. If he did not have it, he could not go on. The astonishing thing is not that humanity is crippled by sin, but that despite this fact it has, or at least Augustine has, a deep and irresistible impulse to praise.

It would be hard to overstate this point, for it is this impulse, the very impulse with which he begins the *Confessions*, that may save him—and perhaps, in his mind, may save us readers as well—from a life of emptiness.

## THE IMPULSE TO PRAISE

The impulse to praise, which moves the writing of the *Confessions*, is in this sense the foundation of Augustine's life, and—we may or may not feel this—perhaps of our own as well. It is obviously of immense importance. Where does it come from?

Augustine goes on to address this question:

*Tu excitas ut laudare te delectet, quia fecisti nos ad te et inquietum est cor nostrum donec requiescat in te.*

1. —*Tu* is "you," of course in this case the *Dominus* to whom everything in the *Confessions* is addressed, from its very first sentence. It is nominative singular, hence the subject of the verb, which follows immediately:

—*excitas*, something like "excite" or "arouse" or "stimulate." Whom does *Dominu*s stimulate? There is no explicitly stated object, but it is clearly the *homo* he has been talking about, who shows up as the unstated subject of the next verb.

—*ut laudare te delectet*: this explains what *Dominus* stimulates in us. We have here a whole clause, beginning with *ut*, a clause-marker, in this case a purposive one, maybe here: "so that." The finite verb of this clause is *delectet*, which means something like "he [the *homo*] should delight." (Why not just "delights"?)[20]

2. —*quia fecisti nos*, Why should we delight to praise you? because you have made us and done so *ad te*, for yourself. That is: you stir us so that we may delight to praise you, who made us for yourself.

3. The sentence could stop here, but instead continues with a clause that is justly famous: *et inquietum est cor nostrum donec requiescat in te.*

—*et* is "and," of course, and *inquietum* can be read as "unquiet," not quite a common English word but clear enough. Maybe "restless" would be best. But what is the noun which that adjective characterizes?

—*est cor nostrum*: "is our heart." Unquiet is our heart.

—*donec requiescat in te*: *donec* here simply means "until"; *requi-escat* is known to us in the famous phrase, *requiescat in pace*, which means "may they rest in peace." It means "rest," but as the "may" in the standard translation shows, it is not what is called indicative, that is a way of describing the way things actually are, but modal, that is a way of describing things as hoped for or feared or expected with uncertainty. Here in the Latin the mode is "subjunctive." So maybe: "until it find its rest in you," where we would be using the rare-ish English subjunctive (in "find") to mirror the Latin.

So perhaps one might translate: "You stir him up so that he may delight to praise you, because you made us for yourself and our heart is restless until it find its rest in you."

\* \* \*

See how Augustine slides from the third person, "he" (referring to the *homo*), to the first person plural, "us," or *nos* (referring, pretty plainly, to both Augustine and his reader, and perhaps to all humanity as well). Thus he brings himself and the reader and all humanity into his sentence: "You made us for yourself and our heart is restless until it rests in you."[21]

Where then does the impulse to praise come from? From God himself, Augustine is saying, from his desire for a relation with us. He made us for himself and wants us to reach out to him, so he has made us restless in heart until we find rest in him. We praise, that is, because God has created in us a hunger or need to connect to him—not just because that is good for us, but because God wants to be connected with us too.

Here there is a significant point: "praise" seems to come from gratitude, an emotion he has not mentioned. But does it suggest an answer to the question, why we should praise *Dominum* (*Dominus* in the accusative), namely, that we should do this in gratitude for the incomprehensible gift of life itself.

As for the restlessness of which he speaks, this is very much the quality of Augustine's life as it is told in the *Confessions*. He is hungry for a kind of coherence in life, for a foundation upon which he can stand, or in his terms "rest," and he attributes this hunger to us as well.

When he does this—as when he says *et laudare te vult homo*, "and man wishes to praise you"—readers are given an opportunity to step back from the book, if they wish, to separate themselves as it were from Augustine, saying something like: "It may be true of you that you wish to praise, that you are restless, but it is not true of me. Maybe I will continue to read what you write, but I will not share this premise on which you proceed."

This opportunity presents the reader with a question. Do you want to separate yourself in this way from what Augustine is saying? Or do you agree that what he is saying about humanity is true of you? If you do accept what he says as true of you, what does that mean for you, as a reader of this book and in your life more generally?[22] If you do not accept it, how do you connect to this book? Or do you just put it down? What does that mean about you?

Can you read this sentence aloud in Latin, with the sense that you understand what you are saying? *Tu excitas ut laudare te delectet, quia fecisti nos ad te et inquietum est cor nostrum donec requiescat in te.*

Try translating it into English and ask what happens when you do that? Can you just put the meaning of the Latin sentence into English? Why not? What can you do?


## LATIN AGAIN

As I said in the Preface and earlier in this chapter, and is obvious from what we have done, I believe that if we wish to engage with Augustine's mind at work, we need to read him, at least in part, in Latin. To read him only in English is a little like trying to fix a watch with mittens on.

Here I shall say a little bit more about the structure of the Latin language and how it works, building on what I said earlier in this chapter. I hope this will make the Latin you have read, and the Latin still to come, a bit less mysterious and daunting. Not that I can fully teach you the language. I do not have full grasp of it myself, and in any event that would require another book.[23]

Here I want to highlight a bit more fully than I did earlier some of the ways Latin is structurally different from English. What I say will be deliberately somewhat repetitive, to save you the task of going back to the earlier passage.

We can start with the nouns, which as I said earlier are all marked for what we call gender and case. Take, for example, the word *anima*, which means, roughly, "soul": it does not have just one form, the way English nouns usually do, but a prescribed set of forms. *Anima* is the nominative, and can be the subject of a verb, as in "the soul exists in me"; *animae* is the genitive, usually marking possession "of the soul," as in the "beauty of the soul"; it happens to be also the dative, roughly equivalent to the English "to," as in "he ascribed to the soul"; *animam* is the accusative, marking the object of a verb, as in "he celebrated the soul"; and *anima* (with a long last syllable) is what is called the ablative, as in "he removed from the soul all its most important qualities." To add richness, and further precision, each of these cases has a different ending in the plural: *animae* in the nominative, *animarum* in the genitive, *animis* in the dative and ablative, and *animas* in the accusative. It is also feminine in gender (rather than masculine or neuter).

The nouns are arranged in a series of patterns, called declensions, five of them, each with its own way of expressing case and number and gender. In addition to the declension of *anima*, that is, the first declension, there are four other patterns or declensions, which have the cases in common but express them with different endings. Roughly the same is true of adjectives. Thus an adjective from the first declension—say *bona*, the feminine nominative singular for "good"—will typically have endings that are identical to those of *anima*. But if they come from a different declension, their pattern will be different but equally marked for gender and case and number (i.e., singular vs. plural).[24] So you cannot simply rely upon similarity of endings to know what words belong together, as in *anima bona*, because when the words are drawn from different declension the markers are different, as for example in *ignis bonus*, "good fire."

This means that every time one uses a noun or adjective in Latin, it is marked with case, number, and gender that tells us what role it will have in the sentence as a whole.

Also: when you see a noun you know that it has an implied relation to a verb, which, unless something is off, will show up somewhere in the sentence.

In Latin, as I said earlier, the noun and adjective may be separated by many words but connected by their grammatical markers. With us, by contrast, the adjective normally has to come right before the noun it modifies, as in "good book," "bad conduct," "lousy lunch." I said earlier, when in Latin you read "*bonus*" ("good" in the masculine nominative singular), you expect a noun also in the masculine nominative singular. That word will come but it may be many words away. When you do come upon it, you will tie it back to the adjective.

What is true of nouns and adjectives, that they are inflected, is also true of verbs, where different word-endings and sometimes changes in internal structures—think "sing, sang, sung"—will mark different functions and meanings of the word. We call these four patterns "conjugations." A verb will by its endings or internal modifications indicate the person acting (that is, whether I, or you, or another), the number of that actor (singular or plural, e.g., I or we, he or they), the time or tense of the verb (present, future, imperfect, perfect, pluperfect, future perfect) and its mood (indicative or subjunctive or imperative), its voice (active or passive), and often its aspect (whether continuing or punctual). For us in English the markers of these features of the verb often require other words. As with nouns, in Latin the verbs establish connections with other words, often objects or subjects, which may be found not next to the verb, as usually in English, but at some distance in the sentence. Even from this brief introduction you may see that in Latin the words are always speaking to each other in ways that are rare in English.

In all these ways the individual Latin word carries much more information than an English word is likely to do. Later in the book you will see this demonstrated very simply, when you see my translation of Latin sentences alongside the originals, for my translations are almost always longer than the Latin original, sometimes much longer.

The English reader looking at Latin words is likely to look for the stem that declares the basic meaning and regard the endings and other transformations I describe above as surplusage, of no real interest. We have to train ourselves to look right away at the endings and other modifications because they shape the way the word can be used. Our habit is to use word order rather than inflection to connect one word with another, in a kind of two-dimensional chain, as opposed to the three-dimensionality of Latin.

Our work has now put us in a certain place. Augustine has brought us here. How would you define that place? How important is the experience of Latin to its nature and quality?

## TRANSLATION

Here, as a way of thinking about that question, I want to return to another: What is it like to translate from Latin into English, as we have been doing? What happens when you try it?

To start with, let me reproduce once more the first four sentences in Latin:

> *Magnus es, Domine, et laudabilis valde. Magna virtus tua et sapientiae tuae non est numerus. Et laudare te vult homo, aliqua portio creaturae tuae, et homo circumferens mortalitatem suam, circumferens testimonium peccati sui et testimonium quia superbis resistis; et tamen laudare te vult homo, aliqua portio creaturae tuae. Tu excitas ut laudare te delectet, quia fecisti nos ad te et inquietum est cor nostrum donec requiescat in te.*

Can you read them in Latin? If so, what have you learned that makes this possible?

Let me encourage you to go back through our discussion and see if your earlier experience helps you read them now. I will ask you to translate but do not do that yet. If you do, the translation will feel like the real text. Instead, try to get to a place where you can read the sentences in Latin.

Now ask: What happens when you read this short passage, not in the Latin in which it was composed, but in translation?

There follow below three translations, all well regarded. How is reading them different from reading the original? How are they different from each other? This is a complex and difficult subject which will be with us throughout the book. It might be a good idea for you to write a response to it when you have read and thought about these passages, as well as you can, and keep it for later review.

\* \* \*

Henry Chadwick, trans., *Saint Augustine: Confessions* (Oxford: Oxford University Press, 1991), 3:

"You are great, Lord, and highly to be praised (Ps. 47:2): great is your power and your wisdom is immeasurable" (Ps. 146:5). Man, a little piece of your creation, desires to praise you, a human being "bearing his mortality with him" (2 Cor. 4:10), carrying with him the witness of his sin and the witness that you "resist the proud" (1 Pet. 5:5). Nevertheless, to praise you is the desire of man, a little piece of your creation. You stir a man to take pleasure in praising you, because you have made us for yourself, and our heart is restless until it rests in you.

Maria Boulding, trans., *The Confessions* (Hyde Park, NY: New City Press, 1997), 39:

Great are you, O Lord, and exceedingly worthy of praise. Your power is immense, and your wisdom beyond reckoning. And we humans, who are a part of your creation, long to praise you—we who carry our mortality about with us, carry the evidence of our sin and with it the proof that you thwart the proud. Yet these humans, due part of your creation as they are, still do long to praise you. You stir us so that praising may bring us joy, because you have made us and drawn us to yourself, and our heart is unquiet until it rests in you.

Sarah Ruden, trans., *Confessions* (New York: Modern Library, 2017), 3:

You are mighty, Master, and to be praised with a powerful voice: great is your goodness, and of your wisdom there can be no reckoning. Yet to praise you is the desire of every human being, who

is some part of what you created; a human hauling his deathless-
ness in a circle, hauling in a circle the evidence of his sin, and the
evidence that you stand against the arrogant. But still a mortal, a
given portion of your creation, longs to extol you. In yourself you
rouse us, giving us delight in glorifying you, because you made
us with youself as our goal, and our heart is restless until it rests
in you.

* * *

A real question: How are we to read translations of this kind?
How are we to think about them?

Here is a question that suggests one approach. Can you read
each of these translations as manifesting a series of decisions by
the translator: decisions about word choice, about the structure
of the sentence, about the tone of voice, and the relation it establishes with the reader, about the expectations the passage creates
and the questions it invites? About the relationship between one
sentence and another? Let me suggest that you think about these
questions energetically with respect to one of the translations.

Next: draft a translation of your own, and ask how you are
making the set of decisions you see the other translators to be
making. What have you been doing? How did you imagine
doing it well? What do you think of what you have done?

Taking as your examples either one of the translations I have
made in the course of the chapter or your own translation, or one
of those given above, ask what the translations leave out; what
they add that does not belong there; what they hide and what
they twist. What is lost here? What does the Latin do and mean
that the English does not? When you try your own translations,
do you do better?

When you look at all these translations, I think it will emerge
that a translation is by its nature its own independent work, the

work of a special kind of writer called a translator, not the work of the original writer reaching out to us. What are the issues you face in reading such a text? In writing it?

Another way to look at these passages—both the original Latin and the translations before you—is to ask of each what comes next. In reading these translations do you find yourself engaged with the text in a way that makes you look forward to the next sentence and paragraph? What expectations are created here? How and why? If you can answer that question more fully of the original Latin text than the others, why would that be? How about your own translation?

You have now read enough so that you may be beginning to get your own sense of the nature and effect of Latin. What do you now think about the relation between the Latin sentences you have read and their English counterparts?

Here is another translation for your consideration, this one by F. J. Sheed and published by Hackett in 1942:[25]

> *Great art Thou, O Lord, and greatly to be praised; great is Thy power and of Thy wisdom there is no number.* And man desires to praise Thee. He is but a tiny part of all that Thou hast created. He bears about him his mortality, the evidence of his sinfulness, and the evidence that *Thou does resist the proud;* yet this tiny part of all that Thou hast created desires to praise Thee. Thou dost so excite him that to praise Thee is his joy. For Thou has made us for Thyself and our hearts are restless till they rest in Thee.

What decisions did this writer make differently from any of the others, and to what effect? You might notice in particular his use of language we think of as Biblical, including the use of the second person singular pronoun in two forms, "thou" and "thee," both of which we have lost. (Latin does have a second person singular, seen in *tu* and *te* and implicit in the verb *es*.)

As you contemplate these various texts let me encourage you to think of them each as offering to its reader a certain experience, or set of experiences, both in the reading itself and in the anticipation of what comes next. In my view at least the meaning of a text worth reading lies not so much in the propositions it advances or the completeness of its argument or the effectiveness of its responses to others, as in the experience it offers its reader, an experience of mind and feeling and imagination.

## DIFFERENCES AMONG LANGUAGES

Now that we have worked for some time reading the *Confessions* in a way that includes the Latin, perhaps we can ask again the question that gave rise to this book: Why does it matter that this book is written in Latin, not English? How and why, that is, does its meaning depend upon its language? In particular: why is it so difficult to give the modern reader an experience in English that at least parallels or imitates or echoes the experience of reading it in Latin?

This is a question presented by every text written in a language other than our own, certainly by all the works written in what we consider the classical languages of Greek and Latin. What is lost when we try to put Homer's *Iliad* into English, for example, or Vergil's *Aeneid*? When we ask that question, what do we hope for: an explanation at a high level of abstraction about the ways texts create their meanings, and about their dependence in doing so upon the language in which they are conceived? Or, at a reduced level of abstraction, do we hope for an explanation of what it is specifically about Greek or Latin, say, that offers resources for meaning that are not available in English?

In Latin, for example, one might think of the ways in which words carry with them syntactic markers, as we have seen, a fact that enables the writer to put words that connect or interact with each other in what feel like remote places in the sentence. The sentence in this language is a naturally complex experience, in which expectations raised at the beginning are kept alive, unresolved, until perhaps the very end, when they close the unit of expression. A language like Latin has much in common with music as we know it, which works by raising expectations, deferring them, resolving them in ways that create new needs or desires in the listener, and so on.

Or to shift to our own language, English, and to ask what is difficult about translating out of it, or into it, we might think about the fact that though it is basically a Germanic language it has a great many terms and locutions that derive from the romance languages, ultimately from Latin. As our language has evolved, Latinate terms, often long-winded, are the mark of much legal and philosophic talk, while Germanic terms, often short, are the mark of ordinary life. What is the difference between a residence (Latin) and a house (Germanic)? Between aspiration and hope? Educating and teaching? A profession and a job?

It might have been possible for us over time to become deaf to these differences, but in fact we are not. The American poet, John Crowe Ransom, maintained that Shakespeare (along with other poets) is responsible for having permanently marked the difference between the two languages that together make up English.[26] Think of Macbeth looking at the blood of Duncan, whom he had just killed, on his hand:

Will all great Neptune's ocean wash this blood
Clean from my hand? No, this my hand will rather
The multitudinous seas inarnadine
And make the green one red.
(MACBETH 2.2.58–61)

Where the writer in English uses this tension productively, as in this brief quotation, we can readily see how difficult it would be to reproduce such an effect in a more unitary language, like French or German.

## SLOW READING

What emerges from what we have done in working with Latin? One thing for sure: when we read it in Latin, not being expert Latinists, we have to do so slowly, with all too acute an awareness that we cannot be sure what the words before us mean, or the exact tone of the gesture or phrase. We are working if not in the dark, in a very dim light indeed, and what we perceive is accordingly uncertain, or at least highly qualified. The sentences naturally inhabit a kind of no-man's-land, between the fluent Augustine and the reader laboring with his language. This very fact is in my view a great merit of what we have been doing. For we have to think, much more than we usually do, about exactly how the sentence is put together, and why, and about the precise meaning of the words, not only in general but in this context. How does the sentence give meaning to its own words?

As I said in an earlier aside, reading in a foreign language in which you are not fluent is a bit like reading poetry in your own language, where the writer will often defamiliarize what she or he writes, with the result that it cannot be skimmed or swallowed with a gulp, but must, if it is to be understood at all, be attended to in a new and deeper way. As I said earlier, our imperfect grasp of Latin is to this degree an advantage to us, for if we were fully fluent we would risk sliding over all the unresolved questions we can see when we read in slow motion.

Another way to put this point is to say that the "meaning" of what Augustine is doing is not perceived in a flash but emerges slowly as a result of the choices made by Augustine the narrator and by ourselves as well. Alternative readings are present in our mind, alternative constructions of what he has done, leaving the whole alive in a deep way.

What is it that we desire when we read the work of another person which we hope will matter in our lives? It is not just the general ideas or concepts, or narratives in outline; we want to engage with the mind and heart of the writer, and to do that we must read what they are writing in the language in which they think it and compose it. A basic question in the reader's mind should be, Why this word? That word? This sequence? In our own language we can approach this question by imagining alternatives from which the writer has chosen, but we cannot do that in a language we do not know.

Another way to put this is to ask what we look for as the meaning of a book. One possibility is to see it as a source of information about the world, presented say in the language of one or another social science. In this context "meaning" is usually thought of as a set of propositions, supported by arguments based on reason, fact, or value. Or it may be thought of as a set of ideas which can be cast in propositional form and transferred to other contexts. A book like the *Confessions* cannot in my view be reduced to propositions or arguments or even the presentation of new data. Its meaning in my view lies in the experience of reading it. What kind of experience is this? How much of the mind and soul does it engage, in what way and to what end? These are the central questions I am pursuing.

The significance of the presence of Latin should be looked at from this perspective. What kind of experience does Augustine offer in Latin, and what relation can it have to the experience of reading a translation?

Here we need to think not only about grammatical and syntactic structures, but other things as well. As one example take the sense that the Latin sentence is built out of blocks that have strong interconnections, blocks that really require each other, which may contribute to a larger sense that a Latin text, or even a sentence, is a little like a work of architecture. As we see a new building, so we see a new sentence, or set of sentences, and can ask: what is it like to live here, to work here? Also, the mere presence of Latin words is in this context the presence of an authority—these are the words Augustine actually used—and since these words often work beautifully with each other, it can be a source of beauty as well. As you look at the Latin words, even if you do not understand them, you will pick up some of this. The words will have a feeling about them, maybe a little as if they were made of varnished wood, connected together by mortis and tenon, while the English words in the translation feel more like bits of wool, not really capable of connection of that kind.

Ultimately of course it is entirely up to you what you make of the Latin this book presents, what you think of it and about it. That is as it should be. But I hope that the experience of living with these Latin words already means something to you, maybe something very hard to express but deeply important.

# 3

# MOVEMENT FROM ONE MODE OF THOUGHT AND EXPRESSION TO ANOTHER (BOOK 1)

IN WHAT WE HAVE READ so far, Augustine has brought us to focus on the desire to praise: where does it come from, and why? What exactly is this desire? What are its conditions, what is its meaning? How is it connected to the restlessness of which he also speaks?

In what follows next, he addresses these questions not by breaking down the impulse to praise into its component parts, or something like that, but by comparing it with other gestures, other psychological and social practices, or what Wittgenstein might call "language games."[1] He asks, that is, how the activity of praising can be located in relation to other activities of mind and feeling in which we engage with respect to God. I think his idea is that if we can see a sequence or pattern among these activities, we may understand more fully what it is we are doing when we feel the desire to praise.

In examining what he does here we will continue to stick close to the Latin.

## COMPARING LANGUAGE GAMES

Here is what Augustine says immediately after the point at which we left him at the end of chapter 2:

> *Da mihi, Domine, scire et intellegere utrum sit prius invocare te an laudare te, et scire te prius sit an invocare te.*

1. —*Da* is the singular imperative of the verb *do*, which means "give." So the first three words mean, "Give me, Lord . . ." Give me what?

—*scire et intellegere*, "to know and understand." To know and understand what?

—*utrum sit prius invocare te an laudare te.* Here *utrum* means "whether," *prius* means "first," and *sit* is the subjunctive form of *est* ("is"), so, keeping the subjunctive in English, "whether it be first to invoke you or to praise you."[2]

2. —Continuing this line of thought the speaker wants to know something else too: *et scire te prius sit an invocare te,* "whether to know you should come first or to invoke you?" That is: should we call upon you without knowing you, or should we somehow know you first, as a condition of calling upon you?

He is now thinking of three things: praising, invoking, and knowing. Which of these activities should come first?

\* \* \*

So far it reads: *Da mihi, Domine, scire et intellegere utrum sit prius invocare te an laudare te, et scire te prius sit an invocare te.*

Or: "Give me, Lord, to know and understand whether it be first to invoke you or to praise you? Whether to know you should come first or to invoke you?"

Can you read this Latin sentence aloud to yourself with the feeling of understanding?

\* \* \*

3. —Notice the puzzle Augustine has created for himself: he began the *Confessions* with a statement of praise—*laudabilis valde*—and here in this very sentence "calls upon" God at least in the sense of asking him to grant him something: *Da mihi...* So he has already spoken as though praising somehow comes first, then invoking. But how does he know? And why is this true?

In this sense he has I think placed himself artfully in the middle of the confusion he sees to exist in the relation between these terms.

4. —He does not stop here, but presses on with more questions, offered as a way of thinking about the questions he has already asked, thus:

—*Sed quis te invocat nesciens te?*, "But who calls upon you, not knowing you?" Here the *sed* is "but," a way of saying you are going to qualify what you have just said; *quis* is "who" in the nominative singular; and *invocat*, roughly "invoke," is the verb of which *quis* is the subject. *Te*, or "you," is the object of that verb. *Nesciens te* is a participle, "not knowing," followed by its object, *te* or "you." Or, more colloquially in English, "Who calls upon you who does not already know you?"[3]

5. —What is more, he goes on, you might call on someone else by mistake: *Aliud enim pro alio potest invocare nesciens.*

Here *Aliud*, in the accusative, is the object of *invocare*, and means something like "another person"; *enim* is a particle, here meaning something like "certainly"; *pro alio* is a phrase that means, "for another"; *potest* means "it is possible"; and *invocare* is of course "to invoke" or "to call upon."

Or: "It is certainly possible in one's ignorance to call on one person rather than another" (i.e., to call by mistake not on God but perhaps on the devil or one of his angels).

6. —Here is the rest of the passage:

*An potius invocaris ut sciaris? Quomodo autem invocabunt, in quem non crediderunt? Aut quomodo credent sine praedicante? Et laudabunt Dominum qui requirunt eum: quaerentes enim inveniunt eum et invenientes laudabunt eum.*

It begins with another qualification, in the form of a question: *An potius invocaris ut sciaris?*

—Here *an* is "or"; *potius* is "rather"; *invocaris* is a passive form of "invoke," i.e., "are you invoked"; and *ut sciaris* is "so that you may be known" (subjunctive). The idea is that maybe we do not need to know God before we invoke him; in fact we may invoke him as a way of getting to know him. So: "Are you called upon so that you may be known?"

This question is followed by another: *Quomodo autem invocabunt, in quem non crediderunt?*

—Here *autem* is "however"; *Quomodo*, "how"; *invocabunt*, "will they invoke"; *quem* "one whom"; *non crediderunt*, "they have not believed."

Or: "How will they call upon one in whom they have not believed?"

Then still another question: *Aut quomodo credent sine praedicante?* Or: "How will they believe without being told (about God)?"

—Here *Aut*, is another word for "or": *quomodo* means "how"; *credent* means "will they believe"; *sine praedicante*, "without preaching."[4]

7. —Finally: *Et laudabunt Dominum qui requirunt eum: quae-rentes enim inveniunt eum et invenientes laudabunt eum.*

The first clause should be clear enough; then *quaerentes*, "searching for"; *inveniunt eum*, "they find him"; *et invenientes laudabunt eum*, "and finding him they will praise him."

Or: "And those who seek him will praise the Lord; seeking him they will find him, and finding him will praise him."

\* \* \*

So here is the whole thing. Can you read it aloud to yourself with understanding?

*Da mihi, Domine, scire et intellegere utrum sit prius invo-care te an laudare te, et scire te prius sit an invocare te. Sed quis te invocat nesciens te? Aliud enim pro alio potest invo-care nesciens. An potius invocaris ut sciaris? Quomodo autem invocabunt, in quem non crediderunt? Aut quomodo credent sine praedicante? Et laudabunt Dominum qui requirunt eum: quaerentes enim inveniunt eum et invenientes laudabunt eum.*

Or, a possible translation:

"Give me, Lord, to know and understand which should be first, to call upon you or to praise you? To know you or to call upon you? But who calls upon you without knowing you? He might unwit-tingly call upon another instead of you. Or, rather, are you called upon so that you may be known? But how will they call upon one in whom they have not believed? And how can they believe with-out preaching [that is, without being told about God]? Yet those who seek the Lord will praise him; seeking they find him, and finding they will praise him."

Go back to the Latin, and ask yourself what it does that my translation does not. How are the voices different, or similar? What expectations does each version create? What does it do with them? Which seems to you most trustworthy, and why? Which seems to lead you into something that follows? Does one seem to stop cold at the end of the passage? In another key, do you have the feeling, as I do, that the English is in this context always an approximation, the Latin always capable of precision? If true, this has the consequence that true close reading is only possible for the original text, not for the translation.

\* \* \*

The psychological and social practices (or gestures or language games) that Augustine thinks about but cannot coherently connect are these: praising God; calling upon God; believing in God; hearing God preached; and searching for God. The questions he is asking here are real ones: which of these should come first? How can you call upon someone without knowing the one whom you call upon? (You may find you are calling upon the wrong one without knowing it.) But how can you know this one, this God, without establishing a relationship with him, through invocation and praise? How can any of this be done without "preaching," that is, without being told about God?[5]

It is important that in tracing out these "language games," and questioning the relations among them, Augustine is making a reference, obvious to the educated Christian of his time, to a similar passage in Paul's Letter to the Romans.[6] Augustine does not merely use it, however; he builds upon it in his own way.

At first there seems to be no way to establish a clear relation among these activities. Augustine seems to be utterly at sea, and to have put us in a similar position. But then he writes a passage in which he finds a way to put some of these practices together, at least enough to proceed with his text:

> *Quaeram te, Domine, invocans te et invocem te credens in te:*
> I would seek you, Lord, calling upon you, and I would call upon you believing in you,
>
> *praedicatus enim es nobis. Invocat te, Domine, fides mea,*
> for you have been preached to us. My faith calls upon you, Lord,
>
> *quam dedisti mihi, quam inspirasti mihi*
> which you gave me, which you breathed into me
>
> *per humanitatem filii tui, per ministerium praedicatoris tui.*
> through the humanity of your son, through the office of your preacher.

To me this passage and the one we just read are astonishing in what they offer the reader. I had certainly never thought of these practices as being in tension in this way, and, at the same time, as being capable of harmoniously acting together. I never asked what conditions make each of them possible, or what relations potentially exist among them, both temporally and substantively.

The reader, like me, is presumably as bewildered as Augustine is. But he is almost always ahead of us, and out of this confusion and uncertainty he discovers something, and with his help so do we: that what makes the invocation possible—the invocation with which this work began—is something called faith: faith not chosen, not invented, not defensible rationally, not deserved, not an aspect of the self we ever wanted or were aware of lacking, but a sheer gift, the deepest part of us and beyond our understanding.[7] It provides the energy with which this book is written, out of which Augustine leads his whole life; but it is not chosen, not deserved, not understood. He says that it is preaching that gave him belief, but how and why did it have that effect? What kind of preaching was it? What is the relation between preaching and faith?

It is faith that permits him to go on. But what exactly is this faith? In our world we can sometimes hear talk about faith that seems sentimental and unreal. How will Augustine talk about it? What connection has it with the kind of careful thought and analysis we see Augustine engage in? What will he tell us about it? How will he display it? How will it be different from some other person's faith?

From what he says we do know this: that the faith of which Augustine here speaks is the rock upon which he builds in making the life he enacts in writing this book. Like the impulse to praise, faith cannot be described or explained except by connecting it with other practices of mind and spirit, and by finding its origin, its saving origin, outside the self in the gift of a God who loves us, despite our defects and failings. This faith, like the impulse to praise, finds its expression in the writing of the book. Like life itself, and the consciousness and intelligence of the writer, faith and the impulse to praise are gifts—unmerited, unchosen, freely given, acts of grace. Once more we can see that Augustine is carefully delineating the boundaries of the clearing that we call the mind, the conscious self that is producing this text, and finding on all sides a mysterious and impenetrable and gracious forest.

When Augustine in this way makes his language and its practices and gestures the subject of thought, something else happens too: he emerges before us as someone different from the language he is using. Unlike us most of the time, he is not just using the only language he knows as if all truth could be expressed in it, as if it were a fact of nature whose words are connected by obvious and certain ties to the world we are given. He does not use his words as though each word had its own certain and singular significance, but seeks to give his words new and deeper meaning as he connects them with others, in compositions of his own. He is present as a mind to whom his language is a problem, as a person who is thinking about what he himself does with that language when he praises, when he invokes, when he knows, when he hears preaching.

Thus he engages in the "language-game" of praising; but no sooner has he done that, than he asks what that practice is, what it depends upon, what relation it has to cognate or similar practices. His language, and the social and intellectual practices in which he engages while using it, are within his visual field, so to speak, and he brings them within the visual (and aural) field of his reader as well, where they can be seen or heard and thought about.

This is a rare quality. Normally when we speak, we use our language in a wholly unselfconscious way, "to say what we think," or "to do what we want." But Augustine knows that what he thinks and what he wants are not just facts, but imply judgments and choices, which are themselves at least partly hidden in the recesses of the self—in one's own self, and the selves of others too. Augustine is interested in what he is doing when he engages in the activities he describes—praising, knowing, invoking, believing, hearing—and he teaches us to be interested in such things ourselves.

We are thus in the presence of a mind that is capable of attending to and thinking about its own language, its own activities of language. This very fact is essential to the meaning of the *Confessions*. One might say that in this way he is exposing to us, and to himself, his very soul—the soul the transformation of which is his deepest subject.

As for us, Augustine is going to ask us to look with fresh eyes at what we ourselves do when we engage in these activities—a looking that leads to questioning, and a questioning that leads to more questioning.[8] This time Augustine ends up on what seems firm ground, the faith that enables him to hear the preaching, to believe, to know, to call, to praise. But where does this faith come from? He does not know. It is simply a gift of God, as he is shortly to say of life itself. Is it possible that this word defines the central objective of the *Confessions*, namely, to explain how it is that this mysterious thing called "faith" happened to him and what it has meant?

## LATIN ONCE MORE

We will soon explore that question, but first I want to come back once more to Latin, and ask you what you think of your experience of that language in what you have read in this book so far. Unless you have studied Latin, I expect that for you it retains a permanent sense of foreignness. You may have little confidence that you could read any Latin sentence on your own, let alone one of the complex constructions we have seen Augustine create. Perhaps you find yourself thinking that all this Latin is really beside the point. "I cannot read it and trying to do so just bogs me down."

That would be completely understandable, but if that is what you are feeling let me suggest that you imagine what this book would have been like without the Latin. Suppose we had in this book just my translations of particular sentences, followed by the questions and thoughts that follow. (Take a look at an actual instance in this chapter and ask yourself whether that would have been possible.)

Are my thoughts and questions generated in part by Augustine's Latin? Is Latin in that sense essential to the meaning of his sentences? If you took away all the Latin, and everything the Latin suggests by way of commentary and question, all that would be left is a translation of a few sentences into English. What could those sentences possibly mean? Here think once more about the translations we considered in the last chapter.

We may well be frustrated, but might that frustration be a crucial part of our coming closer to an understanding, to a real reading, of what Augustine has written?

There is another aspect of what we have done, mentioned in the Preface. To insist on the Latin is to insist on what you cannot understand. It is not just you. I cannot understand Latin in the effortless way I understand much that is written in English. There is before us the mystery of what we cannot quite grasp, the mystery of human expression. That mystery is part of the experience of reading this book. Is the acknowledgement of foreignness really an important part of the text for us?

To think again about translations, imagine that you were asked to write a translation of what we have read so far. How would you define your objective in making the translation? Would it be to create a text in idiomatic English that would read as smoothly or naturally as though it had actually been written by a native English speaker just last year? What would that look like? It is impossible even to imagine I think.

Occasionally one will read a novel translated from another language in such a way that you can imagine the translator wanted it to sound and be completely familiar to us, but it does not work. Other translators, more wisely I think, try to create a text that is intelligible in English, but one in which some of the strangeness, the foreignness, the difficulty of the original is still present. In reading a translation that works this way, say with the text of *War and Peace*, one would never forget that it is a Russian novel one is reading. This is a way of suggesting, for your consideration, that the very opacity of the Latin makes an important contribution to our understanding of the *Confessions* itself.

Likewise, and again as I said in the Preface, an important part of our experience as readers lies in the slowness with which we proceed, as if we were reading parts of a poem. This way of working invites us not only to read, but to reread, with the hope that as we do that particularly with the Latin we will find ourselves discovering more and more who Augustine is and what he is doing.

Our effort here is to bring ourselves into contact with the motions of Augustine's mind and imagination, and his heart too, as he writes this book. The meaning of the writing lies in the experience it offers, and we are trying to tune ourselves in such a way as to have a real access to that experience. My hope is that we have been training ourselves to hear his voice more fully.

Finally let me add a point: this book is written in English, which is the language in which I speak to you as a reader. English has its own structures, its own histories, its own rules of grammar and syntax, and its own things that can be done in it that cannot be done in any other language. It offers its own ways of being and functioning in the world, which are not those of Latin. Just as we cannot translate perfectly from Latin to English, so we cannot put into Latin what we say in our own language. Our experience in this book is not one simply of translation, or of translation and commentary, but of interaction, as the two languages assert themselves in different ways, to different ends, I hope in the process creating a new set of patterns of meaning.

## HOW DOES LANGUAGE WORK?
## BECKER'S VIEW

Another way to come at this is to ask what image of expression is implied in the ways we usually talk about writing. Often the idea seems to be that we have something called an "idea" in our head which we try to express in words as precisely as we can. If we succeed, our reader will have acquired exactly the idea we had, nothing more, nothing less.

This seems to me an utterly impossible view of what goes on when one person talks or writes to another. My late friend, the distinguished linguist Alton Becker, had another way, and I think an admirable one, of talking about what happens when we write or speak, one that greatly complicates his sense of what is going on.

Becker would sometimes demonstrate that sense for a class or audience this way: he would ask each person to write down in a single sentence what happened during the interval between the moment he would say "Now" and the moment he would say "Stop." During that interval he would walk from the side of the room to the table or desk at the front of the room, put down some books, and seat himself.

He would then ask people to read the sentences they had written, one at a time. The most amazing thing, he said, is that the sentences were always different from each other. This means that one thing that is constantly going on in our acts of expression is invention: saying something new or saying it differently. Speaking and writing are in this way akin to poetry. That is true not only for Augustine as he writes this book, but for you and me as we frame our responses to it.

Becker would ask of each sentence how it characterized him, as the subject of the sentence. Common possibilities were "you,"

"Professor Becker," "the teacher," "he," and "Pete." Each of these words implies a different relationship between the sentence-writer and the professor: formal, informal, deferential, familiar, distant, and so on. But in all cases they would create expectations about what comes next and how it is framed. You don't talk to "Pete" the way you would talk to "The Professor."

The definition of one's audience, and the implicit offer of a relationship with that person, is a part of every human expression. Every expression thus reflects or invites the formation of a mini-community. These can have many of the same qualities as larger and more self-conscious communities. We can ask of them: What and who have authority here, and what attitude are we asked to take with respect to that question? Is someone dominant? Is this relation just, or unjust? To what extent is the expression an enactment of the community in question or an invitation to respond in such a way as to confirm its existence? In a sense every sentence is a form of moral and political action.

In this sense every human expression is social. For us the questions this suggests would include: How does Augustine define himself by the way he addresses his two audiences, the God to whom he speaks as a matter of form and his human reader, who is in another sense perhaps his real audience? By the questions he raises, by the way he starts to think about them, by the experience he offers us? This is a complex and important question, and I would encourage you to go back over what we have read, in Latin if possible, and ask what social relation Augustine seeks to establish with you—and with the other audience of his book as well, the Lord he addresses. How fully can you translate this social dimension into English?

A second dimension of all expression is what Becker calls "structural," by which he means the writer's use of the structure of his language looked at as a syntactic and grammatical system.

Thus you can take one of Augustine's sentences and ask what happens when you cast it into another linguistic structure, for example English—or some other language you happen to know. What does Augustine do with that structure? How could you represent that in English? (This is the dimension of meaning that we have been considering when we think of the way in which Latin works as an inflected language.)

A third dimension is what Becker calls "prior texts," that is the writer's use, directly or indirectly, of material from the relevant culture, where he asks: What does that use mean? In what we have read the most obvious use of prior texts is with respect to the Psalms and other scriptural texts, which Augustine uses without citing, sometimes changing them a little, sometimes a lot. This is also a way in which he defines his reader, as someone who will pick up these references, or some of them, and want to see them given meaning and form in a new context. References of this kind will continue, with other texts from the Christian past, especially when we get to the last three books, which are largely about how to read the Scriptures. Here Augustine demonstrates the kind of relation he thinks his readers should have with the sacred texts of the Bible. Indeed, as we have said, we can look at the *Confessions* as itself a kind of psalm for a new era. This theme will become more explicit later on, especially in the last three books, where the question is what Scripture is and how it should be read.

But that is not all. There were biographies and autobiographies in the ancient world, and one question the reader is invited to ask is how this one is similar to the others, how different, and what these things mean. (On this dimension of meaning I am afraid I do not have any relevant knowledge.)

A fourth dimension is what Becker calls "medial," evoking our experience that it matters how things are expressed physically. Compare a marriage proposal on scented purple paper and

"JANE, WILL YOU MARRY ME, LOVE, JEFF" on a sign towed by an airplane over the football stadium.

In Augustine's case, his text was probably oral to start with, copied by stenographer onto papyrus paper, then edited, then turned into a book by being read to a roomful of people held in slavery who would produce either scrolls or the early books called codices. This process of duplication might be repeated several times. The finished product would be sent to people elsewhere in the Roman world who according to custom would gather for group readings of the text. How does our knowledge of this means of production affect the way the text works in our minds? Does it really matter whether product was a set of scrolls or a set of codices?

The next dimension is "silence," which is far more present in our lives with language than we might think. First, there has to be silence sometime, because no one can go on forever, whether in talking or writing. A play has to have a last act, a novel a last chapter. Then, in every single expression we utter we decide to put it this way, not that, and in doing so are being silent about the rejected alternative. Or maybe not so silent, if that alternative is an obvious one, so that the reader or listener will say to themselves, Why did she leave that out? What was she saying? A common example from ordinary life might be: Why did she not say "thank you"? What did that silence say? All our utterances are surrounded by silence, often a speaking or meaningful silence.

The final dimension is what Becker calls "nature," by which he means the world outside the text, including sun and rain, desert and mountain, time and space, but also other things you come up against, such as, in Augustine's case, the violence of religious parties in North Africa.[9] How does Augustine imagine the world, and how does he ask you to do so? As the creation of God? But what does that mean? What is the place of weather in what he writes, or the sea or the mountain, the tree or the garden?

The way all this relates to translation is that to Becker's way of thinking each expression drives its meaning from the way it acts in relation to six different contexts: social, structural, medial, prior textual, silential, and natural. Its meaning lies in what it does simultaneously in each of these contexts, and in the expectations it generates. Speech, oral or written, is never simply the statement of an idea, but always an engagement, or non-engagement, in six different directions at once. He thus offers us a way of seeing speech as both inherently creative and always multivocal.[10]

Becker is attempting to come to terms with the complexity and difficulty of thinking about language. His is not the only approach, to put it mildly. Do you have the beginnings of an approach yourself?

When we now return to Augustine's text, let me suggest that you bring to it whatever thoughts and perceptions this section may have stimulated in you. I hope you are moving in the direction of seeing not only the act of translation but reading itself as a more complex, interesting, and challenging activity than is usually recognized.

Here is a mini-exam to test what you can do. You in some sense know what "LOL" means in a message sent by computer. Can you explain what you know about this expression in ordinary English? Can you translate it into French or German or some other language you happen to know? What happens when you try? Does it work? If so, how? If not, why not?

## THE INVOCATION

Before this digression on the Latin language and translation, we saw that Augustine had arrived at a point where he could see that it was his faith that gave him the impulse to call on God.

That is helpful, but it does not tell him how that calling can be imagined or achieved, nor does it tell him what that faith really is or where it comes from. Maybe we—and he—can only discover what he means as he enacts it in the way he writes—in the way he speaks to and about God, to and about other people, to and about his reader?

In returning now to the text of the *Confessions* we see him moving from one way of thinking and talking, one language game, to another.

> *Et quomodo invocabo Deum meum, Deum et Dominum meum,*
> And how shall I call upon my God, my God and my Lord,
>
> *quoniam utique in me ipsum eum vocabo, cum invocabo eum?*
> because surely I shall call him into myself when I invoke him?[11]

For Augustine it is clear that when he does call upon God he will call him *into himself.* This is not obvious to us, to say the least: Why does "calling upon" mean "calling into"? One answer is built into the Latin verb, *in-voco,* which etymologically means "call into." The word had in fact come to mean pretty much what our version of it means today, namely "invoke" or "call upon." But Augustine revives the original meaning as a way of expressing his sense that calling upon God is not just saluting him from afar, or attracting his attention, or asking him to listen to a plea, but a way of calling him actually into oneself.[12] This way of imagining things presents serious difficulties:

> *Et quis locus est in me quo veniat in me Deus meus*
> And what place is there in me, where my God can come into me,

*quo Deus veniat*[13] *in me, Deus qui fecit caelum et terram?*
where God can come into me, God who made heaven and
earth?

How can God can possibly "come within" him? In thinking
about this question, as we shall see, Augustine represents himself as captured by a way of thinking about God, and himself,
that is fundamentally material and often quantitative. In fact,
Augustine the composer of this text had long ago left behind
this language, this way of thinking, but as the narrator he uses
it here both because he was once taken with it—it is a part
of the story of Augustine, the pilgrim, whose life-story is told
in this book—and because his reader may find it forceful and
familiar.

*Itane, Domine Deus meus*
Is it really so, O Lord, my God?

*Est quicquam in me quod capiat te? An vero caelum et terra,*
there anything in me which can hold you? Or do heaven and
earth

\* \* \*

*quae fecisti et in quibus me fecisti, capiunt te?*
which you made and in which you made me, contain you?

*An quia sine te non esset quidquid est, fit ut quidquid est capiat te?*
or since without you nothing that exists would exist, is it
possible that anything could contain you?

The implied answer is negative, which complicates his prayer of
invocation.

Next he shifts ground, looking now at his own question with critical eyes:

> *Quoniam itaque et ego sum, quid peto ut venias in me,*
> Since I in fact exist, what do I ask when I ask that you should come into me,
>
> *qui non essem nisi esses in me? . . .*
> who would not exist unless you were in me? . . .
>
> *An potius non essem nisi essem in te,*
> Or rather, I would not exist unless I existed in you,
>
> *ex quo omnia, per quem omnia, in quo omnia?*
> from whom is all, through whom is all, in whom is all?
> (1.2.2)[14]

The point here is that in some sense God is already in him, so it makes no sense to call him in; or, looked at the other way around, he is always in God, from whom, by whom, and in whom is everything. This is a line of thought, shaped by a materialistic view of the universe (derived from the Manicheans) that runs out in a kind of impossibility.[15]

This does not keep him from continuing to think in quantitative ways. He quotes the line in Jeremiah where God says, in the Latin text, *Caelum et terram impleo,* "Do I not fill heaven and earth?" (Jer. 23:24). Augustine then asks:

> *Capiunt ergone te caelum et terra, quoniam tu imples ea?*
> Do heaven and earth contain you because you fill them?
>
> *An imples et restat, quoniam non te capiunt?*
> Or do you fill [them] and something remains because they do not contain you?

*Et quo refundis quidquid impleto caelo et terra restat ex te?*
And when heaven and earth are full where do you pour
whatever remains of your self?

*An non opus habes ut quoquam continearis, qui contines omnia,*
Or have you no need to be contained [by something], you
who contain all things

*quoniam quae imples continendo imples?*
because what you fill you fill by containing?
(1.3.3)

The image he is both using and criticizing here is that God is a
substance, like water, that needs to be contained in a vessel, or it
will just run out formlessly. His last question is rhetorical in the
sense that it is clear that the right answer is that the one who
contains everything has himself no need to be contained.[16]

The line of thought we have been tracing out is of great importance in Augustine's life, and in this book, because what he is
performing for us here is the impossibility of conceiving of God
in quantitative or material terms. Augustine's efforts as writer to
rationalize this way of thinking end up in impossible distinctions
and confusions. For us too, as our mind pursues these materialistic
questions it gets hopelessly tangled up in itself.

I think the point of Augustine the narrator here is to engage
us in the tangles and confusions that once beset him, in such a
way as to teach us by our own experience both that the materialistic conception of God is an utter failure yet that the questions
it stimulates are important ones.

This passage is in part a refutation of the Manichees, to whose
religion Augustine was devoted for nearly a decade and who had
a decidedly material and quantitative image of God.

Augustine the narrator refutes this position before it becomes
relevant in the story of the life of Augustine the pilgrim, and

in that sense prematurely; at the same time, he is refuting it in a sense too late, long after the questions he states so forcefully have ceased to become living questions to the actual Augustine. This is a clear instance of the difference among the Augustines we meet in this text: the Augustine who is speaking here as narrator is neither the Augustine who is the main character in the story (Augustine the pilgrim) nor is he Augustine the composer, who creates the whole text, in which the other two Augustines are created characters, and is throughout looking back over his life and his text, as one who has learned what it has to teach; rather, it is the voice of Augustine the narrator who, in our terms a little like a novelist, is enacting before us, and at the same time resisting, a twisted way of thinking by which the young Augustine was to be entranced, but out of which Augustine the narrator had emerged long before the book was begun. There is a deep distance here between the pilgrim and the narrator, both of whom are created by Augustine the composer. It might be called an instance of structural irony.

The larger bearing of this passage is upon Augustine's commitment to his own intellectual capacities, and hence to the activities not only of Manicheism but also of rhetoric, then of philosophy, the limits of which he will in the course of the book discover and explicate. Here Augustine the narrator, is pretending not to know what in fact he knows, in order to give us the experience of being entangled in a kind of reasoning that he thinks will have to be superseded if we are to have a good way of talking about God or indeed ourselves.

## DESCRIBING GOD (1.4.4)

In the few paragraphs we have been examining the Invocation gives rise to the essential question, *Quid es ergo, Deus meus?* or

"What are you, my God?" (1.4.4). Not a quantity, not a container, not something divided up in the creation, not something outside us, but . . . what? His next response is a beautiful prose poem, of which even one who knows no Latin can get some idea, especially from the "*-issime*" words which mark adjectives in the superlative mode:

*Summe, optime, potentissime, omnipotentissime, misericord-issime et iustissime, secretissime et praesentissime, pulcher-rime et fortissime, stabilis et incomprehensibilis, immutabilis mutans omnia, numquam novus numquam vetus, innovans omnia et in vetustatem perducens superbos et nesciunt. Sem-per agens semper quietus, conligens et non egens, portans et implens et protegens, creans et nutriens et perficiens, quaerens cum nihil desit tibi. Amas nec aestuas, zelas et securus es, pae-nitet te et non doles, irasceris et tranquillus es, opera mutas nec mutas consilium, recipis quod invenis et numquam amisisti. Numquam inops et gaudes lucris, numquam avarus et usuras exigis, supererogatur tibi ut debeas: et quis habet quicquam non tuum? Reddis debita nulli debens, donas debita nihil perdens.*

The first unit of this long paragraph is a string of words in what is called the vocative case, which marks the person spoken to, in this case obviously God:

Highest, best, most powerful, most all-powerful, most compas-sionate and most just, most hidden and most present, most beau-tiful and most mighty, stable and incomprehensible, yourself unchanging but changing all things, never new, never old, making all things new, leading the proud to be old without their knowl-edge; always acting, always at rest, collecting and not needing, bearing and filling and protecting, creating and nourishing and perfecting, searching when nothing is lacking for you. You love and do not burn, you love ardently but are unshaken, you regret what you have done,[17] but do not sorrow, you are angry yet at peace, you change your works but never change your plan; you receive what you find yet you have never lost anything; never poor, yet you take joy in wealth, never avaricious yet you demand payment of debts; payment is made to you beyond anything expected, so that you should owe a debt, yet who has anything that is not yours? You pay the debts, though you owe nothing, you give away what is owed you but lose nothing.

(1.4.4)

You might start by reading aloud the first sentence of this passage, maybe after having read the translation, if you need it. Read it aloud not in a mechanical way, but as if you meant every word—as if you were on stage, reading to the people. I hope you can hear and see its beauty. Perhaps you will work your way through the whole poem, and in doing so feel some of the force and power of the Latin.

This is not just a string of superlatives, expressing the sublime qualities of the person of God. For soon after those superlatives there are participles—"changing," "making," "acting," "creating," "nourishing," and so on—and then there are finite verbs of which God is the subject: "You love and do not burn," "You regret what you have done but do not sorrow," and finally a reiteration of the fact that God cannot be thought of in quantitative terms: "You give away what is owed you but lose nothing." There is thus a transformation in this passage, a movement, by which the God whom he is addressing is defined at first by superlative labels, but at the end by his action in the world.

It might be good for you to work through the whole poem, listening to its voices and its movements. In particular, try to see how the tensions and inconsistencies and contradictions work to make it impossible to imagine a set of true propositions about God. He cannot be reduced to a system, even a theological one. If that is right, it means that for Augustine God has to be found somewhere else, I think in the experience of his own heart and mind and soul; and for us, in the experiences in each dimension that he offers his reader.

After writing this prose-poem Augustine asks a question that is crucial to the understanding of the whole of the *Confessions*:

> *Et quid diximus, Deus meus, vita mea, dulcedo mea sancta,*
> and what have we said, my God, my life, my holy sweetness,
>
> *aut quid dicit aliquis cum de te dicit?*
> or what does anyone say when he speaks about you?
>
> *Et vae tacentibus de te,*
> Yet woe to those who are silent about you
>
> *quoniam loquaces muti sunt.*
> Because those who speak [about you] say nothing.[18]
> (1.4.4)

That is, this beautiful paragraph, the best thing that Augustine can write, ultimately fails to express or define or describe God. The effort is doomed to failure. This means that everything Augustine has done, or will do, with words in this book rests on the fundamental truth that the realities with which he is concerned are beyond his mind, his language, his imagination. He is always trying the impossible.[19]

But it is necessary to try, as he says in the next sentence: *Et vae tacentibus de te, quoniam loquaces muti sunt*: "Yet woe to those who are silent about you, for when they talk about you they say nothing." In other words, it is impossible to talk about you, to talk with you, to talk about our inner experience of you; but it is at the same time necessary to do these things as well as we can. This combination of impossibility and necessity defines the essential task he faces both as the writer of this book and as the soul from which it all emanates. The ineffability of God means Augustine cannot describe or explain him, but he continues to speak to him. As for us, he tells us, we must learn to speak not about God but to God.

## WHO WILL GIVE IT TO ME. . . ? (1.5.5–1.6.7)

In this context his next question has real depth and feeling:

> *Quis mihi dabit adquiescere in te?*
> Who will give it to me that I may rest in you?

> *Quis dabit mihi ut venias in cor meum et inebries illud,*
> Who will give it me that you may come into my heart and intoxicate it,

> *ut obliviscar mala mea et unum bonum meum amplectar, te?*
> so that I may forget my evils and embrace my one good, which is you?"

> *Quid mihi es? Miserere ut loquar.*
> What are you to me? Have compassion on me that I may speak.
> (1.5.5)

In the last sentence he is asking God's compassion and help that he may speak to the questions he has just stated, questions which he has come to see are impossible to answer.

He continues this theme:

> *Quid tibi sum ipse, ut amari te iubeas ad me*
> What am I to you that you order me to love you,
>
> *et, nisi faciam, irascaris mihi*
> and if I do not, you are angry with me
>
> *et mineris ingentes miserias?*
> and threaten me with immense sufferings,
>
> *Parvane ipsa est si non amem te?*
> Is it a small suffering [for me] if I do not love you?
> (1.5.5.)

These sentences introduce, quietly and without fanfare, the essential topic of love: God's love for him, his love for God. This is a matter of reality, not theory, and a reality to which no language is adequate. If it is impossible to say where faith comes from, or the desire to praise, it is even more impossible to say where love comes from.

But he is now in a position from which he can ask God to speak to him and to declare that he is his salvation:

> *Ei mihi! Dic mihi per miserationes tuas, Domine Deus meus,*
> Alas for me! Tell me through your compassion, my Lord God,
>
> *quid sis mihi. Dic animae meae, "Salus tua ego sum":*[20]
> what you are to me? Tell my soul: "I am your salvation."
>
> *sic dic ut audiam. Ecce aures cordis mei ante te, Domine.*
> Say it so that I may hear it. Behold the ears of my heart before you, Lord.

*Aperi eas et dic animae meae, "Salus tua ego sum."*
Open them and say to my soul, "I am your salvation."

*Curram post vocem hanc et apprehendam te.*
I will run after that voice and grasp you.

*Noli abscondere a me faciem tuam; moriar, ne moriar, ut eam videam.*
Do not hide your face from me; let me die, lest I die, so that I may see your face.
(1.5.5)

He concludes the Invocation by asking God to allow him to speak:

*Sed tamen sine me loqui apud misericordiam tuam,*
But nonetheless allow me to speak before your compassion,

*me terram et cinerem sine tamen loqui*
earth and ashes as I am,[21] allow me to speak.
(1.6.7)

Augustine has of course been speaking from the beginning of the *Confessions,* so this should be read as a prayer not that he be allowed to address God, but that he be allowed to tell his story, to represent his own life and developing character. He has concluded the invocation of his God, his version of the ancient poets' muse, and is now in a position from which he can begin to tell the story of his life.

# 4

## REMEMBERING EARLY
## CHILDHOOD AND LANGUAGE
## BREAKING DOWN (BOOK 1)

WE HAVE NOW READ TOGETHER the first three sentences of Book 1 and the few pages that constitute what I have called the Invocation. Now, as I said at the end of the last chapter, we are to begin the story of Augustine's life. In what follows we will continue to have the Latin before us, but I shall do much less by way of explication, except occasionally in the footnotes. Let me encourage you still to read the Latin aloud each time, for as you do that I think you will find yourself gradually feeling more comfortable with the language. It will seem less strange. And to this end let me suggest that you acquire a small Latin dictionary, like the excellent *Langenscheidt's Pocket Latin Dictionary*, and use it from time to time, as you find yourself wanting to do that.

The obvious way to proceed would be for me to summarize the story, then focus on some critical moments in it. But in Book 1 of the *Confessions*, as in several, there is not much narrative of a usual kind, which means there is very little story to summarize, which in turn means that the main meaning of the book cannot be in the narrative but must be somewhere else.

If we were to try a summary of the rest of Book 1 (which is about his infancy), it might run like this: Augustine knows that he was born but has no idea where he came from. He does not remember his infancy, but assumes that he was self-centered, as babies normally are. He learned to talk, partly by learning the names of things, partly by engaging in what we today might call "language games"; when he was a little older he went to school, where he was beaten if he did not learn his lessons. He loved to win at games. At one point he fell ill, and begged to be baptized, in case he should die; but he recovered, and no longer wanted baptism.[1] He was trained in Latin literature, which he loved. He hated Greek. He won a prize for a speech, not for the substance of what he said, but for its rhetorical excellence, and was proud of his achievement. He ends Book 1 with heartfelt thanksgiving that he has received the mysterious gift of life.

Such are the bare bones of what we would think of as the "story" of his early life. But what does this story mean? The outline I have given above certainly does not tell us. In fact I think Augustine writes in such a way as to tell us that no such outline could possibly carry the meaning he wishes to express, for that meaning lies not simply in the narrative of young Augustine's existence, but in the shifts and transformations at work in the mind and feelings both of that young person and of the other Augustine, the one who is writing this book.

You might be inclined to think that these early years do not matter much and that attention to them must be much less fruitful than work we do with the older Augustine. I think that in fact the early years are crucial, for they reveal the origins of many of the issues and concerns and problems that run throughout his life.

In this book of the *Confessions*, as in all of them, some digging and thinking is required even to establish the "bare facts" I mentioned above. Augustine often leaves out what we would regard as the details and explanations necessary to make the narrative cohere. In this respect it may seem that he really is writing to God, who knows all these things, not human readers who need that kind of help. But that is not quite right: even to God he does not want to write the kind of text that can be reduced to a narrative outline, as I have just pretended to do. In fact it is an important part of the meaning of what Augustine has written that it cannot be reduced to a story in such a way.

So how do we read it? Maybe not as a story at all, but rather as if it were a piece of music, in which what matters are the melodies and harmonies, the developments, the transitions, and ultimately the shifts and transformations it achieves, in itself and in us—especially the shifts and transformations in Augustine's relation to the God to whom he is speaking, to his reader, and to the language that seems to break down in his hands as he uses it.

It is important, as I have said, to remember that there are at least three dramas here, each with a different Augustine as its central figure: the drama of the life of Augustine the pilgrim, as it is told from his birth to his departure for Africa after his conversion; the drama expressed in the voices and shifts of Augustine the narrator; and the drama of Augustine the composer, who creates these other dramas from their starting point in the sentences with which the *Confessions* begins to an ending point we cannot now foresee.

What are the questions and difficulties out of which the text emerges, and how far, and in what way, can we expect them to be resolved? Based on the Invocation, we can imagine that these will have to do in part with the nature of the gestures or motions Augustine is able to make in his language, their appropriateness and adequacy (or not), and the relations and sequences he establishes among them. Implicit in these gestures—since he is speaking to God—are immense questions having to do with the way he conceives of God and himself, and the relation between them, in the story itself, in the way the story is told, and in the composition as a whole. Likewise, since he is speaking to us, his readers, similar questions are raised about the way he conceives of himself, and us, and of the relation between us.

It is a fact to be welcomed that these questions, difficulties, and issues run straight through to the end of the whole of the *Confessions*, where they are advanced but still imperfectly resolved.

How then are we to approach what Augustine does here? It is important to see that his way of responding to these issues is not to describe them, much less their resolution, in words, but in the activity of language in which he, and we as his readers, engages. What cannot be described can be enacted.

## SPEAKING TO GOD (1.6.7)

Augustine begins this portion of Book 1, as we saw at the end of the last chapter, by asking God's leave to speak:

> *Sed tamen sine me loqui apud misericordiam tuam, me terram et cinerem*
> But allow me to speak before your compassion, I who am dust and ashes

Followed by an explanation I did not include before;

> *quoniam ecce misericordia tua est, non homo, inrisor meus, cui loquor.*
> because it is your compassion, not man, my mocker, to which I speak.[2]

*Et tu fortasse inrides me, sed conversus misereberis mei.*
though perhaps you deride me; but having turned you will
have compassion on me.
(1.6.7)

Notice the power of the word *conversus* ("having turned"), with
all of its overtones of "conversion." Augustine is saying, in effect,
"Though you are indeed mocking me now, you will in time turn
toward me and treat me with compassion"—in this gesture
reversing the usual roles of God and his follower.

Here, as often, Augustine's text makes discernible references to scriptural texts. The phrase "dust and ashes" goes back
to Genesis 18:27, the idea that God "mocks" him goes back to
Psalm. 2:4, the image of God "turning and having compassion"
goes back to Jeremiah 12:15.[3] In this weaving of the Scriptures
into the background of his text Augustine is not simply speaking the language of his culture—trying to reach God across an
abyss—but speaking, or at least alluding to, what he regards
as God's own language, as we saw him do in the opening
sentence of the *Confessions*. In this sense he creates a text that
is partly his, partly God's, and in doing so mirrors his awareness, expressed in the Invocation, that God is within him, he is
within God, all the time.[4]

This opening is an extraordinary act of trust[5] on Augustine's
part. He is saying what he knows could be ridiculed—what
would surely be ridiculed by a certain kind of person—to the
God who does deride him, but will turn and have compassion on
him. This is a God whose *misericordia* is utterly dependable, and
Augustine is a person who knows this about him. That is why he
can speak to him as he does.

His deepest definition of God is perhaps implicit in these
words, as it is in the opening lines of the *Confessions* itself,

namely, that he is the one to whom Augustine can speak, and, so far as he is able, can speak the truth. It is his sense that his God is a God of compassion that makes it possible for him to speak to him as he does, to write this book. This knowledge—where does it come from?—is the foundation of all that happens here.

Think how far this is from the kind of religious life that conceives of its central feature as something called "belief," and then, on the basis of appropriately reasoned arguments, concludes that a God indeed exists. If this is what someone does, they will feel the need to describe this God, almost by definition an impossible task. By contrast Augustine does not claim to be able to define or understand God; but he can talk to him, as he shows throughout the *Confessions*.

He starts with the knowledge of God's reality and presence and compassion, which is obviously an immense gift to him. In doing so he reverses the common order in which this kind of knowledge is acquired, which begins with the self, and the knowledge of the self, then through reason and experience finds its way to God, or to some other ultimate truth. Augustine starts with the God to whom he knows how to speak.

But this fact presents a question: Why is the knowledge of God's trustworthy compassion not enough for him? If Augustine knows that, why does he have to say or write anything more? Or, as we asked earlier, why is it not enough to praise him, as the opening words so eloquently do: *Magnus es, Domine, et laudabilis valde.*

One way to try to find an answer would be to look at the ways in which Augustine in fact speaks to God as he continues from that opening. How might we characterize what he does?

Here the title of his work, *Confessions* (or, in Latin: *Confessiones*), is of some help, for this title is derived from the verb, *confiteor*, which means something like: "confess," "admit," "assert," "own," or "acknowledge." But what is Augustine confessing or acknowledging, and to what end is he doing so? What is this act of confession? Why in fact is he writing this book?

This is the question to which the whole *Confessions* is a response. But one thing is already clear, that in the world Augustine is creating in this book, the person to whom he speaks when he engages in the activity of confession is God. As he writes his book, that is, he is simultaneously defining the activity of confession and the God to whom he confesses, all in relation to each other. The character of God shapes the practice of confession; the practice of confession gives definition to the God to whom he is speaking.

Is it in fact the central aim of Augustine's book to establish this relation with God, to give it shape and meaning in his own experience, and in this text? Is it a sense of this possibility, of this as yet imperfectly defined relationship, that makes the relation of trust he already has in some way not enough?

## INFANCY (1.6.7)

As we have seen in the Invocation, Augustine established himself as speaking to God, as praising God. But what exactly does he wish to say, and why? We know it will be a life story, but what kind of life story? In a sense this is the beginning of the *Confessions* proper.

> *Quid enim est quod volo dicere, Domine,*
> What is it that I wish to say, Lord
>
> *nisi quia nescio unde venerim huc,*
> except that I do not know whence I have come here

*in istam dico vitam mortalem an mortem vitalem? Nescio*
into this mortal life, as I call it, or living death? I do not
know.

(1.6.7)

Augustine starts with what he does not know, and can never
know, which is how he came to exist at all. He shows us that
the "I" that is expressed in the speaking voice we hear as we read
has a deep hunger, a hunger it can express—or confess—without
embarrassment or defense, a hunger to know who he is.

This Augustine does not understand God—no one can do
that—but he does in some sense know him, knows him well
enough to speak to him. We have seen that he knows that God
is worthy of praise and that his compassion is beyond question.
But he does not know who he himself is. Part of the purpose
of the *Confessions*, then, seems to be to help him discover what
emerges only as he writes it: who he is—not only who he was
as a child or young man, but, more important, who he is now as
the person engaging with God and his reader in this book, as
the person he is making himself as he writes. We can se that this
person is not a wholly independent or autonomous being, but
one who lives constantly in relation to the God he addresses and
who is fully defined only in that relation—a relation between
two persons, God and Augustine, our sense of neither of whom
can be reduced to intellectual understanding.

\* \* \*

There is a danger that we will think of Augustine in twenty-
first-century terms, as though he lived in a world in which self-
discovery and self-fulfillment are among the most validated
cultural activities—as though he were engaged in a great contemporary quest to discover the self, the self that is the essential

unit of reality. Likewise, we might make the mistake of reading his time as a Manichee, for example, as if it were just like a certain sort of modern person's term as a Zen Buddhist, or a vegan, before he or she became wise and found fulfillment—that is, as an expression of a generally accepted set of impulses having to do with the discovery and expression of the "self."

This means that we have to be careful, as we read, not simply to see Augustine in terms that are easy for us, but to try to perceive what he is actually saying and doing—to the extent we can do so over the cultural and linguistic and temporal chasm that divides us. For you as a reader it means that you have to be alert to catch me when I make this mistake, and correct me as well as you can.[6]

As Augustine thinks about his early life, then, his starting point is that he does not know where he came from, and that he wishes he did. Most of us have probably wondered about where we came from, and why, but we usually put the question aside. (Why do you suppose we put it aside? Why does Augustine not do so? Why it is important to him that he does not know where he came from?)

Again and again in his treatment of his early life Augustine will say that he does not know, or does not remember, and as I suggested in chapter 1, the things he does not know will grow more numerous and important as the *Confessions* proceeds, until almost all he really does know is that God exists and is within him. This gradual recognition of fundamental ignorance and failing understanding is one of the great movements of the *Confessions* as a whole. Here we get a taste of it, but only a taste. As we proceed through this work, Augustine's confessions of ignorance will gradually take on new and deeper significance.

Another way to put this point is to say that the sentence, *nescio*, "I do not know," changes its meaning over the course of the *Confessions*. If we were to read the whole thing together, we would find that the same is true of many other sentences and their key terms.

## LIFE AS A GIFT (1.6.7–1.6.10)

Though Augustine cannot remember, he in a sense knows—by inference, not directly—from his parents, that

> *susceperunt me consolationes miserationum tuarum*
> the consolations of your compassion have sustained me
>
> *sicut audivi a parentibus carnis meae,*
> as I heard from the parents of my flesh,[7]
>
> *ex quo et in qua me formasti in tempore: non enim ego memini.*
> from whom and in whom you have formed me in the world
> of time—I do not remember this.
> (1.6.7)

Thus when he was fed by milk from his mother or a nurse, it was not they who decided to produce the milk, but God who brought it forth in them; similarly, God gave Augustine the capacity to know when he had had enough, just as he gave the nurses the instinctive wisdom to give him the milk they had been given. This seemingly trivial fact will come to have great significance in the *Confessions* as a whole, for Augustine is revealing here that he and the nurses both have a kind of knowledge—how to nurse and when to stop—that cannot be explained or rationalized. This is not the kind of knowledge that his formal education and training will give him, knowledge as a kind of power, or knowledge as the result of intellectual work, but something much deeper, more intimate and mysterious. It is in fact knowledge of this kind that will carry him into his conversion, and into his knowledge that God exists and is within him.

He was surrounded with goodness, goodness from God, of which milk is offered as an example, milk that was itself a gift from God.

> *Nam bonum erat eis bonum meum ex eis,*
> For the good for me that came from them was good for
> them too,
>
> *quod ex eis non sed per eas erat.*
> which came *from* them, but not *through* them.[8]
> (1.6.7)

The world that he does not know and cannot understand is here defined as a source of blessing, of gifts, to him and to others—including the gift of life and all that is required to support it. Then this central statement:

> *Ex te quippe bona omnia, Deus,*
> All good things surely come from you, O God,
>
> *et ex Deo meo salus mihi universa*
> and from my God is my whole well-being [or salvation].[9]
> (1.6.7)

He thus begins by recognizing his complete dependence as a created being upon the goodness of God, of the world, and of other people.

Next, he believes, he began to smile: *post et ridere coepi, dormiens primo, deinde vigilans,* "Afterward I began to smile, at first while sleeping, then when awake" (1.6.8). He makes little of this, saying only that this is one of the things he does not remember but knows by report from others, confirmed by his experience of watching other babies.

But I think it is significant. First, ask yourself this, as every parent must have asked himself or herself: What is happening when the baby smiles when asleep? One view is that this is only a mechanical response to digestive processes, without any affective or expressive elements. But no parent ever believed this about their baby. It is clear at least to the parents that the baby is having interior experiences of some kind, perhaps a kind of dreaming, perhaps something else, maybe a kind of memory. In the context of the *Confessions* this is another image of a person having a kind of knowledge, a kind of life, that is not apprehensible by what is usually called the mind. This kind of life, which cannot be remembered, cannot be reasoned, cannot be understood, is foundational for human experience. Without it we would not exist. It is who we are at the core. It is the kind of knowledge that will ultimately lead to Augustine's conversion, knowledge that he celebrates in his great passages about the nature of time and memory.

Then, as his awareness increased, he developed clearer desires and the wish to express them:

*Et ecce paulatim sentiebam ubi essem,*
And lo! By small steps I became aware of where I was

*et voluntates meas volebam ostendere eis per quos implerentur*[10],
and I wished to display my desires to those by whom they might be fulfilled

*et non poteram, quia illae intus errant,*
but I was not able, for those (desires) were within me

*foris autem illi, nec ullo suo sensu valebant introire in animam meam.*

and those people [*illi*] were outside me, and in no way were they able to enter into my soul.

(1.6.8)

He is imagining, or remembering, a gap between his inner life and other people, a gap he had no way of bridging. His way of defining this gap echoes what he earlier said about invocation, that he was calling God into his soul, for here the sort of understanding he wishes he had is put in similar terms: "in no way were they able to enter into my soul," that is, the grown-ups could not discover on their own what he was wishing and feeling and thinking.

How is such a gap ever to be closed? Never completely, most of us believe; but valuable relations can be established by making connections, sometimes intimate ones, through language and other gestures. (Is it one of the purposes of the *Confessions* to close this gap with us as readers, to bring us within his soul, not his childish soul but his mature one? Or to bring him within our souls?)

At the stage of life Augustine is talking about here he still cannot speak. But look at how much he already has: he knows how to suck at the breast, he knows how to stop when he has had enough. He has desires and wishes, arising within him, not coming from outside, and he has the larger desire to communicate these, but is unable. All this he has by nature, as a gift of his being. None of it is his creation.

When he was frustrated he would get fussy and cry, and like other infants demand what he wanted by throwing himself about:

*Et cum mihi non obtemperabatur*
And when I was not obeyed

*vel non intellecto vel ne obesset,*
either because I was not understood or lest something
should injure me,

*indignabar non subditis maioribus et liberis non servientibus,*
I was indignant with the grown-ups who were not
submissive and the children who did not obey me,

*et me de illis flendo vindicabam.*
and I avenged myself on them by weeping.
(1.6.8)

He says all this on the basis not of his own memory but of what
he was told by his parents, or has observed in other children:
*Nam ista mea non memini,* "For I do not remember these things"
(1.6.8). What kind of knowledge is this, then?

This question is important in part because it has a connection to an activity that may seem very different, the reading of
Scripture. For here too we are asked to believe something not
because we were there, or remember, but because the witnesses
and scribes reported in Scripture are reliable and authoritative.[11]
Yet, as Augustine confirms what he is told by his parents when
he sees other children behaving as they say he behaved, so too
with him and with us as readers of Scripture: our faith is not
blind or empty, but can often be confirmed by our own experience of the truth and vitality of what we read there—a fact
that is demonstrated for us by Augustine's own use of Scripture
throughout the *Confessions,* connecting directly both to his present thoughts and to his past experiences.

Instead of proceeding with an account of his growth and
what it meant, Augustine pauses to reflect on what he has just
said. *Et ecce infantia mea olim mortua est et ego vivo,* "Behold my
infancy is long dead and I am alive" (1.6.9).

Here he is stepping back to look at what he has just said, a move that is familiar to us from the Invocation and is highly characteristic of Augustine throughout the *Confessions*. As I said earlier, he has the rare ability of being able to say something, then to look at what he said with fresh eyes, and in this way put into question his assumptions, his language, and his mind.

Here his point is to capture a sense that as we pass through our lives, we leave behind what is now inaccessible and look forward to what cannot be known. This sense, gently adumbrated here, will gradually be intensified until he tells us later (in Book 11) that we are always in motion, moving from the past that has gone by to the future that is unknown, and experiencing only the infinitesimal moment that exists between what has passed out of existence and what is still to come. As we are living we are dying. This will become one of his grand themes.

Now he returns to a question he intimated above, namely, where he came from: *Dic mihi, utrum alicui aetati meae mortuae successerit infantia mea?*, "Tell me whether my infancy succeeded to some other state of my life, then dead" (1.6.9). Of course, he knows about pregnancy, but:

> *Quid ante hanc etiam, dulcedo mea, Deus meus?*
> Before that what was there, my sweetness, my God?
>
> *Fuine alicubi aut aliquis? Nam quis mihi dicat ista, non habeo;*
> Was I anywhere or anyone? For I have no one to tell me these things;
>
> *nec pater nec mater potuerunt, nec aliorum experimentum nec memoria mea. . . .*
> neither father nor mother could do it, nor my experience of others nor my memory. . . .

*Unde hoc tale animal nisi abs te, Domine?*
Where does such animal come from, if not from you, Lord?

*An quisquam se faciendi erit artifex?*
Or will anyone be the artisan of his own making?
(1.6.9–10)

From his ignorance about his own origins—his possible prior
existence, what his life in the womb was like—combined with
his awareness that he did not create himself, comes the beginning of what will be a profound intensification of his recognition
that his life is a sheer gift.

From this in turn comes a perhaps surprising humility, a sense
of severe limit on what we would call the ego. He, the smart-
est man in any room, had nothing to do with the creation of
his own existence. It is completely founded in grace. I think we
are to understand that it is in part this sense of life as a gift that
gives rise to the impulse to praise, to give thanks, with which he
begins the *Confessions*. Without it he could get nowhere. It is the
elemental fact of his existence. To put his last sentence in slightly
different terms: "No person makes their own soul." That we exist
is a foundational fact of our lives that we cannot comprehend.

He closes this section with a mystical celebration of the timelessness of the unchangeable God.

*Tu autem idem ipse es*
You however are always the same

*et omnia crastina atque ultra omniaque hesterna et retro*
beyond all tomorrows and back before all yesterdays

*hodie facies, hodie fecisti.*
you will make today, you have made today.

*Quid ad me, si quis non intellegat?*
What is my task, if someone does not understand?

*Gaudeat et ipse dicens, "quid est hoc?"*
Let him rejoice saying, "What is this?"

*Gaudeat etiam sic, et amet*
Let him thus rejoice and let him love you,

*non inveniendo invenire potius quam inveniendo non invenire te.*
finding you by not finding you, rather than by finding you
not to find you.
(1.6.10)


# THE SINS OF THE INFANT (1.7.11–1.7.12)

Augustine starts to tell us what he thinks to be a second foundational fact, namely, that he was never free from sin. But as he
does this, his account gets complicated in interesting ways.

He begins with a lament to God:

*Vae peccatis hominum! Et homo dicit haec, et misereris eius,*
Woe for the sins of man! A man says this, and you have
compassion for him

*quoniam tu fecisti eum et peccatum non fecisti in eo.*
because you made him and did not make the sin in him.
(1.7.11)

Here he establishes a basic theological position, that God creates humanity, but not the sin of humanity. Where then does sin
come from?

Instead of pursuing that question explicitly Augustine focuses on what he regards as the inherent self-centeredness of the baby, who can think only of their own needs. Most of us would not call this kind of selfishness a sin, but rather perhaps an age-appropriate disposition of the self. It is the sensible result of natural selection, essential to the successful growth and life of the child. Who can even imagine an infant having concern for others of the kind that we try so hard, often with little effect, to develop in ourselves as grown-ups?

*Quis me commemorat peccatum infantiae meae,*
Who reminds me of the sin of my infancy,

*quoniam nemo mundus a peccato coram te,*
because no one is pure of sin before you,

*nec infans cuius est unius diei vita super terram?*
not even an infant whose life is a single day on earth?

*Quis me commemorat?*
Who reminds me?

*An quilibet tantillus nunc parvulus, in quo video quod non meminimi de me?*
Or does any tiny little child [do this], in whom I can see what I do not remember about myself?
(1.7.11)

But in another mood Augustine himself denies that the baby's greed is in fact a kind of sin, although it would be in a grown-up.

*Tunc ergo reprehendenda faciebam,*
Then, therefore, I did things that were in principle reprehensible,

*sed quia reprehendentem intellegere non poteram,*
but because I was not able to understand the person
correcting me,

*nec mos reprehendi me nec ratio sinebat.*
neither custom nor reason permitted me to be blamed.
(1.7.11)

But in still another mood he says that he has himself seen a jeal-
ous baby looking with a bitter face at his sibling at his mother's
breast. This is sin, and it is everywhere.

*Sed blande tolerantur haec, non quia nulla vel parva,*
These things are tolerated readily, not because they are little
or nothing

*sed quia aetatis accessu peritura sunt.*
but because with advancing age they disappear.
(1.7.11)

This is proved by the fact that if older people behave this way
we know they are doing wrong: *Ita inbecillitas membrorum
infantilium innocens est, non animus infantium,* "The innocent[12]
part of a baby is not their will but the weakness of their limbs"
(1.7.11).

All this amounts to a claim that sin begins in infancy, and is
universal. He knows his own infantile sins because he sees them
in others. This fits with the dogmatically repressive vision of
Augustine that exists in popular understanding even today.

Augustine does not rest on this claim, however, but goes on
to counter it with the affirmation that he does not remember
his experience as a baby and that therefore he does not really
include it in his life on earth. It is like the time in the womb.

He can see that he was selfish, but does not accept that as his responsibility.

*Sed ecce omitto illud tempus:*
But look, I leave that time out

*et quid mihi iam cum eo est, cuius nulla vestigia recolo?*
and what can it be to me, a time of which I remember nothing?
(1.7.12)

In these paragraphs, then, he slides around the issue of infantile sin in what seems a slippery way: he affirms it on the basis of the selfishness he sees, but does not really face the obvious argument that what is wrong in a grown-up is not necessarily wrong in a baby. He reaffirms the presence of sin in the child, but then, in the passage just quoted, says that because it is not remembered it is as though it had not happened. He thus is saying and unsaying, in a text that is marked by an internal conflict or inconsistency that is not resolved, but left open.

Where are we then? This writing seems confused, even incoherent. You could cite different segments of the same paragraph to support directly opposed positions about human nature and the presence of sin in the infant. Is this incoherent writing? How can it be explained?

\* \* \*

I once asked a friend who was a distinguished art critic about the meaning of a Jackson Pollack painting. He said, "That's easy. The meaning is that we do not know where we are." I was struck by this remark and realized that in many paintings one of the central aims of the art is to do the exact opposite, to give us a sense—an

artificial sense—that we know with certainty where we are. Think
of a Dutch interior by Pieter de Hooch, for example: the patterns of the tiles receding away in perspective, the massive walls,
the window letting in light, the view through an open door of
the street and a canal beyond it, all these things tell us where we
are. In writing too it is one of the standard tasks to tell us where
we are, not so much physically as intellectually, ethically, socially.
Think of the first sentence of the *Confessions*: *Magnus es, Domine,
et laudabilis valde.* We seem to know where we are. But this is no
longer true or not yet, or not entirely. We are being exposed to
the fact that as Augustine uses his language to express and make
sense of his experience, it begins to collapse, to break down.

This inconsistency is meant I think to capture something of
the mental and moral state of the Augustine whose life is being
presented here: not so much the infant Augustine as Augustine
the narrator, who as he tells these stories about his life is shown
to be himself in a kind of confusion—a confusion out of which
we naturally hope he will grow and change as the work proceeds.
Will that happen? If so, how? This question is one of the true
subjects of the *Confessions*.[13]

Such things will of course happen later, too, for example in
the famous story of the theft of the pears in Book 2, which is
told in many different ways at once: as a proof of Augustine's
serious depravity, as a pointless and inconsequential prank, as an
instance of his susceptibility to being led by others into things
he would on his own never do, and so on. It is also true, as I said
earlier, that as he tells the stories of his life he does not tell us
much that we want to know, or not clearly: who the people are,
by name or background or history; exactly where the remembered Augustine is physically, and in what company; in what
sequence the events occurred (since he is frequently jumping
from one place or time to another); and so on. As I suggested

earlier, this may be a way of saying that he is really talking to God, who does not need to be told the things that Augustine does not say.

But the effect, and a useful one, is that the reader is in this way put in a position of incomplete or inconsistent knowledge, of puzzlement, that parallels Augustine's own, and with which they have to live just as Augustine does. I hope to show that as we proceed things will become gradually clearer and firmer. Perhaps paradoxically, this is achieved in large part by the process in which Augustine recognizes more and more fully the expanding zone in which he knows nothing.


## LANGUAGE (1.8.13)

As the Augustine whose life is told here becomes a boy, *puer*,[14] new experience does become accessible through memory to Augustine the narrator. He remembers being able to talk, but only later does he remember how language was learned. This turns out to be a complex subject for him.

Grown-ups did not teach him language, in a systematic way, giving him the meaning of one bit, then another, all in proper order,[15] as they would later do with letters:

*Sed ego ipse mente quam dedisti mihi, Deus meus,*
But I myself, with the mind you gave me, my God,

*cum gemitibus et vocibus variis et variis membrorum motibus*
by groans and different voices and different motions of my limbs

*edere vellem sensa cordis mei,*
would try to express the senses of my heart,

*ut voluntati pareretur,*
so that my will would be obeyed,

*nec valerem quae volebam omnia nec quibus volebam omnibus,*
*prensabam memoria.*
nor was I able to express all the things I wanted or to reach
all the people I wanted, I grasped all this with my memory.
(1.8.13)

That is, language learning was an active and creative process on
his part, the work of his own mind, not merely a matter of being
fed information by others.

Then follows the passage made famous by Wittgenstein—
who quoted it on the first page of the *Philosophical Investiga-*
*tions* as setting forth a view of language and its learning that he,
Wittgenstein, found both familiar and hopelessly inadequate:
a view of language as a set of names, applied to things, which
established the main activity of language-learning as learning
names.

*Cum ipsi appellabant rem aliquam*
When they [the grown-ups] named something

*et cum secundum eam vocem corpus ad aliquid movebant,*
and when, after making the sound, they moved the body
toward it,

*videbam et tenebam hoc ab eis vocari rem illam quod sonabant*
*cum eam vellent ostendere. . . .*
I saw and remembered that this thing was called by them
what they sounded when they wished to point it out. . . .

*Ita verba in variis sententiis locis suis posita et crebro audita*
Thus when these words were put in their places in different
sentences and frequently heard

*quarum rerum signa essent paulatim conligebam*
I gradually acquired understanding of the things of which
they were the signs

*measque iam voluntates edomito in eis signis ore per haec
enuntiabam.*
and as my mouth was trained to these signs [*edomito ore*] I
expressed my wishes through them.[16]
(1.8.13)

As others have pointed out,[17] Wittgenstein's selection of this
single passage distorted Augustine's far more complex view, that
language learning is not simply acquiring names, as if words were
merely "signs" of "things," but requires the work of the individual person engaged in learning how sense is made in the range
of social and cultural circumstances in which they find themselves. It is plain from our reading of the opening of the *Confessions*, for example, that Augustine knows that language does not
simply work by naming, but consists of identifiable gestures, at
once social, intellectual, and ethical in kind—such as "praising
another," "calling upon another," "knowing another," "believing
in another"—among which the responsible speaker or writer has
to establish appropriate relations. He has in fact a clear sense
of what Wittgenstein called "language games," perhaps a richer
sense than Wittgenstein himself had.

For our purposes what is most significant is that here once
more what Augustine says is marked by inconsistency. To what
extent was he just learning words as he had learned letters, to
what extent was he half-creating the language that he learned,
making it his own? There are in this passage strands of both possibilities, as we have seen, and they are unreconciled. In this sense
his present language is proving its own inadequacy to explain
what language itself is and how he learned it.

## SCHOOLING (1.9.14–1.10.16)

Augustine's account of his schooling presents another version of the same kind of inconsistency. He begins by saying that the purpose of his education was to equip him to succeed in the world by the manipulation of others:

> *ut in hoc saeculo florerem et excellerem linguosis artibus*
> so that I should flourish in the world and excel in the arts of language
>
> *ad honorem hominum et falsas divitias famulantibus*[18].
> serving the purpose of acquiring honor among men and false riches.
> (1.9.14)

This is a statement not only about what we would call his primary education, but his training all the way through to his role as imperial rhetor. You might say that he was trained to be something like a propagandist or an advertising executive, or a lawyer, and as such a manipulator of others through linguistic skill. That is the negative; the positive is that this very training, of which he now so deeply disapproves, was also an essential part of his education in a good sense. We might find something comparable in the life of a child today who is sent to an elite boarding school. In retrospect he believes this schooling was meant to train him to become a success in the dominant culture and society—to become rich and powerful and maybe famous—but he also sees it as having given him experiences that have enabled him to criticize his world, to discover or create his own values, and to build a life on that basis. They pretended to be teaching virtue and excellence; they were in fact teaching modes of success; but perhaps what one learned was essential to virtue and excellence after all. Something like this is what I think Augustine is saying.

In his account of his schooling Augustine faces another issue on which he expresses strongly inconsistent views, namely, the matter of his own inherent sinfulness—or not. His early school experience, for example, included beatings, which seem to have been regarded by everyone as perfectly normal. His parents laughed about them. To him they were brutal and terrible, a source of acute fear. But he goes on to say, not exactly that the beatings were justified, but that he, and his fellows, were at fault: *Peccabamus . . . minus scribendo aut legendo aut cogitando de litteris quam exigebatur a nobis,* "We sinned . . . in writing less and reading less and thinking less about the works assigned than was demanded of us" (1.9.15).

This does not exactly justify in his mind the cruelty of the beatings, but he repeats that he was at fault.[19]

What then are we to think of the beatings? That they were monstrous cruelties, that they were appropriate punishments of vice, or what? He does not resolve this uncertainty, as it were suspending judgment. Once again, we are exposed to an inconsistency, or even incoherence, in the way Augustine is thinking as he remembers these events. He cannot put them into an organized whole. He cannot tell us where he was or where we are.

He concludes this section with a prayer:

*Vide ista, Domine, misericorditer,*
Behold these things, Lord, with compassion

*et libera nos iam invocantes te,*
and free us who are calling upon you

*libera etiam eos qui nondum te invocant,*
free also those who do not yet call upon you

*ut invocent te et liberes eos.*

that that may call upon you and you may set them free.
(1.10.16)

Notice that in this prayer Augustine can see and sympathize with those who are different from him, indeed keep them in his prayer.

\* \* \*

Let us now look at this passage a little differently. What happens if you put the Latin passage and my translation together, and ask what you think has been lost, or added, or obscured in the English version? For example, you have already heard the word *invoco* used in ways that do not have a parallel in English, as meaning not only "call upon," as the translation reads, but something far more radical: "call to enter us," as we saw in our discussion of the first three sentences. Would the use of that phrase solve the problem? What else would you have to say to make clear what you meant?

How about *misericorditer*? Its roots are in a word for "suffering" and the word for "heart." You have seen this word, and how well do you think "with compassion" expresses what it means? How about *libera* and *liberes*: does "set free" do the job? What about the difference between those two terms: how adequately is that expressed in English?

Let me encourage you now to write out your own translation, and ask how satisfactory it is? What else would you need to be confident in your judgment?

## ILLNESS AND BAPTISM (1.11.17–18)

A similar set of inconsistencies are at work in his account of his illness and baptism. The story begins with an account of an illness he had as a boy, during which he pled with his mother Monnica that he might baptized, and hence saved, before he died. She was concerned for his salvation and made all the necessary arrangements, but he recovered his health before the baptism occurred. He says: *Ita iam credebam et illa et omnis domus, nisi pater solus*, "Thus I already believed, and she believed, and so did all the house except my father alone" (1.11.17). But in what sense did he "believe"? Certainly not as he will come to "believe" later in life.

It was then decided (by Monnica? by Augustine?) to defer his baptism, on the ground that he was bound to sin and it was better for him to be washed clean of his sins late in life, not early on. If he were baptized now, that is, he would naturally build up a record of sinning that would be held against him; if he deferred, at least some of that record would be wiped out by his later baptism.

This may seem to us a rather strategic and manipulative way to think about this sacrament, though I am told some of his contemporaries also thought this way. To his credit Augustine is troubled, and asks God, was this decision really for his good?

*Rogo te, Deus meus:*
I ask you, my God:

*vellem scire, si tu etiam velles, quo consilio dilatus sum ne tunc baptizarer,*
I would like to know, if you also are willing, by what plan my baptism was then delayed,

*utrum bono meo mihi quasi laxata sint lora peccandi. An non laxata sunt?*
whether it was for my good that the reins restraining sinning were, as it were, relaxed. Or were they not really relaxed at all?
(1.11.18)

His own present judgment is that it would certainly have been better, *melius vero*, not to delay, he has no doubt about that. But whom is he criticizing: his mother, who in her own view made this plan for his sake, or God himself, who is after all at work in all things? And does his later life bear out his judgment that it would have been better not to delay the baptism? He did commit sins, after all.

All this is of real significance, because the baptism he finally undergoes at the hands of Ambrose is a key moment in his whole life.[20] If he had been baptized as a child, as he here wishes he had, he would never have had that experience. Would he have been fully converted as a child? Then he would not have needed what happened at the hands of Ambrose. But he was now headed into a kind of rebellion against the faith of his mother, and his mother personally, and would baptism as a child really have changed that? It is very hard to believe this.

Once again, a topic is raised on which Augustine defines alternative possibilities, triggering conflicting feelings and judgments which he does not resolve. Once again, we do not know where we are in relation to these essential questions. But we do know that the baptism he would have had as a child was not the same thing as the baptism he did have as an adult.

## LATER EDUCATION (1.12.19, 1.13.22)

In the next stage of his education, we are told, he did not love his schoolwork, but was urged to it by his teachers, and their urging was good for him.

But what did this work really mean? Why was it good for him? Now an important sentence:

*Nec faciebam ego bene*
Nor was I doing well

*(non enim discerem nisi cogerer;*
(for I would not learn unless forced;

*nemo autem invitus bene facit, etiamsi bonum est quod facit;,*
and no one does well against his own will even if what he
does is good),

*nec qui me urgebant bene faciebant, sed bene mihi fiebat abs te,
Deus meus,*
nor did those who urged me on do well; but what was good
for me was done by you, my God.
(1.12.19)

The teachers were not "doing well," for they were training him
only *ad satiandas insatiabiles cupiditates copiosae inopiae et igno-
miniosae gloriae,* "for the satisfaction of insatiable desires for
abundant emptiness and shameful glory" (1.12.19). He was not
"doing well" because he did not want to do it at all, and worked
against his own reluctance.

Somehow, out of all this mistaken activity did come good, but
this was only at the hand of God:

*Ita de non bene facientibus tu bene faciebas mihi*
Thus by those who were not doing well you did well to me

*et de peccante me ipso iuste retribuebas mihi.*
and you justly punished me, as I was sinning;

*Iussisti enim et sic est, ut poena sua sibi sit omnis inordinatus animus.*
You commanded it, and thus it is, that every disordered
spirit is its own punishment.
(1.12.19)

The disorder which Augustine perceives in his younger self is being enacted for us in his language and the way he uses it. Thus this chapter is full of a sense of injustice, with anger and contempt for his bullying teachers; but it is also full of the humanity and reality of the child's world, with real appreciation of what the education actually did for him in the end—which was, among other things, to help him become the person who could write the *Confessions*. The child was imperfect but not fallen as far as his superiors.

I will pass over his discussion of the rest of his education, except to say that he found the training in the basics of grammar, reading and writing, of great value. But the next stage, a reading of fictions in the form of the *Aeneid* or the plays of Terence, inflicted a distortion. In reading the *Aeneid*, for example, he says he wept for Dido's imaginary death, but not for his own death of the spirit, which was caused by his failure to love "you, my God" (1.13.20). What bothers him is that the death of Dido is fictional, imaginary, and what he should have been paying attention to was the real damage done to his own soul. Thus he was shaped by the approval of his teachers and peers—misshaped really—into having what he regards as a twisted set of values.

In this criticism of his education Augustine is resisting universal Roman assumptions about what an education should be, what a life should be. The sort of education he had was the mark of privilege. Success in mastering the literary culture of Rome was the key to the success and prestige he was himself to seek. Those who flourished in this educational system were proud of their achievements, and felt superior to those who did not have these advantages. (Think here of our friend the all-star law student.) Augustine is aware that people who have achieved this kind of success—the success for which he was trained and of which he was capable—will despise what he saying now, about his longing for the Christian God:

*Non clament adversus me quos iam non timeo,*
Let them not shout out against me, those whom I no longer fear,

*dum confiteor tibi quae vult anima mea*
when I confess to you what my soul desires[21]
(1.13.22)

## LANGUAGE AGAIN (1.14.23–19.30)

Augustine hated Greek, partly because of the difficulty of learning any foreign language, but he loved Latin, which he had of course learned painlessly without threat or punishment from his teachers. In the following passage he complicates deeply, without saying so, the image of language learning reproduced above, of which Wittgenstein made so much:

*Nam et latinam aliquando infans utique nulla noveram,*
At one time I knew no Latin [*infans*, not yet speaking]

*et tamen advertendo didici sine ullo metu atque cruciate,*
yet by paying attention I learned without fear or pain

*inter etiam blandimenta nutricum et ioca adridentium et laetitias adludentium.*
from the coaxing of my nurses, from the jokes of people laughing, from the pleasures of those playing games

*Didici vero illa sine poenali onere urgentium,*
I learned without the painful burden of those urging me on,

*cum me urgeret cor meum ad parienda concepta sua,*
since my heart urged me to express[22] what it understood.

*et qua non esset, nisi aliqua verba didicissem non a docentibus sed a loquentibus,*
which could not have happened unless I had learned some words not from teachers but from speakers,

*in quorum et ego auribus parturiebam quidquid sentiebam.*
into whose ears I expressed whatever I was feeling or thinking.

*Hinc satis elucet maiorem habere vim ad discenda ista liberam curiositatem quam meticulosam necessitatem.*
From this it is clear enough that free curiosity is a greater force for learning than meticulous necessity.
(1.14.23)

He is saying, that is, that he learned the language not as a set of names, not as a set of signs that stood for things, not as an intellectual system, but as a set of gestures at once intellectual and social, many of which gave him great pleasure. It is also important that a crucial part of his learning to speak was his coming to have things he himself wanted to say or do in language. He was the center of his own learning.

In reading this passage one might well say, "Where has the knowledge you now reveal been lurking all this while? Or are you discovering something as you write?" For, as we have repeatedly seen, in the *Confessions* there are frequent unmarked shifts or changes in Augustine's understandings and expressions, assertions that are inconsistent with other assertions. As I have suggested, this is his way of placing us as readers where he once was, not knowing where we are.

He turns now from his account of his education to God, a move that puts him in a place in which he can see the meaning of his education, or potential meaning, differently.[23] He asks: *Tibi serviat quidquid utile puer didici, tibi serviat quod loquor et scribo et lego et numero*, "Let whatever useful I learned as a boy serve you; let what I say and write and speak and count serve you" (1.15.24). He is asking, that is, that the complex process of good and bad that was at work in his education be turned now to God's service, not the service of those who wanted him by his education to become rich and powerful.[24]

In this context Augustine now confronts in a new way the force of his culture, and the language through which it worked. The culture irresistibly imposed its values, its ways of thinking and talking, on those who grew up in it. This has been a theme throughout his treatment of his education, but here it becomes explicit: in his world, for example, acculturation meant learning about the god Jupiter, who was an adulterer, and beholding, in a play by Terence, a young man using the example of Jupiter to justify his own sexual misconduct. Some say that this education is necessary to teach people how to use language well, that is, to increase their power and advance their career. The idea is that the culture itself can turn bad into good. But this, Augustine says, is simply not true. In his own case, he says, he learned this passage from Terence well and for doing so, he sardonically says, *bonae spei puer appellabar*, "I was called a boy of good hope" (1.16.26).

Likewise, he won a prize for his translation of a speech by Juno from the verse in which it was composed into prose, a speech that was of course completely fictional. This was a training in the skills of language without any regard to the use to which they were put, to their actual meaning in anyone's life, and it cannot have been a good thing. *Nonne ecce illa omnia fumus et ventus?*, "Was not all this smoke and wind?" (1.17.27). So he says, but as readers we cannot help thinking that it was partly this training, defective in his view as it was, which helped him develop the extraordinary capacities of thought and language that we see before us on each page of the *Confessions*.

In all of this he was of course influenced by the praises he earned, which encouraged him to more and more perfect work. But this, he says, was a dislocation of praise. He could have been turned away from these trivial and vicious subjects to better ones:

> *Laudes tuae, Domine, laudes tuae per scripturas tuas*
> Your praises, Lord, your praises through your Scriptures
>
> *suspenderent*[25] *palmitem cordis mei,*
> would have held up the vine-branch of my heart
>
> *et non raperetur per inania nugarum turpis praeda volatilibus.*
> and it would not have been snatched by empty trifles, as a foul prey for the birds.
>
> *Non enim uno modo sacrificatur transgressoribus angelis.*
> There is not just one way in which sacrifice can be made to the wicked angels.
> (1.17.27)

But would it really have been better for him to have spent his time competing with other boys to see who can frame better praises of God? The context of the classroom would almost certainly have led to praise for the ornate, the sophisticated, the well-formed, not for the deeply felt or emotionally true. If that were not the emphasis, there would be the danger of dullness and boredom that would alienate the children from religion forever. Think of some Sunday schools today.[26]

Thus it was not surprising that he says:

> *A te, Deus meus, ibam foras, quando mihi imitandi proponebantur*
> *homines*
> I went far away from you, my God, when the men who were
> held up to me for my imitation,
>
> *qui aliqua facta sua non mala, si cum barbarismo aut soloecismo*
> *enuntiarent,*
> who if in giving an account of their own deeds, not evil ones,
> used a barbarism or solecism,
>
> *reprehensi confundebantur,*
> were mortified at the reproach;
>
> *si autem libidines suas integris et rite consequentibus verbis*
> *copiose ornateque narrarent,*
> but if they told the stories of their lusts in well-composed
> prose, copiously and ornately,
>
> *laudati gloriabantur?*
> they were praised for it and gloried in the fact![27]
> (1.18.28)

When he says he "went far" Augustine of course does not mean
that he went on foot, or through physical spaces, but went far
from God's face, led by his teachers and the culture into which
they initiated him.

> *Et certe non est interior litterarum scientia quam scripta conscientia,*
> Certainly the knowledge of letters is not deeper within the
> person than the writings of the conscience

*id se alteri facere quod nolit pati.*
namely, that one does to another what one would not like to
experience. (Mt. 7:12)
(1.18.29)

Here he affirms that beneath the mind that is being trained and
educated by such teachers as he describes is a deeper part of the
self, which is learning things that can serve as a corrective to the
mind.

Such were the moral practices and conventions, the ways of
life, on the threshold of which he lay as an unhappy boy,

*ubi magis timebam barbarismum facere*
where I was more afraid to commit a barbarism

*quam cavebam, si facerem, non facientibus invidere.*
than I was watchful to avoid envying those who did not do
so, if I did.
(1.19.30)

\* \* \*

Can you translate this Latin passage into English? First let us
see if you can put the Latin together. *Timebam* means something
like: "I (continuously) feared"; *magis* is "more"; *facere barbarismum* is "commit a barbarism"; *quam cavebam*, "than I was (continuously) alert not to"; *invidere*, "envy"; *non facientibus*, "those
who did not do it." Do you understand the Latin enough to read
it aloud with an awareness of its structure and meaning?

Now: can you write out your translation? What are its merits,
its weaknesses? Can you improve it?

To think this way is to generate questions. What is Augustine saying here? That he was conforming himself to this

competitive and false culture? Could he have avoided that given its pervasiveness and the commitments of his teachers? Is the implication that he could hardly be blamed for it? He was just becoming what the system was meant to produce? Could he have protected himself against that outcome? And if in fact did he do so, how?

But he then goes on in a different vein, describing things he did for which his responsibility is unavoidable: he stole food and drink from his parents to give to his friends, and he both cheated in games and at the same time denounced others if he caught them at it. *Istane est innocentia puerilis? Non est, Domine, non est,* "Is this the innocence of a child? It is not, Lord, it is not" (1.19.30).

In all of this what stands out most, for me at least, is his complex and tension-ridden attitude toward his own education. He sees that it cannot be a foundation or ground for the life of the soul; he sees that it replicates a culture it cannot examine; and he sees its essential emptiness, cruelty, and stupidity. But it is part of what made him who he is and gave him the extraordinary capacities necessary to the writing of this very book.

In almost every aspect of his education he finds himself without a language in which he can make sense of his experience. Good and evil are intertwined in a way neither his culture nor the language it has given him can straighten out.

## A MOMENT OF STABILITY (1.20.31)

The last paragraphs of Book 1 are in a sense a response to the invocation with which it began. Having given us a complex web of changing and contrasting truths about himself and his world, he sums up his situation in a language that achieves some real clarity and firmness.

*Sed tamen, Domine, tibi excellentissimo atque optimo conditori
et rectori universitatis,*
But to you, Lord, the most excellent and best founder and
ruler of the universe,

*Deo nostro gratias, etiamsi me puerum tantum esse voluisses.*
to you our God I give thanks, even if you wished me only to
be a boy.[28]
(1.20.31)

Why does he begin with the adversative "but" (*sed* strengthened
by *tamen*)? Because he has been talking about his own weaknesses, sins, and susceptibilities to the values of his culture. This
may sound as though he was not good, his life was not good (as
indeed many people read Augustine as saying). But this is wrong:

*Eram enim etiam tunc, vivebam atque sentiebam*
Even then I existed, I was alive, I had feelings

*meamque incolumitatem, vestigium secretissimae unitatis ex qua
eram, curae habebam,*
I took care of my own safety (itself a trace of the secret unity
from which I arose),

*custodiebam interiore sensu integritatem sensuum meorum*
I took care, by an interior instinct, of the integrity of my
experiences

*inque ipsis parvis parvarumque rerum cogitationibus veritate
delectabar.*
and in my little thoughts about little things I was delighted
by the truth.

*Falli nolebam, memoria vigebam, locutione instruebar, amicitia
mulcebar, fugiebam dolorem, abiectionem, ignorantiam.*

I did not wish to be deceived, I flourished in my memory, I was instructed in speech, I was softened by friendship, I fled from sorrow, depression, and ignorance.

*Quid in tali animante non mirabile atque laudabile?*
What in such a being was not wonderful and worthy of praise?
(1.20.31)

Having stressed difficulty, selfishness, and sin, in himself and those who taught him, he now stresses the opposite, the sense he has of wholeness and life within. This is a passage affirming the self he was able to become even in the fallen and conflicted world he inhabited.

I have spoken of the shifts and transformations that take place in Augustine's prose, and this is perhaps the most dramatic, from finding fault with his education, his teachers, and himself, to celebrating what he became. He recognizes that this is not the result of his own efforts or skill or virtue, but a sheer gift of life from God.

He begins this short passage by thanking God, and ends it by declaring that he himself is *laudabile*, praiseworthy, the very word he used of God in the opening sentence of the *Confessions*. What does this reversal mean? How is it explained? (Or are we to understand God as the one who is *laudabile*?)

He provides something of an answer in the way he goes on to articulate the relation between himself and his Creator in a new and powerful way:

*At ista omnia Dei mei dona sunt.*
But all these things are gifts of my God.

*Non mihi ego dedi haec, et bona sunt, et haec omnia ego.*
I did not give them to myself, and they are good, and all of them are me.

*Bonus ergo est qui fecit me, et ipse est bonum meum, et illi exulto*
*bonis omnibus quibus etiam puer eram.*
Good therefore is the one who made me, and he himself is
my good, and to him I rejoice for all the good things with
which I was even when a boy.
(1.20.31)

What about the sins and failures and deficiencies of which we
have been hearing so much?

*Hoc enim peccabam, quod non in ipso sed in creaturis eius me*
*atque ceteris*
In this I sinned, that, not in God himself but in his
creatures, both myself and others,

*voluptates, sublimitates, veritates quaerebam, atque ita*
*inruebam in dolores, confusiones, errores.*
I was seeking pleasures, loftiness, and truths, and thus I ran
into sorrows, confusions, and errors.
(1.20.31)

He closes the book this way:

*Gratias tibi, dulcedo mea et honor meus et fiducia mea, Deus*
*meus, gratias tibi de donis tuis:*
Thanks to you, my sweetness and my honor and my trust,
my God, thanks to you for your gifts.

*sed tu mihi ea serva.*
But preserve these things for me.

*Ita enim servabis me, et augebuntur et perficientur quae dedisti mihi,*
Thus you will preserve me and what you have given me will
increase and be perfected

*et ero ipse tecum, quia et ut sim tu dedisti mihi.*
and I shall be with you, because you have given to me that I
might exist.

(1.20.31)

To me, all of this feels in its own terms solid and firm, unlike
anything else we have read in Book 1. I think that one point of
Book 1 has in fact been to carry him, and us, from its beautiful
but uncertain beginning through a welter of events, character-
izations, and attitudes, to a moment, perhaps only a moment, of
clarity and truth, a point where he knows where he is and who
he is, and his language works.

It is important to add that the image of the human self at
work here is not as a complete, independent, integrated entity,
but as a person in relation to others—especially to the God he
addresses here, who is both the creator of the self and the giver
of its blessings; to his culture, and its necessarily defective language of fact and value, in which he was raised; and to his reader
as well.

In this he speaks for all of us, for we have all been raised
in a defective world, a defective culture, speaking a defective language. His simultaneously critical and creative task is
to remake the language he has inherited and in so doing to
remake himself in relation to the one who is in the first place
the creator of the self—no man made his own soul[29]—and in
the second place the giver of blessings to the soul he has created. In the course of Book 1 he moves from praising God to
thanking him. This is itself a manifestation of a change within
his being, the development of an awareness that makes this
shift possible.

As I said earlier, when Augustine makes his language and
its practices the subject of thought, something else happens: he
emerges before us as someone different from the language he is

using. He is present as the mind to whom the language is a problem and as the person who is thinking about what he himself does with that language when he praises, when he invokes, when he knows, when he hears preaching. One might say that in this way he is exposing to us, and to himself, his soul—the soul, the transformation of which is his deepest subject.

# PART II

# 5

## ADOLESCENCE, SEX, AND THE
## STOLEN PEARS (BOOK 2)

WE HAVE NOW SPENT a lot of time and energy on Book
1 of the *Confessions*, trying to read it with special attention to
the way the Latin works in each of a series of passages. Obviously we cannot continue at that pace, so the chapters that
follow will focus for the most part on relatively short passages
taken in order from later books of the *Confessions*. In each case
I will try to give some sense of the narrative or other context in
which the passage appears. The point will be to continue to ask
what kind of life Augustine's text offers us as his readers and to
discover ways in which that life shifts, and grows, and changes
as the *Confessions* proceeds. In all of this I shall continue to
give particular attention to the role of Latin in the experience
it offers us. I hope this language will seem increasingly familiar
to you.

In Book 1, as we have seen, Augustine talks about his early
childhood, the stages in Latin called (for a boy) *infantia* and
*pueritia*—in our terms "infancy" and "boyhood." In Book 2 he
turns to adolescence, *adulescentia*, focusing mainly on what happened when he was sixteen.

## ADOLESCENCE (2.1.1)

He begins this way:

*Recordari volo transactas foeditates meas et carnales corruptiones animae meae,*
I wish to remember my foul deeds and the carnal corruptions of my soul,

*non quod eas amem, sed ut amem te, Deus meus.*[1]
not because I may love them but so that I may love you, my God.
(2.1.1)[2]

This important sentence defines one central purpose of the whole *Confessions*, which is to learn to love God. Think of the sentence with which the *Confessions* begins, *Magnus es, Domine, et laudabilis valde*, which, as we saw, presents the question: "Why does Augustine want to praise God, when God, whoever he is, seems beyond all praise?" The sentence quoted above provides one answer: not to please him, not to give him something he needs, not for God's sake at all, but for Augustine's own sake: that he may learn to love God.

In the course of the *Confessions* Augustine often finds in himself an uncertainty about various theological propositions, an uncertainty which could be boiled down to the question: How do we know the truth about who God is? Augustine's elaboration of these concerns is intelligent and energetic; in his account of himself he comfortably acknowledges sin and failure, again with energy, and he reaches conclusions in which he is confident. But what he is saying in the quoted sentence, beneath this intellectual surface, raises a question of a very different kind: Can he learn to love God? To accept God's love of him? Why is it so hard?

The Augustine who has this desire includes both the pilgrim whose life story is being told and Agustine the writer. Though Augustine the pilgrim may not have known it at the time, I think we are being told here that his great concern was to learn to love God, no easy thing to do or to understand. Likewise I think that for Augustine the narrator, one object he may have in writing the book is, by writing it, to deepen his own capacity to love God, now. To say this is to suggest that even at the time of writing he is aware that he does not yet love God as he wishes he did.

Why does he not say this explicitly? What are the ways in which his love falls short? How does he imagine the love he might have? Or, even more basically: What does he mean by loving God? How does his experience help him answer these questions?

Perhaps one hope he has in writing the *Confessions* is for us, not for him, namely, that our experience of this book as readers may teach us how to love God as well. If so, how does he seek to reach us and teach us, in what we have already read? How do you suppose will he do so in what follows?

In this context it may help to remember that the whole teaching of Christianity is often summed up this way: "Love God and your neighbor."

Here is another point. When Augustine says at the beginning of this book that he wants to remember his foul deeds, *non quod eas amem, sed ut amem te, Deus meus*, "not so that I may love them but so that I may love you, my God," he is talking about the practice of confession. He does not just want to remember these deeds, he wants to confess them, that is, to share his memory of them with God as a penitent. If I am right, he is here defining in a new way not only the purposes of the *Confessions* as a whole, for himself and for us, as I have been saying, but also the purpose of confession itself—including the sacrament of confession—which, he is impliedly saying, is not to secure forgiveness or excuse, or to trigger acts of penitence that may wash sin away, but to learn to love God. When Augustine writes, *ut amem te* ("so that I might love you"), he is saying: so that I might learn to love you—not what I have been loving. All this raises for us as readers the question: How well will he engage in this activity, and with what results? And: How is he trying to teach us to love God? What does it mean to love God, for him and for us, as his readers?

When we put ourselves in the story in this way, even more disturbing questions rise to the surface: Whom or what do we love, and why? Are these loves good for us? Are they good for the objects of our love?

The negative language Augustine uses to describe his defects, in the sentence quoted above, is very strong indeed: *foeditates* and *corruptiones*. Why do you suppose he speaks with such loathing of conduct that is likely to appear, at least to us, not very disturbing at all—especially when we get to the famous story of the stolen pears?

\* \* \*

He goes on to say:

*Amore amoris tui facio istuc,*
I do this out of love of your love

*recolens vias meas nequissimas in amaritudine recogitationis meae,*
reliving my wickednesses in the bitterness of my rethinking

*ut tu dulcescas mihi, dulcedo non fallax, dulcedo felix et secura,*
so that you might treat me sweetly, [you who are] sweetness itself, never deceitful, sweetness happy and untroubled,

*et conligens me a dispersione, in qua frustatim discissus sum*
and binding me together from my disintegration, in which I
was painfully split into pieces,

*dum ab uno te aversus in multa evanui.*
while, turned from the One, you, I disappeared into many
things.
(2.1.1)

We are told here that learning to love God truly is not merely a
choice and decision, like turning on a light switch, but requires,
and invites, the deepest kind of work, in this case the reintegra-
tion of a soul he feels to be fragmented.

* * *

What would a soul be like that was not split or self-divided, but
an integrated whole? Will Augustine achieve such a state and
present it to us? Will he show us what such a soul is like? How?
In the way he writes to us? In his voice? In what ways are our
own souls divided, or integrated?

* * *

Next he defines the state from which he has moved a little, and
from which he wishes to move more securely and completely:

*Exarsi enim aliquando satiari inferis in adulescentia,*
Sometimes in my adolescence I burned to satiate my desire
for hell

*et silvescere ausus sum variis et umbrosis amoribus,*
and dared to grow wild with various dark loves

*et contabuit species mea, et computrui coram oculis tuis*
and my appearance wasted away, and I rotted before your eyes

*placens mihi et placere cupiens oculis hominum.*
pleasing myself and desiring to please the eyes of men.
(2.1.1)

## SEX (2.2.2–2.2.8)

In the next several pages Augustine deplores his own sinfulness
as a teenager, mainly with respect to sex. His feelings of self-
revulsion are clear, but he does not explain in any detail what he
actually did, or with whom, or how often. His burning sexuality
is the object of feeling, not specification.

He does say that as he fell into what seems to have been a
kind of addiction, God was silent, a fact that is not explained in
any way.

> *Tacebas tunc,*
> You were silent then,
>
> *et ego ibam porro longe a te in plura et plura sterilia semina*
> *dolorum*
> and I was going far from you into more and more sterile
> seeds of sorrows,
>
> *superba dejectione et inquieta lassitudine.*
> in my proud dejection and restless apathy.
> (2.2.2)

Though God was in one sense silent, Augustine says he was not
entirely absent, revealing himself in Augustine's internal experience, as he found that the pleasures he sought were marred by
bitterness and self-shame (2.2.4). This too is an important statement, for it defines God as acting within him, for his own good,

by creating experiences of shame and sorrow. In this important way, though incompletely, he sees that God is within him.

Why were his parents not helpful? His father did make sacrifices to send him to school, but his concern was only with his son's success there, not with *qualis crescerem tibi aut quam castus essem,* "what I was becoming in relation to you or how chaste I was" (2.3.5). In fact, when he saw Augustine in the baths, and could see that he was becoming sexual, he rejoiced that he would be having grandchildren, *nepotes* (2.3.6).

Augustine's mother Monnica was a Christian, with a deep fear for his soul, and, being afraid of his possible or actual fornication, and especially adultery, told him so. But these to him

*monitus muliebres videbantur, quibus obtemperare erubescerem.*
seemed womanish warnings, which I would be embarrassed to obey.
(2.3.7)

Though these warnings came from her, he goes on to say to God:

*Illi [monitus] autem tui erant*
These warnings were really yours[3]

*et nesciebam, et te tacere putabam atque illam loqui*
and I did not know and thought you were being silent and that it was she who spoke,

*per quam mihi tu non tacebas,*
through whom you were not being silent [but speaking]

*et in illa contemnebaris a me, a me, filio eius,*
and in her you were treated with contempt by me, by me, her son,

*filio ancillae tuae, servo tuo.*
by the son of your handmaiden, by your servant.
(2.3.7)

* * *

Let me suggest that you look at this passage, which is really just one sentence, with care. Read it aloud, if possible with understanding. Then look at the structure of the sentence, beginning with his rejection of his mother's warnings and ending with his awareness that in treating her with contempt he was treating God with contempt. In what spiritual condition does he begin, in what condition does he end? Can you see how he gets from such a beginning to such an ending? What are the movements by which he does this? Now the hard part: can you translate this sentence in such a way as to bring home to the English speaker what you have just discovered?

* * *

In this passage there is an expansion of Augustine's sense of the way God works: not only within him, as we just saw, but within other people too, in this case his mother, in relation to him. Her concern for him was a way in which God was working through her, for his benefit. This is an important step, for it breaks down the image, common in our own world, of the individual person as an autonomous and distinct self, choosing and shaping their own independent life. This passage helps us see that we live and move in and through each other, a fact that is immensely important to Augustine.

Augustine got into a bad crowd of young men, or older boys, who bragged about their sexual conquests. His mother had warned him to protect his virginity, *pudicitiam* (2.3.8), but she did not realize the force of what his father had seen in the bath, namely, that he was ready for sex. Marriage might have been a partial solution, but she did not favor it because she thought marriage would interfere with his progress, through education, toward God.

Is he overreacting in his self-condemnations here? We may think so, but who of us, of either sex, does not know and remember the difficulty human beings almost always have in integrating their sexuality with the fuller sense they have of themselves?

Despite all his self-accusations and feelings of misery, it is really not at all clear, to me at least, what his behavior actually was. At one point, he says that he pretended to have done things he had not, in order to maintain what we would call his "street cred" with the crowd he hung out with (2.3.7). What is clear is that he felt torn by his sexuality.

Are we to regard this as a particular burden or blessing, or is it for him simply playing out in real time the larger fact of "original sin"—perhaps another word for self-division? We shall return to this topic.

## THE STOLEN PEARS (2.4.9–10.18)

Here is the famous story:

*et ego furtum facere volui et feci,*
and I wanted to commit a theft, and I did so,

*nulla compulsus egestate nisi penuria et fastidio iustitiae et sagina iniquitatis.*
compelled by no need except an absence of justice and loathing for it, and a fullness of wickedness.

*Nam id furatus sum quod mihi abundabat et multo melius,*
For I stole what I had in abundance, and much better too.

*nec ea re volebam frui quam furto appetebam, sed ipso furto et peccato.*
nor did I wish to enjoy by theft a thing that I was desiring, but simply the theft itself, the sin of it.

*Arbor erat pirus in vicinia nostrae vineae*
There was a pear tree in the neighborhood of our vineyard

*pomis onusta nec forma nec sapore inlecebrosis.*
loaded with pears, enticing in neither beauty nor taste.

*Ad hanc excutiendam atque asportandam nequissimi adulescentuli perreximus nocte intempesta . . .*
We worthless adolescent boys proceeded to shaking the pears down and carrying them away in the dead of night . . .

*et abstulimus inde onera ingentia, non ad nostras epulas sed vel proicienda porcis,*
and now we took away from there a huge load, not for our own eating, but to throw to the pigs

*etiamsi aliquid inde comedimus, dum tamen fieret a nobis quod eo liberet quo non liceret.*
though we did eat some, claiming we were fully free only in that which was forbidden.

*Ecce cor meum, Deus, ecce cor meum, quod miseratus es in imo abyssi.*
Behold my heart, God, behold my heart, on which you had compassion in the deep abyss.

*Dicat tibi nunc, ecce cor meum, quid ibi quaerebat,*
Let it say to you now, behold let my heart say, what it was seeking there,

*ut essem gratis malus et malitiae meae causa nulla esset nisi malitia.*
that I should be gratuitously evil, the cause of my malice being none other than malice itself.

*Foeda erat, et amavi eam. Amavi perire, amavi defectum meum,*
It was foul and I loved it, I loved to be destroyed, I loved my own defect,

*non illud ad quod deficiebam, sed defectum meum ipsum amavi,*
I loved not that for which I was defective but my defect itself,

*turpis anima te dissiliens a firmamento tuo in exterminium,*
my disgusting soul bursting from your foundation into utter destruction,

*non dedecore aliquid, sed dedecus appetens.*
not acquiring something by shame, but desiring shame itself.
(2.4.9)

This is perhaps the most famous story in the *Confessions*, told as a confession itself, spoken to God. With a bunch of rowdy teenagers, with whom he had already been disorderly in many ways, he stole pears from a neighbor's tree. His account of this, and his feelings about his conduct, summarized above, seem to many modern readers wildly exaggerated. Why is it so important to him, why so negative?

As he puts it at first, what was so bad about this act was that it was done for the love of the wickedness of it. He and the others had no need for pears, and these were not of the highest quality. They did not even eat most of them, but threw them to the pigs. He goes on to say that there are many beautiful and good things in life for which people will wrongfully commit crimes. In those cases the sinner is choosing a lesser good over a greater one. He says that even the monster Catiline,[4] the personification of evil, did his crimes for the sake of other things, which were in some way good. There was nothing good in Augustine's motives or desires. The pears were good, as part of the creation, but he did not take them for the sake of their goodness (2.6.12).

This is a perceptive self-analysis, explaining that to love evil for its own sake is bad, even if it seems on the surface a trivial matter.

But is his reaction to all this excessive? Many people think so, but I am myself not at all sure. Love of evil even in something small is a bad thing. It can capture the mind and soul and lead to many worse things.

Then he sums up:

*Et nunc, Domine Deus meus, quaero quid me in furto delectaverit,*
Now Lord, my God, I ask what there was in the act of theft that delighted me

*et ecce species nulla est*:
and behold, there was no beauty

*non dico sicut in aequitate atque prudentia,*
I mean beauty not as in justice or prudence,

*sed neque sicut in mente hominis atque memoria et sensibus et vegetante vita,*
nor as in the mind of man and memory and in the senses and in growing life,

*neque sicut speciosa sunt sidera et decora locis suis et terra et mare plena fetibus, qui succedunt nascendo decedentibus—*
nor was it beautiful like the stars, beautiful in their places, or the earth or the sea full of newborn beings, which, being born, follow the dying,

*non saltem ut est quaedam defectiva species et umbratica vitiis*
*fallentibus.*
nor even like the defective and shadowed beauty in
deceptive vices.
(2.6.12)

This lovely sentence does much to catalogue the blessings of the
life we have been given in the creation, against which his trivial
and not so trivial wrongdoings stand out as valueless.

What was it that led him to steal the pears, then? He reports
toward the end of Book 2 that he would never have done it
alone, concluding that it was the very sense of the group, and
their boldness, that led him to do it. This is a way both of sharing
guilt and shifting his sense of his own wrong. He concludes:

*in illis pomis voluptas mihi non erat,*
my pleasure was not in the pears themselves,

*ea erat in ipso facinore quam faciebat consortium simul peccantium*
it was in the wrong that a consort of sinners committed
together.
(2.8.16)

Finally, in the last paragraph of the book, after much self-examination, and explanation, and self-blaming, he in a sense throws
up his hands:

*quis exaperit istam tortuosissimam et implicatissimam nodositatem?*
who will untie this twisted and complicated knot?

*Foeda est; nolo in eam intendere, nolo eam videre.*
It is foul, I don't want to pay it any attention, I don't want to
see it.

*Te volo, iustitia et innocentia, pulchra et decora, honestis luminibus et insatiabili satietate.*
I desire you, because of your justice and innocence, beauty and elegance, wholesome splendor, and abundance that cannot be sated.

*Quies est apud te valde et vita imperturbabilis.*
Peace is with you, and untroubled life.

*Qui intrat in te, intrat in gaudium Domini sui et non timebit et habebit se optime in optimo.*
whoever enters you enters the joy of his Lord and will not be afraid and will live best in the best.

*Defluxi abs te ego et erravi, Deus meus,*
I flowed away from you, my God, and wandered,

*nimis devius ab stabilitate tua in adulescentia, et factus sum mihi regio egestatis.*
I was too much off the right road of your stability when I was an adolescent, and I made myself a region of neediness.
(2.10.18)

We may still have the feeling that he is making a mountain out of a molehill in the way he feels and thinks and talks about the theft of the pears. However he puts it, his feelings of guilt and shame may seem like too much.

If that is where you are, it might help to think about an imagined wrong of another kind, taking place in our own culture, our own lives.

Imagine that you are a young man married to a wonderful woman. She is kind, trusting, open, amusing, deeply honest, all in ways only she can be. She is precious to you beyond words. She knows you and loves you. Now you are at dinner with two other couples, and the other two guys begin to needle and tease their wives in ways the men think amusing, and the women seem to affirm by laughing—though you now recognize that this response was forced. Led on by the other men, you tease your wife in ways that hurt her, not very much, but enough to see her pained, and you do it on purpose. You try to back off a little, the dessert comes but is quickly eaten and the party breaks up.

At home your wife tells you how deeply hurt she feels. What do you feel? Not good things. The "minor" injury is actually not so minor at all, especially when seen as part of a continuing and intimate relationship. You now realize that it is no defense to call it "just teasing," and you also realize that you would never have done this on your own.

So what does it mean about you that you joined those who were teasing their wives? There are real parallels with Augustine's situation. Like him, you have work to do.

The genders could be reversed, if that helps: imagine a similar scene in which you are the wife, making fun of your husband's (very slight) speech impediment. Or if you are a reader of Jane Austen, think of the moment when Emma, at Box Hill, says something brief but cruel to a highly vulnerable woman. This event, tiny as it is, becomes the turning point of the whole novel.

Thinking this way may help us see a little more clearly that Augustine imagines his God not as a source of fear and thunder, not as a rigid rule-enforcer, not as demanding obeisance and obedience, but as a center of trusting love, a center than can be injured by us, even by our minor failings—none of which is in fact minor. He is imagining God's love as tender and vulnerable.[5] Augustine has injured God as the man in my example injured his wife. Does this perception help explain other moments in which he talks about God?

To sum up. Book 2 offers us an extraordinary experience of Augustine's mind: wrestling simultaneously with his own mind and feelings and with the language he has been given to make sense of them; trying hard to understand what he was doing with his sexual desires, what he was doing when he stole the pears and did other rowdy things with his pals; full of intense self-loathing at the beginning, but much less so at the end; making moral and practical distinctions that seem real, but in the end turning away from what was a sort of exposition of moral philosophy, away from analysis and explanation, and toward the God he is learning to love.

# 6

## LOVE, PHILOSOPHY, AND
## MONNICA'S DREAM (BOOK 3)

IN THE NEXT FEW CHAPTERS what we read may seem less organized than what we have been reading, where we had the story of Augustine's early life to give it structure. In what follows now, up to his final conversion, Augustine is not really telling such a story, nor is his material organized thematically or as a single project. Rather, what he offers us as readers is a set of experiences that are like his own: as he moves from topic to topic and back again, finds clarification then loses it, often returning to a state of puzzlement, so do we. This is his gift.

Most people seem to work this way when the work is deep. In Augustine's case, this means that we can look for progress less in connection with ideas than with relations: his relation to God, his relation to the language in which he talks to him, and his relation to us, his readers. In reading these chapters it is especially important for us to be open to the reality he creates for us in his writing, for it is there that we can learn something of what his life was actually like.

Certain issues will surface at a variety of moments, then withdraw, then come back to the center of attention. These include the whole subject of sexuality, love in various forms, the nature of true friendship, what philosophy can and cannot do, the place of Scripture in the life he is making, charity as a central value (sometimes in surprising ways), his relation with Monnica, the practices of confession and praise, the Manichees, the desire for impossible certainty, the tension between eloquence and truth, the nature and origin of evil, divisions within the self, the tension between internal and external experiences, the search for people who could be guides and mentors, literal versus imaginative interpretation of Scripture, baptism, and the nature of the Christian community, among many others.

He comes to a kind of clarity on many of these issues, but the process by which he does so is not for the most part a form of reasoning in the usual sense, but a much more complex process, much of which he shares with us. Another way to put this point is to say that it becomes increasingly clear that for him the ground of life is not belief but knowledge, and that it rests not on reason but experience. I think it is his object to make that true for us as well. A good question to keep in mind is how confidently each of us as a reader can understand where he comes out on these issues, and how well, if at all, we could express what we perceive.

A related point: I realized in revising these chapters that I often find myself saying that something is what I call "central" to Augustine's life and character—a discovery, a way of thinking, a sense of a relationship—but I say this about different things. This is in a sense an impossible reading of the word "center": there can logically be only one, and in geometry it is reduced to a dimensionless point. I thought at one time that I should figure out what was truly central, and confine my remarks to that, but after thinking further I decided to allow these competing centers to remain, for they capture an element of our experience of Augustine, namely, that he seems to have many centers, important and shifting.

In all of this our attention should be on what Augustine himself says, and how he says it, certainly not on anything I might say. We might read the passages I reproduce from Augustine a little as if they were poems and it was our goal to try to make them available, and to learn how they might best be read. As the title of this book suggests, the project on which we are here launched together is learning to read the *Confessions* of Augustine. That is where our attention should be focused.

\* \* \*

Book 3 begins this way:

> *Veni Cartthaginem,*
> I came to Carthage

> *et circumstrepebat me undique sartago flagitiosorum amorum.*
> and there resounded around me on all sides a frying pan of shameful loves.
> (3.1.1)

This defines his opening theme, which will run through Book 3. It is significant that he does not here tell us why he went to Carthage in his early twenties (which was at least in part to continue his professional education in rhetoric). What I think he is saying by his silence on such matters is that his distress about love was and is much more important to him than his education.

> *Nondum amabam, et amare amabam,*
> I did not yet love, yet I loved to think of loving,

> *et secretiore indigentia oderam me minus indigentem.*
> and in a secret longing I hated myself for longing so little.
> (3.1.1)

What does he mean by this? Perhaps he is saying that his hidden longing was to love an actual person, or relationship, which he was unable to attain. Another possibility is that the secret longing is actually a longing for God, which is swamped at the moment by his other desires. A third possibility is one we might see today: a person who desperately wants to love, to be loved, to express himself or herself sexually, but has no idea how to do these things. Such a person is not incapable of love but does not know how to get from here to there. (Which is Augustine, do you think?)

> *Quaerebam quid amerem, amans amare,*
> I was seeking something to love, loving love itself as I did,
>
> *et oderam securitatem et viam sine muscipulis,*
> and I hated safety and a path free of snares,
>
> *quoniam fames mihi erat intus ab interiore cibo, te ipso, Deus meus,*
> because there was an inner hunger within me for inner food—for you yourself, my God,
>
> *et ea fame non esuriebam,*
> but this hunger I did not really want to satisfy;
>
> *sed eram sine desiderio alimentorum incorruptibilium,*
> but I was without desire for incorruptible food,
>
> *non quia plenus eis eram, sed quo inanior, fastidiosior,*
> not because I was filled with it, but the more I was empty the more picky I became.
> (3.1.1)

Such are the themes and issues with which he begins, very similar to the main topics of Book 2.

## PERVERSE LOVES (3.1.1–3.3.5)

He elaborates his sense of his condition by describing the poor
state of his soul, desperate for physical stimulation and connection,
bringing his own lust into friendships where it did not belong.

*Rui etiam in amorem, quo cupiebam capi* . . .
I rushed into love, by which I desired to be seized . . .

*ut caederer virgis ferreis ardentibus zeli*
so that I was beaten with burning iron rods of jealousy

*et suspicionum et timorum et irarum atque rixarum.*
and of suspicions and fears and rages and brawls.
(3.1.1)

We need to remind ourselves here that despite its urgency this is
all past tense. The Augustine who is writing this book is not living the life he portrays but remembering what that life was like
for the young Augustine, confused as he was by his own internal
conflicts and misunderstandings.

Suppose the earlier Augustine came to you as his therapist,
revealing this array of conflicting and unhappy feelings. What
would you say to him? What would you hope for him? What
would you ask him? One possibility would be: "Why do you
continue to do things that make you so unhappy?"

That is in fact the question that Augustine addresses next, in
connection not with his sexual or romantic life but with his love
of the theater—which we were told in Book 2 was problematic
even when he was reading plays in school. Now he goes to see
plays, a lot, and the question he asks is: why is it pleasurable to
behold the imagined misery of others, as one so often does at the
theater? But that is what a person does:

*et dolor ipse est voluptas eius*
and sorrow is his pleasure.

*Quid est nisi mirabilis insania?*
What is this but wonderful insanity?
(3.2.2)

Is the reason we take pleasure in this pain that there is pleasure in compassion itself? I sympathized with lovers who were acting wrongly, he says, and was sad for them when they paid the price, but at the same time I experienced delight. But he sees perceptively that there is potential wrongdoing here, certainly if we want others to suffer, even in imagination, so that we can feel compassion (3.23).

These are matters of relevance today, where someone might well say, with Augustine, *At ego tunc miser dolere amabam*, "But then I, unhappy as I was, loved to be in sorrow" (3.2.4). He then describes his life as a loathsome disease, scratching the itch of desire, and desire for sorrow—not compassion—and goes on: *Talis vita mea numquid vita erat, Deus meus?* "Was such a life as mine really life at all, my God?" (3.24). [I was] *amans vias meas et non tuas, amans fugitavam libertatem*, "loving my ways and not yours, loving a fugitive liberty" (3.3.5).

## PHILOSOPHY, SCRIPTURE, AND SIN (3.3.6–3.9.17)

A top student of rhetoric and proud of it, Augustine makes a point of saying that he distanced himself from a rowdy crowd of students who were more mature and more violent than those with whom earlier he stole pears: these are the *eversores*, "the overturners" (3.3.6). He is saying that he could now resist that kind of destructive appeal.

At about this time he came upon a now lost work of Cicero, the *Hortensius*, which asserted the priority of philosophy over rhetoric. This led him to become obsessed for a time with philosophy.

> *Viluit mihi repente omnis vana spes,*
> Suddenly all my empty hope [of love?] became of no value
>
> *et immortalitatem sapientiae concupiscebam aestu cordis incredibili,*
> and I found myself desiring the immortality of wisdom with an incredible burning of the heart,
>
> *et surgere coeperam ut ad te redirem.*
> and I began to rise up so that I might return to you.
> (3.4.7)

Augustine describes the effect of philosophy as a kind of obsession or passion, and in a sense this was true for him; but it is a different kind of obsession from the loves we have seen, because it is intellectual, not physical, in nature. Of course there are false philosophies, as Cicero made plain. What captured Augustine was the idea of wisdom itself to which he gave himself wholeheartedly. But he found something missing here:

> *quod nomen Christi non erat ibi . . .*
> that the name of Christ was not there . . .
>
> *hoc nomen salvatoris mei, filii tui,*
> that name of my savior, your son,

*in ipso adhuc lacte matris tenerum cor meum pie biberat et alte*
*retinebat*
which my soft heart had piously imbibed with the very milk
of my mother, and preserved deeply within
(3.4.8)

Notice that the fact that he had taken in the name of Jesus with
his mother's milk—that is, in his relationship with her from the
very beginning—was the result of no decision or plan by him.
He did not choose it in any way. I think he is necessarily saying
that it was an act of pure grace, and one of great importance.
Where would he have been had that not happened?

His understanding of human life is not that we start as *tabu-*
*lae rasae* upon which we inscribe our experiences and thoughts
and desires, but that at every stage we interact both with each
other—teaching and changing each other for better or for
worse—and with the God who is within us.

He then decided to turn to Scripture itself:

*attendi ad illam scripturam,*
I gave Scripture my attention

*sed visa est mihi indigna quam tullianae[1] dignitati comparem*
but it seemed to me unfit that I should compare it with the
worthy writings of Cicero.
(3.5.9)

That is, Scripture as an intellectual or literary matter just did not
measure up to the work of the best Roman thinker and writer.
(It is important to know that by the end of the *Confessions* he
will have completely reversed himself on the reading of Scripture, which became the basis of his work in the last three books.)

\* \* \*

But for now the next stage of his story:

> *Itaque incidi in homines superbe delirantes, carnales nimis et*
> *loquaces*
> And so I fell among men delirious with pride, thoroughly
> physical, and full of talk
> (3.6.10)

These, here unnamed, were the Manichees, among whom
Augustine was to count himself for nine years. One appeal
of the sect was that it had a way of explaining evil in the
world which avoided the paradox of a God who was at once
perfectly good and the creator of a world with lots of evil
in it. They imagined not one but two deities—one good, one
bad, each responsible for works of his own kind. Another key
doctrine was the idea that God, like everything real, was a
physical reality. Augustine was absorbed by this theology for
years, but ultimately came to see what he came to regard as
its errors.

As for the physicality of God, Augustine the writer tells us
that the Manichees were wrong:

> *nec ista corpora es quae videmus quamquam in caelo. . . .*
> nor are you those bodies [sun, moon, stars], which we see
> sometimes in the sky. . . .

> *Sed nec anima es, quae vita es corporum . . .*
> But nor are you a soul, which is the life of bodies . . .

> *sed tu vita es animarum, vita vitarum, vivens te ipsa, et non*
> *mutaris, vita animae meae.*
> but you are the life of souls, the life of lives, yourself living,
> you are not changed, life of my soul.
> (3.6.10)

In all my false beliefs, I was searching for you, he says,

> *sed secundum sensum carnis. . . .*
> but according to the awareness of the body.

> *Tu autem eras interior intimo meo et superior summo meo.*
> You however were deeper within the deepest part of me and
> higher than the highest part.
> (3.6.11)

As the end of the book approaches, he sums up what he did not
know:

> *non noveram malum non esse nisi privationem boni. . . .*
> I did not know that evil was nothing but the absence of
> good. . . .

> *non noveram Deum esse spiritum, non cui membra essent per
> longum et latum nec cui esse moles esset. . . .*
> I did not know that God is a spirit, not one whose parts have
> length and breadth, not one which existed as a mass. . . .

> *Et non noveram iustitiam veram interiorem,*
> And I did not know of that interior true justice,

> *non ex consuetudine iudicantem sed ex lege rectissima Dei
> omnipotentis,*
> not judging by custom but by the most righteous law of
> omnipotent God,

> *qua formarentur customs regionum et dierum pro regionibus et
> diebus,*
> by which the principles of different regions and times could
> be formed on behalf of those regions and times

*cum ipsa [lex] ubique ac semper esset, non alibi alia nec alias
aliter*
While the law itself was always the same, not different in
one place or time[2]
(3.7.12–13)

Next a sentence to which I wish to draw special attention.

*Sed inter flagitia and facinora[3] et tam multas iniquitates sunt
peccata proficientium,*
But among the serious sins and outrages, and so many
wrongs, are the sins of those who are making progress,

*quae a bene iudicantibus et vituperantur ex regula perfectionis*
which by those who judge well are both blamed by the rule
of perfection

*et laudantur spe frugis sicut herba segetis.*
and praised for the hope of fruit, like the plants of the field.
(3.9.17)

It is to me an astonishing statement that some sins, in some circumstances, can be a ground of hope. I think this is true, but I
would not have thought of it on my own. This attitude of generosity and kindness in Augustine, really a species of *caritas*, is
consistent with what we just saw him say respecting the moral
customs with which the actors in the Old Testament were raised
(and by implication doing the same with other actors, raised
in other cultures), namely, that in essential matters virtue and
justice are the same for all people, though with respect to less
important matters it is important to tolerate, or even learn from,
diversity of opinion. This is consistent too with the position he
takes at the end of the *Confessions*, where he devotes Books 11

and 12 to his interpretation of the opening verses of Genesis, and then says in effect that while what he has written is what he really thinks, after a lot of work, if someone else pays the Scripture similar attention, in a spirit of good will, his reading is as entitled to as much respect as Augustine's own.

In our passage he goes on to say that proper judgment about the true wrongfulness of conduct depends a lot on context and motive, which may be simply unclear or unknowable.

> *Multa itaque facta quae hominibus improbanda viderentur*
> *testimonio tuo approbata sunt,*
> many things are done which seem to men to be the proper object of strong rejection, but which in your judgment are approved,

> *et multa laudata ab hominibus te teste damnantur,*
> and many things praised by men are condemned in your judgment,

> *cum saepe se aliter habet species facti*
> since often the appearance of the deed is different to different observers

> *et aliter facientis animus atque articulus occulti temporis.*
> and the same is true of the intention of the actor and the structure of the hidden time.
> (3.9.17)

The charity and humility and trust in God that Augustine expresses here seem to me extraordinary, miles away from the rigidity and punitiveness which are often attributed to him.

* * *

To get a better sense of what Augustine means here, let me suggest that you read the Latin aloud to yourself as something you mean. *Multa itaque facta* (many things are done) *quae hominibus improbanda viderentur* (which seem to men to be the proper object of strong rejection) *testimonio tuo approbata sunt* (but which in your judgment are approved), *et multa laudata ab hominibus* (and many things praised by men) *te teste damnantur* (are condemned in your judgment) *cum saepe se aliter habet species facti* (since often the appearance of the deed is different to different observers) *et aliter facientis animus* (and the same is true of the intention of the actor) *atque articulus occulti temporis* (and the critical nature of the moment [which is a possible meaning of the difficult phrase, "the structure of the hidden time"]).

\* \* \*

Can you divide the sentence into clauses and explain the sequence and pattern they make? Is it like a little dance?

\* \* \*

## MONNICA AND THE BISHOP (3.11.19–3.12.21)

All of this time, Monnica was full of fear and anxiety about her son's future. Distressed and weeping she repeatedly prayed to God for his soul, at one point apparently refusing to let Augustine live in her house, as he had been doing, but then changing her mind. Then she had a vision in which she saw a young man standing on the far end of a kind of board or ruler, seemingly in great health. When he asked her why she was weeping every day, she said that she had seen an image of his damnation. The young man told her to remember, *ubi esset illa, ibi esse et me,* "where she was, I was there too" (3.11.19).

She was reassured, though he continued in his shameful ways.

One final story. She went to a bishop to ask him to intercede with Augustine and teach him a proper way of being. He refused to do that on the grounds that it would be of no use. He himself had been a Manichee and had to work his way out of it and knew how hard it can be. Instead, he said:

> *"Sine illum ibi.*
> Let him be.
>
> *Tantum roga pro eo Dominum.*
> Only pray for him to the Lord.
>
> *Ipse legendo reperiet quis ille sit error et quanta impietas.*
> By reading he will learn what an error it (Manicheism) is and how great an impiety."
> (3.12.21)

Still she pestered him constantly until he said in frustration,

> *"Vade . . . a me!*
> "Get away . . . from me!
>
> *Ita vivas: fieri non potest, ut filius istarum lacrimarum pereat."*
> As you live: it cannot be that the son of these tears should perish."
> (3.12.21)

But Augustine was to stay with the Manichees for nine more years. We can imagine Monnica's distress.

# 7

## FRIENDSHIP AND STRUGGLES
## WITH MANICHEISM (BOOK 4)

BOOK 4 IS LENGTHY and important, covering the nine years Augustine spent as a Manichee, from his nineteenth to twenty-eighth year.

He begins by representing his spiritual condition (using the first person plural to mark that he was not alone[1] but part of a group of Manichees who behaved together in the way he describes):

> *Per idem tempus . . . seducebamur et sedebamus,*
> In this time . . . we were being seduced and seducing,

> *falsi atque fallentes in variis cupiditatibus,*
> [we who were] deceptive and deceiving in our everchanging desires

> *et palam per doctrinas quas liberales vocant,*
> openly [doing so] through teachings they call liberal,

> *occulte falso nomine religionis,*
> secretly by using the false name of religion,

> *hic superbi, ibi superstitiosi, ubique vani,*
> here proud, there superstitious, and everywhere empty,[2]

*hac popularis gloriae sectantes inanitatem,*
in the one activity [i.e., the liberal arts] seeking the
emptiness of popular fame

*usque ad theatricos plausus et contentiosa carmina et agonem
coronarum faenearum*
including theatrical applause and song contests and a
struggle for crowns of straw

*et spectaculorum nugas et intemperentiam libidinum,*
and the triviality of spectacles and the intemperance of lusts,

*illac autem purgari nos ab istis sordibus expetentes,*
in the other [i.e., Manicheism], desiring to be cleansed from
these foul things—

*cum eis qui appellarentur electi et sancti afferemus*
when we brought to those called "elect" and "holy"

*escas de quibus nobis in officina aqualiculi sui fabricarent
angelos et deos*
food by which they would then fabricate for us, in the
workshop of their bellies, angels and gods

*per quos liberaremur.*
through whom we would be liberated.[3]

*Et sectabar ista atque faciebam cum amicis meis per me ac mecum
deceptis.*
I was pursuing these things and doing them with my
friends, who were deceived by me and deceived with me.
(4.1.1)

This is an exercise in skillful and amusing mockery, leaving no
doubt where Augustine the narrator stands and at the same time

making clear that Augustine the pilgrim is at this point leading a twisted and empty life.

There follows an important completion of the thought:

*Inrideant me arrogantes*
Let the arrogant ones mock me

*et nondum salubriter prostrati et elisi a te, Deus meus,*
and those not yet prostrate and dashed to pieces by you, my God,

*ego tamen confitear tibi dedecora mea in laude tua.*
I may nonetheless confess to you my shameful things in your praise.
(4.1.1)

Here the Augustine the narrator is undertaking to confess now the follies and sins he committed as Augustine the pilgrim.

You may remember that in chapter 1, which described the shape of the *Confessions,* I said that Augustine's movement was not from triumph to triumph to triumph, as one might expect in the autobiography of a famous person today, but from failure to failure, in a process one might call benign humiliation. That is what he is talking about in this sentence, which looks forward to the rest of the *Confessions* and the many ways in which the successes that once most gratified him were taken away.

It is crucial that he speaks of the activity of mind and heart and imagination in which he is engaged as a form of confession. This sentence is part of the armature by which the whole text is given structure. Remember here what he said in Book 3, that the purpose of his confession was to learn to love God.

*Quid enim sum ego mihi sine te nisi dux in praeceps?*
What indeed am I to myself without you, except the one
who leads myself off a cliff?
(4.1.1)


## RHETORIC (4.2.2–4.2.3)

Here is a brief version of the story told in Book 4. Augustine was
now in Carthage, by profession a teacher of rhetoric—which he
defines as selling eloquence itself:

*victoriosam loquacitatem victus cupiditate vendebam . . .*
I, conquered by desire, was selling victorious loquacity . . .

*et eos sine dolo docebam dolos*
and I was teaching trickery to those without trickery.
(4.2.2)

He hoped his students would not use as lawyers the skills he
taught them to harm innocent people *contra caput*, "against principle," but sometimes, when, *pro caput*, "consistent with principle," to help the guilty.

During those years he lived with a woman, by whom, despite
their prayers to the contrary, he had a son, "Adeodatus" (meaning "given by God"), whom Augustine loved deeply until his
death in early adulthood. As in his account of the experience of
the nursing child in Book 2, I think Augustine is giving us an
example, in the love he has for his son, of the benign force of our
living physical and emotional nature.

Someone offered to ensure Augustine victory in a poetry recita-
tion competition if he gave him a bribe, which he refused to offer

him. As part of his exploration of the world he consulted astrologers, whom he thought less poisonous than the seers who sacrificed animals—a practice prohibited to Manichees—or invoked evil spirits. But the astrologers tended to excuse moral or behavioral fault by saying that it was fated or determined by one or more of the gods, which was to Augustine what we would call a copout. Augustine was attracted by horoscopes as well, a practice he would not abandon entirely because he was not wholly persuaded that they had no value at all—an example of his overly fastidious insistence on perfect knowledge, a trait of which we shall see more.

Two things emerge here. First that Augustine is seeking something outside himself, greater than himself, which will make living itself manageable and intelligible. Second, it is clear from these briefly described aspects of his life that Augustine was by no means as bad or wicked as he now says (though not especially admirable either). Augustine the narrator tells us that the problem was this:

*non enim amare te noveram,*
I did not know how to love you,

*qui nisi fulgores corporeos cogitare non noveram.*
I who did not know how to imagine radiance[4] except in a physical form.
(4.2.3)

As I have said, it was the doctrine of the Manichees that all reality was physical. Augustine's acceptance of this doctrine prevented him from imagining any God as a spiritual being, let alone one with a presence within his own heart.

Augustine the narrator is here not defining a state of sinfulness or wickedness in Augustine the pilgrim so much as a state of essential confusion, arising both from his professional role as a teacher of rhetoric and from his religious life, where he was committed to the principles and practices of Manicheism. As I said earlier, the great attraction of this sect seems to have been that it provided a way of explaining the existence of evil in the world, by positing an evil God as well as a good one, neither of whom was omnipotent. In its belief, just mentioned, that all reality was physical it had the additional simplifying appeal of a kind of reductionism that has over the years been all too familiar in many other forms than this.

## FRIENDSHIP (4.4.7–4.9.14)

When Augustine was teaching in Thagaste—probably when he returned from Carthage to spend a year in his hometown, for reasons we are not told[5]—he formed a friendship with an unnamed young man he had known since they were boys together. He tells us that this was at first not the wonderful kind of friendship it came to be later on, indeed that even at its best it was not true friendship, *vera amicitia*:

> *quia non est vera [amiticia] nisi cum eam agglutinas inter haerentes tibi*
> because friendship is only true if you make a bond among those adhering to you

> *caritate diffusa in cordibus nostris per spiritum sanctum, qui datus est nobis.*
> by the charity spread in our hearts by the Holy Spirit, who is given to us.[6]
> (4.4.7)

In fact, when it came to religion, Augustine persuaded him to give up Christianity.

Here Augustine the writer sees what that other Augustine, whose life he is telling, does not see, namely, that despite his feelings at the time, it was far from a perfect or truly loving friendship. In fact, it fits the same pattern as the other aspects of the life he has been describing, namely, that it is in some ways good, very good in fact, but ultimately confused or defective, not because there was anything wrong with the friend, but because Augustine did not then have the psychological center that was to be the gift of God. This friendship, he says, was *suavis mihi*, "sweet to me," *super omnes suavitates illius vitae meae*, "over all the other sweetnesses of that life of mine" (4.4.7).

Then the friend was struck with illness; while unconscious he was baptized; when he recovered, Augustine wanted to make a joke of the baptism—what could it possibly mean?—but his friend told him not to talk that way if he was to be his friend. He then had a relapse and died, at which Augustine was inconsolably wracked by grief.

*Quo dolore contenebratum est cor meum,*
With what sorrow was my heart overshadowed

*et quidquid aspiciebam mors erat.*
and whatever I beheld was death. . . .

*Et si dicebam, "spera in Deum" iuste non obtemperabat,*
And if I said [to my soul] "Hope in God," the soul rightly would not obey,

*quia verior erat et melior homo quem carissimum amiserat*
because the beloved person I had lost was truer and better

*quam phantasma in quod sperare iubebatur.*
than the fantasy in which the soul was being told to hope.
(4.4.9)

Here Augustine is honoring his own experience of love and grief, and using it to criticize his immature religiosity, which is reduced here to a *phantasma*, "fantasy." This gave him a ground for doubting and ultimately rejecting Manicheism, which offered him no adequate way of imagining or speaking to God. He now realizes that though the sense of loss and grief was real, the friendship itself was not based on mature mutual love. Consistently with what we have read so far in Book 4, it was good but confused. In all of this Augustine the pilgrim was in passionate and obsessive distress.

This is how he thought and felt about it:

*Mirabar enim ceteros mortales vivere,*
I was amazed that other mortals still lived

*quia ille, quem quasi non moriturum dilexeram, mortuus erat,*
because he whom I had loved as though he would never die was dead,

*et me magis, quia ille alter eram, vivere illo mortuo mirabar.*
and I was the more amazed that I lived when he was dead, when I was another him.

*Bene quidam dixit de amico suo: "dimidium animae" suae.*
Well did someone say of his friend that he was "half of his soul."

*Nam ego sensi animam meam et animam illius unam fuisse animam in duobus corporibus,*
For I felt my soul and his soul to be one soul in two bodies.

*et ideo mihi horrori erat vita, quia nolebam dimidius vivere,*
and for this reason life was to me a horror, that I did not want to live as half a person

*et ideo forte mori metuebam, ne totus ille moreretur quem*
*multum amaveram.*
and for this reason I strongly feared to die, that he would
then be wholly dead whom I had loved so much.
(4.6.11)

Augustine's merged identity with his friend is a destructive or
incomplete or immature version of the important experience
in which one recognizes the presence and activity of another
person—most of all of course God himself—within one's self.
In the modern jargon one would say that he lost his sense of
boundaries.

Not surprisingly he found life without his friend unendurable.

*Ad te, Domine, [anima mea] levanda erat et curanda,*
That to you, Lord, [my soul] should have been raised up and
cured,

*sciebam, sed nec volebam nec valebam. . . .*
I knew, but I did not really wish it nor was I able do it. . . .

*Non enim tu eras, sed vanum phantasma*
For you did not exist [for me], but were an empty
imagining,

*et error meus erat deus meus.*
while my own mistaken religious belief was my actual god.

*Si conabar eam ibi ponere ut requiesceret,*
If I tried to put my soul where it might rest

*per inane labebetur et iterum ruebat super me,*
it would slide off through an empty space and again it
descended on me,

*et ego remanseram infelix locus,*
and I remained in an unhappy place

*ubi nec esse possum nec inde recedere.*
where I could neither exist or from which depart.[7]

*Quo enim cor meum fugeret a corde meo?*
Where could my heart flee from my heart?

*Quo a me ipso fugerem?*
Where could I flee from myself?
(4.7.12)

Augustine left Thagaste and went to Carthage, where in time he developed other relations and practices, which, along with other things, took the place of his sorrows:

*non quidem dolores alii causae tamen aliorum dolorum.*
not indeed certain other sorrows, but the causes of other sorrows.

*Nam unde me facillime et in intima dolor ille penetraverat,*
For how could that sorrow have pierced me so easily,

*nisi quia fuderam in harenam animam meam diligendo moriturum acsi non moriturum?*
had not I poured out my soul on the sand by loving a person who was to die as though he was never to die?
(4.8.13)

This is where he comes out:

*Beatus qui amat te et amicum in te and inimicum propter te.*
Blessed is the one who loves you, and loves his friend in you, and his enemy on account of you.

*Solus enim nullum carum amittit cui omnes in illo cari sunt qui non amittitur. . . .*

He alone loses no one beloved to him to whom all are beloved in the one who cannot be lost. . . .

*Te nemo amittit nisi qui dimittit*

No one loses you unless they send you away

(4.9.14)

This is Augustine the narrator telling us what Augustine the pilgrim should have learned about the love of another person, in Christian terms about love of his neighbor.

## STRUGGLES WITH MANICHEISM
### (4.12.19–4.16.31)

Most of the rest of Book 4 is about the struggles Augustine had with his chosen religion, Manicheism, especially with the two central doctrines I have mentioned: that all reality is physical, and that there are two deities in constant tension, the good one and the bad one. His struggles are hard to reproduce, but are deeply moving, capturing beautifully what it is like for a person with a set of fundamental beliefs to begin to question them seriously and comprehensively. It is not merely a matter of changing one principle or idea, because everything is connected to everything else. If you read the *Confessions* on your own, do not skip these pages but allow yourself to live in them.

By the end of the book Augustine the narrator has worked out for his earlier self a set of arguments and perceptions that will ultimately lead him to the Christian orthodoxy, as he will define it:

*Et descendit huc ipsa vita [Christus] nostra,*
And our life itself [*i.e.*, Christ] came down here,

*et tulit mortem nostram et occidit eam de abundantia vitae suae,*
and bore our death and killed it with the abundance of his
life,

*et tonuit, clamans ut redeamus hinc ad eum in illud secretum
unde processit ad nos,*
and he thundered, proclaiming that we should return to
him from where we are, into that secret place from which he
emerged to us

*in ipsum primum virginalem uterum ubi ei nupsit humana
creatura, caro mortalis, ne semper mortalis.*
in that first virginal womb where the human creation wed
him, mortal flesh, so that it would not longer be mortal.

*Et inde velut sponsus procedens de thalamo suo exultavit ut
gigans ad currendam viam.*
And he came forth like a bridegroom coming out of his
chamber, like a giant running his course.

*Non emin tardavit, sed cucurrit clamans dictis, factis, morte,
vita, descensu, ascensu, clamans ut redeamus ad eum:*
He did not hesitate, but ran, proclaiming with words, with
deeds, with death, with life, with descent, with ascent,
proclaiming that we should return to him;

*et discessit ab oculis, ut redeamus ad cor et inveniamus eum.*
and he left our sight so that we might return to our own
hearts and might find him there.

*Abscessit enim et ecce hic est.*
He has gone away, but behold: he is here.

*Noluit nobiscum diu esse et non reliquit nos.*
He did not want to stay with us long, but he has not left us.
(4.12.19)

Having said these things, and more besides, he soon adds:

*Haec tunc non noveram*
Then I did not know these things
(4.13.20)

That is, the person who has just set forth the essentials of the Christian life is Augustine the narrator, providing a basis for looking now at what was happening then.

Next he talks about his captivation by the idea of beauty as the ultimate good, and the book he wrote, his first, *De pulchro et apto*, or *The Beautiful and the Fitting*, written out of a kind of ambition he now disowns. He wrote because he wanted to be praised as much as Hierius, a skillful orator, whom he loved in the particular sense that he wanted to be like him, and whose approval he somewhat desperately sought (4.14.23).

He struggled with the idea that evil was a physical reality.

*Non enim noveram neque didiceram nec ullam substantiam malum esse*
I did not know nor had I learned that evil was no substance

*nec ipsam mentem nostram summum atque incommutabile bonum.*
nor that our mind was not the highest and unchanging good.
(4.15.24)

The idea that evil is the absence of good, not an independent reality, is one he had been struggling toward but not yet achieved.

Likewise, as the high-powered intellectual he was, interested deeply in philosophy and religion, it was difficult for him even to begin to rank the mind below the soul.

Then a series of questions, which for the sake of space, I will edit and shorten. I will also be freer than usual in moving from one language to another:

> *Quid mihi proderat*, what good did it do me, that I read and understood Aristotle's *Ten Categories* by myself?
> (4.16.28)

> And: *quid hoc mihi proderat*, what good did it do me, that I tried to reduce you, my God, to those ten categories?
> (4.16.29)

> And: *Et quid mihi proderat*, what good did it do me
> *quod omnes libros artium quas liberales vocant* [*legi*]
> that [I read] all the books which people called the liberal arts?[8]
> (4.16.30)

> And: *quid mihi proderat*, what good did it do me, that I did not use my property well?
> (4.16.30)

> And: *Sed quid mihi hoc proderat*, what good did it do me,
> *putanti quod tu, Domine Deus veritas, corpus esses lucidum et immensum*
> But that I was thinking of you, Lord God, the Truth, as a luminous and immense body,
> (4.16.31)

*et ego frustum de illo corpore?*
and I a tiny piece of it?
(4.16.31)

And: *quid . . . mihi proderat ingenium per illas doctrinas
agile*
what . . . benefit to me was my intelligence, which [had been
made] agile through those teachings [of the Manichees]

*et nullo adminiculo humani magisterii*
that without any aid from a human teacher

*tot nodosissimi libri enodati,*[9]
those most knotty books explained [*enodati*],

*cum deformiter et sacrilega turpitudine in doctrina pietatis
errarem?*
when in a way that was disfigured, sacrilegious, and foul I
erred in the understanding of piety?
(4.16.31)

This is the voice of one who has himself worked through these
problems and is now talking about the confused and torn state
of his earlier self, who had begun but not finished that process.

\* \* \*

He concludes Book 4 with a lovely prayer:

*O Domine Deus noster, in velamento alarum tuarum speremus,
et protege nos et porta nos.*
Oh Lord our God, let us hope in the covering of your wings;
protect us and carry us.

*Tu portabis et parvulos et usque ad canos tu portabis,*
You will carry us when we are small, as far as old age you
will carry us,

*quoniam firmitas nostra quando tu es, tunc est firmitas,*
because when you are our firmness, then there is real
firmness,

*cum autem nostra est, infirmitas est.*
when our firmness is our own, it is weakness.

*Vivit apud te semper bonum nostrum,*
Our good always lives in your presence

*et quia inde aversi sumus, perversi sumus.*
and because we turn from it, we are perverted.

*Revertamur iam, Domine, ut non evertamur,*
Let us return [to you], Lord, in such a way that we are not
overturned

*quia vivit apud te sine ullo defectu bonum nostrum,*
because our good lives with you without defect,

*quod tu ipse es,*
because you are that good

*et non timemus ne non sit quo redeamus, quia nos inde ruimus.*
and we are not afraid that there may be no way for us to
return[10], because we have fallen into ruin.

*Nobis autem absentibus non ruit domus nostra, aeternitas tua.*
Even while we were away from you our house did not fall
into ruin, for our house is your eternity.[11]

(4.16.31)

# 8

## FROM THE MANICHEES TO
## AMBROSE (BOOK 5)

AUGUSTINE BEGINS BOOK 5 with a plea to God—his
audience throughout the *Confessions*—a plea to accept *sacrificium confessionum mearum*, "the sacrifice of my confessions." This
is a way of keeping before us the fact that the whole work is a
single great confession, or a series of confessions. As we saw at
the beginning of Book 4 he has discovered that the aim of confession is not to admit one's sins in the hope of redemption, but
to help the confessor himself or herself come to love God in a
new and richer way. Accordingly he now says:

> *Sed te laudet anima mea ut amet te,*
> But let my soul praise you so that it may love you,
>
> *et confiteatur tibi miserationes tuas ut laudet te.*
> and let it confess to you your acts of compassion, so that it
> may praise you.
> (5.1.1)

* * *

Look at the vocabulary at work in this sentence: *te laudet anima
mea*, "let my soul praise you," *ut amet te*, "so that it may love you,"

*et confiteatur tibi miserationes tuas,* "and let it confess to you [or "recognize"] your acts of compassion," *ut laudet te,* "so that it may praise you." We have soul, praise, love, confess, and compassion, and all the verbs are subjunctive ("may it happen that"). This is a substantial part of what could be called his foundational vocabulary. Each of these terms has been used over and over, and in the process developing a sense of depth and richness. Have the English terms had similar deepening? Can you describe the deepening of words in Latin? In English?

\* \* \*

In this passage Augustine is recalling the very beginning of the *Confessions*, when he first called God, *Magnus . . . et laudabilis valde,* then launched into an examination of a cluster of related language games—praising, invoking, knowing, believing, seeking—asking what relation each bore to the others, but never finding an answer. Now the language games he joins together—in a sense each being the cause of the other—are praise and love. He is seeing these activities, different though they seem to be, as in a deep sense the same, or at least as implying one another.

This raises a question for us: What does he think is the proper relation between love and praise? What do we think? What does our experience of reading this book tell us? Our experience of life outside the book?

Following the theme of praise, he first says that the whole creation praises God, but then quickly turns to a part of the creation that does not do so, i.e., wicked human beings: *Eant et fugiant a te inquieti iniqui,* "let the restless wicked leave and flee from you."

But then, almost immediately:

*Quo enim fugerunt, cum fugerent a facie tua*[1]?
Where did they flee when they tried to flee from your face?

*Aut ubi tu non invenis eos?*
Or where have you not found them?

*Sed fugerunt ut non viderent te videntem se*
But they fled so that they would not see you seeing them,

*atque excaecati in te offenderent. . . .*
and, blind as they were, they blundered into you. . . .

*Videlicet nesciunt quod ubique sis, quem nullus circumscribit
locus. . . .*
Surely they did not know you are everywhere, you to whom
no place gives limits or bounds. . . .

*Convertantur ergo et quaerant te,*
Let them be converted and seek you,

*quia non, sicut ipsi deseruerunt creatorem suum, ita tu deseruisti
creaturam tuam:*
because you have not deserted your creation as they have
deserted their creator.

*ipsi convertantur.*
May they be converted!
(5.2.2)

As the ellipses show, I have for reasons of space omitted some
of this paragraph, but the basic movement is clear and important: Augustine starts by talking of the wicked ones who have
fled from God as though they are different forms of human life.
But quickly he humanizes them, saying that their fear is the terrible feeling they will have if they behold God looking at them
in their wickedness—a kind of moral shame undercutting the
idea that they are really wicked after all. He tells us next that
they really do not understand that God is always where they are,

always within them in fact, so that wherever they flee they stumble upon him. Augustine asks that they be converted.

This passage thus reflects by stages a generosity of spirit, a living *caritas*, which is one of deep dispositions of Augustine's mind and heart, realized here in his compassion for the wicked and his understanding of their condition. He moves from being a kind of goody-goody looking down on the wicked ones to recognizing their common humanity. Here we may remember the way Augustine talked about himself as a young man torn by his sexuality and by the theft of pears from a neighbor, where he demonstrated his own internal experience of what he calls wickedness.

Is it possible that this prior "wickedness" is what enables him to have the understanding and feel the compassion that he does? If so, does this mean that the former wickedness was in the end a form of goodness? A real question I think, not only here but elsewhere in the *Confessions*, suggested but not stated.

Next he turns to one of the most fundamental of his discoveries and beliefs, namely, that God is within him, a fact known to Augustine the narrator, but not yet to Augustine the pilgrim.

*Et ecce ibi es in corde eorum, in corde confitentium tibi*
And behold you are there in their hearts, in the hearts of those confessing to you

*et proicientium se in te*
and throwing themselves upon you

*et plorantium in sinu tuo post vias suas difficiles. . . .*
and crying aloud on your breast after their difficult passages. . . .

*Et ubi ego eram, quando te quaerebam?*
And where was I when I was seeking you?

*Et tu eras ante me, ego autem et a me discesseram nec me
inveniebam: quanto minus te!*

You were right before me, but I had forsaken myself and did
not find myself—much less find you!

(5.2.2)

The question "Where was I?" implies a related, even deeper
question: "Who was I?"—a question for us as readers as well:
Who do we think Augustine was, and why? We have had a lot of
exposure to him by now. What do you think? And: Who are we
in relation to Augustine and his book?

## MANI AND FAUSTUS (5.3.4–5.7.13)

Augustine was becoming less and less infatuated with the Manichees but out of his characteristic desire to be certain before
he did anything rash, he awaited the arrival of a famous Manichee bishop, one Faustus, who was an eloquent and skillful
orator. Perhaps he would explain away what has been troubling
Augustine.

But when he arrived in Carthage, during Augustine's twenty-
ninth year, Augustine was interested more in what Faustus said
than how he said it, and, as we shall see, was not impressed. In
response he turned to the Neoplatonic philosophers, who were
full of knowledge about the heavens and the heavenly bodies.
They could explain all sorts of heavenly phenomena, especially
eclipses of the sun. Augustine the narrator admires what they
could do with their intelligence, *ingenium*, but: *non enim religiose
quaerunt unde habeant ingenium quo ista quaerunt*, "they do not
seek in a religious way the source from which they had the intelligence by which they seek these things" (5.3.4).

That is, in an important sense their scientific impulse faltered, for it did not lead them to the next question, about the source from which their own capacity of intelligence came to them.

The philosophers did not offer Augustine all that he was seeking. But as far as it went, their science worked, and when he compared the work of the philosophers with the Manicheans, the latter failed every test of rationality. It was thus paradoxically the non-Christian philosophers who provided the knowledge and impetus to save him from the false religion of the Manichees.

As for the writings of Mani himself, he found them pretty much hopeless, in part for their narcissistic grandiosity. Speaking of Mani he says:

> *Non enim parvi se aestimari voluit,*
> He did not wish to be of no account,
>
> *sed spiritum sanctum, consolatorem et ditatorem fidelium tuorum.*
> but the holy spirit, the consoler, the enricher of your faithful,
>
> *auctoritate plenaria personaliter in se esse persuadere conatus est.*
> he tried to persuade others that all these actually existed within him, with plenary authority.
> (5.5.8)

You would think this might be enough to justify a breach, but it was not. Augustine was not yet 100 percent certain that the celestial events the Manichees claimed to predict could not be predicted accurately by them:

> *ut, si forte posset, incertum quidem mihi fieret utrum ita se res haberent an ita,*
> so that, if that could be so, it was made uncertain to me whether this side or that held the truth,

*sed ad fidem meam illius auctoritatem propter creditam*
*sanctitatem praeponerem*
but I could still because of my belief in his holiness put his
authority in support of my faith.[2]
(5.5.9)

Here he reveals once more his habitual insistence on proof beyond
a reasonable doubt before moving on from what he in some way
sees to be defective positions. This is a kind of intellectual perfectionism, and we will see it again at least twice more in Book 5.

When Faustus finally appeared in Carthage during Augustine's ninth year as a Manichee, he had little to recommend him
except an elegant style. And by now Augustine had learned to
distinguished between what is said and how it is said:

*iam ergo abs te didiceram ne eo debere videri aliquid verum dici,*
By then I had learned from you that nothing ought to seem
to be truly said

*quia eloquenter dicitur,*
because it is said eloquently

*nec eo falsum, quia incomposite sonant signa labiorum*
nor should anything be thought falsely said because the
messages of the lips have a disorderly sound
(5.6.10)

This division between eloquence and truth, for him the natural, even necessary, consequence of his education in rhetoric, is
a theme throughout the *Confessions*. As he talked with Faustus
his opinion of him fell precipitately. Faustus was simply not able
to engage in constructive conversation about the differences in
their views and he turned out as well to know very little about
the books of liberal arts for which he was famous.

On the other hand, he willingly admitted that he did not know enough to defend the claimed expertise of the Manichees in astronomical knowledge. Augustine, charitable once more, found this very fact appealing.

> *Noverat enim se ista non nosse nec eum puduit confiteri.*
> He knew he did not know these things and was not
> ashamed to admit it.

And:

> *Pulchrior est enim temperantia confitentis animi quam illa quae*
> *nosse cupiebam.*
> More beautiful is the disposition of the confessing spirit
> than the things I desired to know.
> (5.7.12)

A remarkable thing to say about the man whose position he is at last beginning to reject. Another instance of his charity.[3]

By now his enthusiasm for the Manichees had been destroyed. He separated himself from them, though not completely:

> *sed, quasi melius quicquam non inveniens,*
> but as if not finding something better

> *eo quo iam quoquo modo inrueram contentus interim esse*
> *decreveram,*
> I had determined to be content with what I had rushed into,
> in whatever manner,

> *nisi aliquid forte magis eligendum esset eluceret.*
> unless perhaps something should appear to be more worthy
> of choice.
> (5.7.13)

This is another example of his characteristic insistence on certainty before moving on.

## ROME (5.8.15–5.10.18)

With the support of a patron, Romanianus, from Thagaste, Augustine decided to leave Carthage for Rome. The reason, as he describes it, was not ambition so much as the desire to escape from the rude and disorderly students at Carthage, who made it nearly impossible for him to function as a teacher. But part of the appeal of Rome was the set of Manichees there, who, it turns out, would subject him to pressure to remain one of them.

His mother beseeched him in the strongest way to return home, and failing that urged him to take her with him to Rome. In an astonishing gesture, Augustine falsely pretended to her that his departure had been delayed by the visit of a friend, then sneaked off to embark without her, and without explaining what he was doing and why. While for him the land was disappearing from view, she was left behind, heartbroken, weeping, and praying (5.8.15).

This seems brutal, and is almost certainly a manifestation of the huge cost of his incapacity to maintain what we would call proper boundaries with Monnica. It seems that he needed to assert his independence from her and that this, however costly to her, was the only way he could manage to do that.

Speaking to God he says:

*In quo mane illa insaniebat dolore,*
In the morning she went crazy with sorrow

*et querellis et gemitu implebat aures tuas*
and with complaints and groaning filled your ears

*contemnentis ista,*
but you had contempt for these things

*cum et me cupiditatibus meis raperes ad finiendas ipsas
cupiditates*
when you took me by my desires for the purpose of ending
them

*et illius carnale desiderium iusto dolorum flagello vapularet.*
and her physical desire was beaten down by the just whip of
sorrows.

(5.8.15)

This is tough stuff, seemingly heartless, but it is hard to judge
without knowing more than we do about Monnica's deep and
deliberate involvement in the most important aspects of her
son's life. Maybe it really was something he had to do.

In a more general way, he expresses great confidence that it is
God who is leading him to Rome, a movement that will lead to
his salvation. Here he is resisting the view common among very
smart people that we are to get the whole credit for what we do
and who we become, because it is all our work. For Augustine,
however—who, as you remember, received with his mother's
milk the knowledge of Christ—that is not true. In his world we
all live in and for each other, in the company of the active presence of God.

In Rome he continued to associate with the Manichees, now
including not only the "Hearers," as before, but the "Elect." He
was very much taken with their idea that active in us were two
different forces, one good, one bad, because this meant that
when we do something wrong it is not we who do it, but the
evil force. But, he says immediately below, this in turn means
there is no necessity for confession of sin, a temptation of

immense significance in this book which consists of one long
confession.

> *Adhuc enim mihi videbatur non esse nos qui peccamus*
> To this point it still seemed to me that it was not we who sin
>
> *sed nescio quam aliam in nobis peccare naturam,*
> but some other nature, I don't quite know what, within us.
>
> *et delectabat superbiam meam extra culpam esse et,*
> and it delighted my pride that it was beyond any blame
>
> *cum aliquid mali fecissem, non confiteri me fecisse,*
> and, when I did something wicked, that it was not necessary
> for me to confess,[4]
>
> *ut sanares animam meam, quoniam peccabat tibi,*
> in order for you to save my soul, that I had sinned against you,
>
> *sed excusare me amabam et accusare nescio quid aliud quod*
> *mecum esset et ego non essem.*
> but I loved to excuse myself and to accuse I don't quite know
> what that was with me, yet I was not it.
>
> *Verum autem totum ego eram et adversus me impietas mea me*
> *diviserat*
> However I was in fact the whole thing, and my impiety had
> already divided me against myself
> (5.10.18)

He flirted with the school of Academics who were committed
to the view that all things should be doubted, *nec aliquid veri*
*ab homine comprehendi posse*, "nor could anything of the truth
be understood by a human being." He became convinced that
truth could not be found in the church, in part because it seemed

out of bounds to believe God could ever be reduced to a human body, in part because he could still only think of God as a material mass, on the Manichean grounds that all reality was material. Likewise, evil had to be material too, a conviction that led back to the idea of two different forces in the world, one good, one bad. He could not believe that Christ could be born of a woman without being defiled by the flesh.

His efforts to establish himself as a teacher of rhetoric were utterly frustrated by the students who to avoid paying for their tuition would skip from one teacher to another.

Such was his state in Rome. We can see that it is increasingly unsatisfactory to him, yet it is not clear what else he might do.

## MILAN (5.13.23–5.14.25)

Then a message came from Milan to one Symmachus, also a patron of Augustine, asking him to choose a teacher of rhetoric for that city. Augustine applied, was accepted, and moved to Milan, where he was warmly greeted by Ambrose, Bishop of Milan, who was to become immensely influential in Augustine's future.

> *Et eum amare coepi, primo quidem non tamquam doctorem veri,*
> At the beginning I began to love him, at the beginning, not in fact as a teacher of truth,

> *quod in ecclesia tua prorsus desperabam, sed tamquam hominem benignum in me.*
> for I despaired utterly of your church, but as a man kindly disposed to me.
> (5.13.23)

He listened to his disputations among the people, but with attention to his eloquence (*facundiam*) much more than the substance of what he said—in this confirming a theme we have seen before.

> *Et dum cor aperirem ad excipiendum quam diserte diceret,*
> Yet while I opened my heart to grasp how eloquently [*diserte*] he spoke,
>
> *pariter intrabat et quam vere diceret, gradatim quidem.*
> at the same time it gradually entered (my mind) how truly [*vere*] he spoke.
> (5.14.24)

In other words, while he consciously focused his attention on the rhetorical skill Ambrose manifested, he unconsciously became aware of the issues Ambrose addressed and his ways of thinking about them. In this way Ambrose was teaching him that the Catholic faith could be explained and defended, including against the attacks of the Manichees.

Finally he was introduced by Ambrose to nonliteral ways of reading the Old Testament, which exploded many of the Manichean objections to their sanctity. (We shall come back to this topic in a big way when we read Books 11 and 12, both of which are in large measure about the first two verses of Genesis, which Augustine reads in a decidedly nonliteral way.)

In a final burst of effort he decided to see if he could refute the Manichees with absolute certainty. He was not yet able to do this, as Augustine the narrator tells us:

> *Quod si possem spiritalem substantiam cogitare,*
> If I had been able to imagine a spiritual substance or reality,

*statim machinamenta illa omnia solverentur et abicerentur ex anima meo:*
immediately all those devices [of the Manichees] would have been brought to an end and thrown from my soul:

*sed non poteram.*
but I could not do it.
(5.14.25)

At this point he decides finally that he must leave the Manicheans, and join the Catholic Church with the intention of being baptized, which he does. It is crucial that he does not get there simply by intellectual means, by proving that the Manichees cannot do science, for example, or by showing that one cannot live under the injunction of the Academics to admit nothing as true. He puts his powerful mind to work at the process of conclusive proof, but finds in the end that there is no such thing, a fact that liberates him and opens up his other capacities of imagination and thought.

What brings him into the church is not a set of arguments, but experience of a very different kind, most notably his experience of his mother, Monnica, who loved him, and of his new mentor, Ambrose, whose essential gift was species of kindness. As Augustine is learning more fully that God is within him he is at the same time moving in the direction of discovering what love can be.

# 9

## CERTAINTY AND UNCERTAINTY
## (BOOK 6)

BOOK 6 BEGINS WITH AN expression of Augustine's sense of loneliness and despair early in his time in Milan.

> *Spes mea a iuventute mea, ubi mihi eras et quo recesseras? . . .*
> You, who were my hope from my youth, where were you for me, and where had you withdrawn yourself? . . .
>
> *Et ambulabam per tenebras et lubricum et quaerebam te foris a me,*
> and I was walking through darkness and slipperiness, and I was looking for you outside of myself
>
> *et non inveniebam Deum cordis mei*
> and I could not find the God of my heart.
> (6.1.1)

We are quickly given a different perspective on his spiritual condition, that of Monnica, his mother, who has followed him first to Rome, then to Milan. When he said that he was no longer a Manichee but not yet a Catholic, she responded, not with anxiety or urgency, but with confidence that the next step, baptism, would indeed take place. But she continued to pray, and was in constant attendance at the sermons of Ambrose.

> *Diligebat autem illum virum sicut angelum Dei,*
> She loved him [Ambrose] as an angel of God

> *quod per illum cognoverat me interim ad illam ancipitem*
> *fluctiationem iam esse perductum*
> because she had recognized that in this time I had been
> led by him into the wavering fluctuation that I was
> experiencing.
> (6.1.1)

She was sure God would help him the rest of the way.

As an example of her devotion to Ambrose, Augustine tells us that she had a practice, known elsewhere in the Christian world, of bringing food and wine to the shrines of the saints (usually martyrs), where the food would be given to the poor. She is told by an official at one of the shrines that she is not to do this, and when she understands the reason is to discourage drinking she readily accepts the constraint. But—and this is the interesting part—Augustine goes on to say that he thinks she would not have been willing to give it up *si alio prohiberetur quem non sicut Ambrosium diligebat*, "if it had been prohibited by someone whom she did not love as she loved Ambrose" (6. 2).

I think the point of Augustine's remark is to draw our attention away from rules and practices to another dimension of life entirely, the way one person imagines, relates to, and feels about another. The fact that she loves the person of Ambrose, "as an angel of God," not a set of ideas or rules, is what governs her conduct.[1] This is among other things an important recognition that deep emotions, at best the emotion of love, move the human soul more deeply than careful reasoning or authority.

As for Augustine, he greatly admired Ambrose, at first not for his greatness of heart or mind nor for his remarkable character, but for his success, as measured by honor and esteem. He was one *quem sic tantae potestates honorarent*, "whom so many powerful people honored" (6.3.3). Augustine's admiration for honor and esteem itself reveals a motive of ambition in him that is meant I think to be compared, to its disadvantage, with the feeling of love that moves Monnica.

Augustine wanted a special relationship with Ambrose, but it was not forthcoming. Ambrose was constantly busy with other men, or at meals, or reading—which he did silently, often with many people around him whom he would not permit to interrupt him. Augustine could not break through this pattern, but he could go to church and listen to Ambrose preach. As he did this he became increasingly clear that the attacks made on the books of the Old Testament by the Manichees, mainly on the ground that they told unbelievable things, *posse dissolvi*, "could be refuted" (6.3.4).

Likewise he learned that the fact that we are made in God's image does not mean that we should believe that God is himself bounded by the form of the human body.[2] Augustine the writer tells us that Augustine the pilgrim should have understood God not as a physical being, as the Manichees thought, but as a spiritual one:

> *tu enim, altissime et proxime, secretissime et praesentissime*
> you [God] are both the farthest away and the nearest, the most hidden and the most open

*cui membra non sunt alia maiora et alia minora,*
whose members are not some bigger and some smaller,

*sed ubique totus es et nusquam locorum es*
but all of you is everywhere, and nowhere are you defined by
one place.
(6.3.4)

But Augustine was then not able to conceive of God as a spiritual being. He should have addressed this failure, he says, as
Jesus invites his believers to do: "Ask and it shall be given you;
seek, and ye shall find; knock, and it shall be opened unto you"
(Matt. 7:7).[3]

## CERTAINTY (6.4.6–6.5.8)

Augustine found Ambrose's way of dealing with the Scriptures,
especially those of the Old Testament, immensely helpful. He
did not read them literally, Augustine says, but was restrained
and responsible in the way he came to terms with them. The way
Ambrose put it was to quote Paul: *littera occidit, spiritus autem
vivificat*, "the letter killeth, but the spirit giveth life" (6.4.6).
Augustine came to accept the Catholic teaching *ut crederetur
quod non demonstrabatur*, "that what could not be demonstrated
might nonetheless be believed" (6.5.7).

In his response to Ambrose, Augustine was beginning to recognize what we have noticed, that one of his major failings was
a kind of insistence on, or hope for, certainty beyond what it is
possible for human beings to enjoy, an insistence that was perhaps a species of intellectual pride. Ambrose helped him move
away from the frame of mind that demanded that everything he

thought or said should be demonstrable to a degree of certainty that is simply not possible:

*Volebam enim eorum quae non viderem ita me certum fieri*
I wanted to be made as certain about those things I could not see

*ut certus essem quod septem et tria decem sint.*
as I was certain that seven and three make ten.
(6.4.6)

Augustine was torn and unhappy in his beliefs:

*Sed id credebam aliquando robustius, aliquando exilius,*
But this I did believe, sometimes robustly, sometimes exiguously,

*semper tamen credidi et esse te et curam nostri gerere*
always I believed that you existed and cared for us
(6.5.8)

As he thought about how empty his sort of perfectionism could be, he began to recognize that he already did believe in lots of things of which could not be certain—as he did, you may remember, with respect to what he was like as a baby, which he could not recall himself but as to which he relied on what his parents told him and what he himself later saw in other children. Likewise: historical events to which he was not a witness, things learned from doctors and other professionals, the reported experience of friends. Insistence on certainty renders impossible forms of belief that are good for us to hold, in ordinary life and in religion as well. The world is full of things we rightly believe but cannot demonstrate beyond doubt.

The passage quoted above is a statement of what Augustine seems to have regarded as the most basic and simplest Christian belief. It may not sound like much, to say that God exists and cares for us, but compared to living without those beliefs it was for Augustine a crucial step.

As for Scripture, he was shown ways in which apparent absurdities could be explained, in different ways to people of different intellectual capacity. The result was:

> *mihi illa venerabilior et sacrosancta fide dignior apparebat*
> *auctoritas,*
> the authority [of Scripture] appeared to me to be more
> venerable and more worthy of sacred faith,

> *quo et omnibus ad legendum esset in promptu*
> by the way it could be read openly by everyone

> *et secreti sui dignitatem in intellectu profundiore servaret,*
> yet preserve the worth of what it kept secret for profounder
> minds;

> *verbis apertissimis et humillimo genere loquendi se cunctis et*
> *praebens*
> by offering itself to everyone in the most open language and
> in the most humble fashion

> *et exercens intentionem eorum qui non sunt leves corde,*
> and at the same time challenging the understanding of those
> who were heavy-weights in the heart

> *ut exciperet omnes populari sinu.*
> so that they [the Scriptures] might take all people to their
> breast.
> (6.5.8)

Here we get a foreshadowing of the position Augustine takes toward the close of the *Confessions* when he says that the meaning he has given to the first two verses of Genesis is only one possibility, and there may be others just as good. Here he is saying that the range of meanings of which the Scriptures are susceptible is itself a virtue, because it means that a very wide range of people can be brought to the Scriptures in ways that are good and beneficial.

## THE HAPPY BEGGAR (6.6.9–6.6.11)

Augustine is now at a point where he has made progress away from the Manichees but has not yet found his home. He sees a drunken beggar in the street, who seems to be happier, more cheerful, than he is, and this disturbs him. He was educated, as the beggar was not, but:

> *non inde gaudebam, sed placere inde quaerebam hominibus,*
> I did not rejoice on this account, but sought on its basis to please other people,

> *non ut eos docerem, sed tantum ut placerem.*
> not that I might teach them, but only that I might please them.
> (6.6.9)

He talked with his friends about this and other important matters:

> *et inveniebam male mihi esse et dolebam*
> and I found myself to be in a bad case full of sorrow

> *et conduplicabam ipsum male et, si quid adrisisset prosperum,*
> and I [in this way] multiplied the sorrow and if anything good smiled on me,

*taedebat apprehendere, quia paene priusquam teneretur*
*avolabat.*

I hesitated to accept it, because it flew away when I had
nearly grasped it.

(6.7.11)

## ALYPIUS AND NEBRIDIUS (6.10.17–6.16.26)

Now he tells the story of two of the friends with whom he discussed these things, Alypius and Nebridius. The first of these two
passages is so long and complete that it reads a bit like a short
story, a story based on a life. One question is: What is friendship
for him—as the pilgrim?—as the writer?

The outline of the story is this: Alypius, a few years younger
than he, grew up with Augustine in Thagaste and their friendship continued in Carthage, Rome, and Milan. In Carthage he
studied with Augustine (against the wishes of his own father)
but he also became addicted to the "games" at the circus—
games not identified, but not healthy or productive of good.
He was present at a seminar run by Augustine, who happened to speak about the circus in harsh terms, without any
consciousness of its meaning for Alypius. But Alypius heard
him and changed his ways immediately, abandoning the circus entirely. His father gave up his objection and Alypius followed Augustine to Rome. Augustine saw this as an instance
in which God was working through him, and he took no personal credit for it.

But in a crucial moment, when Alpius was walking by the
Roman circus with his friends, hearing the roars of the crowd
as gladiators fought to the death, his friends urged him to

come in, trying to break down his claimed moral superiority to them with respect to this issue. He claimed he could go in and close his eyes and not be affected by what he heard. So in he went. But at the first roar from the crowd he opened his eyes, and his obsession returned in full force. Only much later was he to give it up.

Alypius's experience in this scene mirrors in one respect Augustine's experience of the theft of the pears. Augustine tells us that he would never have done it alone, but was influenced by his friends to join them. Here it is clear that Alypius would not have gone to see the gladiatorial fights if it were not for the challenge his friends put to him. In both cases, but in different ways, it is the connection with the actor's friends, if that is the word, that leads to the mistaken, indeed sinful, behavior.

A second crisis in Alypius's life arose when he was wrongfully arrested for a theft committed by someone else. He was to be legally charged, a very serious matter, but the chance emergence of a witness led to a cessation of the proceedings. He later became a lawyer in Rome with a high position. Once he was tempted with a bribe, which he resolutely refused to accept, despite lots of pressure from other officials.

These details about the moral and successful man he becomes give us some sense of who the man was and why Augustine could love him. You might say this story as a whole, and the story about the pears as well, are demonstrations of the way in which character and morality are to Augustine's mind formed by a combination of initial disposition and experience that is understood.

When Augustine moved to Milan, Alypius went with him, where he was part of the small group Augustine had built around himself. And when Augustine and the others later moved back to Africa, Alypius was to come too.

As for Nebridius, he came from Carthage to be with Augustine in Milan:

*Nullam ob aliam causam Mediolanium venerat,*
For no other reason did he come to Milan

*nisi ut mecum viveret in flagrantissimo studio veritatis et sapientiae,*
than to live with me in the most burning study of truth and wisdom,

*pariter suspirabat pariterque fluctuabat,*
equally with me did he pant, equally did he waver,

*beatae vitae inquisitor ardens et quaestionum difficillimarum scrutator acerrimus.*
a burning examiner of the blessed life and the sharpest analyst of the most difficult questions.

*Et erant ora trium egentium et inopiam suam sibimet invicem anhelantium*
So there were the mouths of three needy men, gasping their shared helplessness to each other,

*et ad te expectantium, ut dares eis escam in tempore opportuno.*
and waiting for you, [in the hope] that you would give them the food they needed in time.
(6.10.17)

The three friends were all suffering from much the same kind of uncertainty and confusion and certainly did not seem to be moving in the direction of clarity and understanding and trust.

What is more, they collectively continued Augustine's habit of insisting on perfection before making a shift of commitment:

*dicebamus, "Quamdiu haec?"*
we were often saying, "How long?"

*et hoc crebro dicebamus, et dicentes non relinquebamus ea,*[4]
and this we said frequently, and even in saying it we did not
release those things we had received

*quia non elucebat certum aliquid quod illis relictis*
*apprehenderemus.*
because nothing certain shone forth that we might hold
onto after the other things were given up.
(6.10.17)

Perhaps Augustine the narrator is here recognizing that one of
the chief errors they needed to give up was the insistence on perfect understanding, perfect knowledge.

These three friends, along with some others, clearly felt themselves to be a community—intellectual, personal, and religious.
They would soon form a Christian community at an estate
near Milan, and several of them would return to Africa with
Augustine.

But sex figures largely in their lives in ways that complicate
their plans. Augustine himself accepted in principle a marriage
arranged largely by Monnica, and to that end broke off all relations with the nameless woman—really a wife—with whom he
lived in harmony and fidelity for more than ten years and with
whom he shared their son Adeodatus. This was traumatic for
both of them: Augustine says his heart was cut and wounded
and dragged through blood, *cor . . . concisum et vulneratum mihi*
*erat et trahebat sanguinem* (6.15.25), while she went back to Africa,
vowing never to take another man.

As for his friends, when they were on the verge of establishing
a community, the men found that their wives and other women

would not stand for it. In the last paragraph of Book 6 Augustine says, speaking of the friends:

> *Quos utique amicos gratis diligebam*
> I loved those friends I loved and without any sense of reward
>
> *vicissimque ab eis me diligi gratis sentiabam.*
> and in turn I felt that I was loved by them in the same way.[5]
> (6.16.26)

The *Confessions* is not a book of concepts, nor is it ideas that drive its movements. As I have said before, at its deepest it is a book of love, the discovery of love.

# 10

## IMAGINING GOD AND THE ORIGIN OF EVIL (BOOK 7)

BOOK 7 IS DIFFICULT TO SUMMARIZE. It has almost no straight narrative material and it only names one person in addition to Augustine himself. It is an account by Augustine the narrator of the experience of Augustine the pilgrim as he engaged in the early stages of his conversion to Christianity.

This was not a straightforward or logical process, to say the least. He began with his own complex way of imagining the world, based largely on Manicheism, and it had to be undone, bit by bit, before he could begin to see and accept the ways of thinking that characterize Christianity—as he imagined it into existence. In all this there is understandably a lot of movement back and forth, and sideways, as in fact one would expect of a responsible and intelligent person engaged in the transformation of his or her life.

As you may remember, at the end of Book 5 Augustine had decided to engage in the extensive education and training that was preparatory to baptism in the Catholic Church.[1] But at the end of Book 6 we saw that he was still in considerable confusion and uncertainty, shared with the small group of important friends he had collected around himself. It would have been hard to predict a future for that little society.

At the beginning of Book 7 he is still struggling with the basic question, How is he to imagine God?

It is significant that he asks this question at all. The roots of conversion are often deep within the self, and cannot be made the object of intellectual analysis. But Augustine consciously engages in a great struggle to find a way to imagine God that—well, that what? That satisfies him? That pleases him? That he thinks adequate? That is true?

By what imaginable criteria can he, in his internal conversation with himself, approve or disapprove his own conception of God? Maybe in fact God is real, but not omnipotent, or not omniscient, or even not strong on truth or love? This would be an unsatisfactory God, but not an unreal one. He has to think both about the God he wants and the God he has. And this thinking has to take place against the background of his own long-term commitment to Manicheism, which has its own attractions. And "thinking" is too weak and limited a term for the process in which he is engaged, for the kind of feeling and intuition he reveals, for his sense of hope, and for his deep need for something he does not have. The root of his conversion lies in experience, experience which cannot be fully identified or expressed, even to himself. To the extent this is true, Augustine is enacting for us an essential characteristic of our own religious—or other deeply important—experiences or impulses or hopes, namely, that they cannot be reduced to propositions or descriptions.

I think the reader is here called upon by Augustine's example to address the questions I posed above on their behalf. It is not enough, that is, to read this as a kind of psychological novel, in which the reader watches Augustine move from one state to another, in a process that one might observe in an intellectually neutral way, from a distance as it were. No. The *Confessions* is written to engage us, the readers, in our own version of the

activity it exemplifies. I think Augustine is writing, as I said earlier, to help us learn to do what he learns to do, that is, to love
God—whatever that we might make that mean.

The minute you say that, all the questions raised above
become real for us as they are for him. His questions are offered
to us as our questions too, and he asks that we live with them
and think about them, not only in the terms he uses, but in our
own way, for ourselves. This book asks its reader: How will you
come to terms with what Augustine is, what Augustine does?

A related way to think about the *Confessions* is to look at what
Augustine is and does, and what he calls upon us to be and do, as
ways of creating a community with us—a community that is his
best definition of the life about which he wishes to teach us and to
which he wishes us to belong—a community that is for him ultimately the life of the church. How does he do this? Who is he in
his writing, and how does that define the life of the church? Who
are we, as he writes to us, and what kind of life does he offer us?

Indeed, on this view what is the church? It is a community,
or set of relations, in which someone can talk as Augustine does,
and someone else can listen as we do, or as we come to do, for we
are responsible for who we are in this interactive life. For him the
church is defined and created by the experience he offers us as
readers of his book.

## IMAGINING GOD

Augustine the writer has of course already come to a certain way
of imagining God and believing in him, that of what he calls the
Catholic Church.[2] He is telling the story, and can see Augustine
the pilgrim moving toward what he regards as right understanding and the right kind of faith. In this sense it is Augustine the

narrator who is defining the theological and spiritual state that Augustine the pilgrim should and does enter.

What are we to think of the various stages the pilgrim goes through? What are we to think of the end point approved by the narrator, and why? Does Augustine the pilgrim end up in the right place? If so, why do we think so? If not, where does he go wrong? What does this mean for us?

Who, that is, do we become as readers of this text, and what are we to think of it? A hard and crucial question: Is it possible for us to engage with this book on its terms, openly and honestly, without ourselves becoming in a sense members of the church, as by our agreements and disagreements we help create and maintain the relation established with us by Augustine the narrator, and in the process make it our own? What would it be like to read the book and then turn our backs on it? These are questions to keep in mind.

## A PHYSICAL GOD (7.1.1–7.1.2)

Augustine tells us at the beginning of Book 7 that he has come to a point where he no longer needs to think of God as having a body like ours, with weight and height and mass and form, but he does not know how to imagine him as a purely spiritual being either. He cannot get away from the idea that God has to have some kind of body, for he is still caught by the Manichean insistence that only physical things can be real.

This may seem an odd place to be stuck, but if you think about our own world, and the way it is often imagined by scientists, you will see I think a clear parallel to what Augustine faces. There is a sense in which many people in our culture, including sophisticated people, do seem to believe that whatever is real must be physical, in the sense that it can be seen, touched, examined under a microscope, quantified, photographed, or demonstrated through the process of experimentation. In addition our culture largely believes that this material universe, ranging from sub-atomic particles to the farthest reaches of the universe billions of light years away, is all governed by a process of cause and effect, a process that can in principle be studied and understood; and, once understood, can be the ground for the prediction of future changes and transformations. Physical cause-and-effect is *the* mechanism by which all movement and change take place in our imagined universe, including in what is called the human brain—and soul? To think otherwise, some would say, would be fanciful and irrational and unproductive. In this sense we are all heirs of the Manichees, and when Augustine is struggling with them he is struggling with us as well.

Augustine tells us that at age twenty-nine or so he has now left his adolescence, and entered into *juventus*, the stage that would carry him into his forties:

> *quanto aetate maior, tanto vanitate turpior,*
> the older I got, the more I was foul in my vanity,

> *qui cogitare aliquid substantiae nisi tale non poteram, quale per hos oculos videri solet.*
> I who was able to think anything of real substance only when it was the kind of thing that could regularly be seen by my very eyes.
> (7.1.1)

As for God, Augustine did not think he had a human form, as per-haps he once thought, but was still compelled to imagine him as

> *corporeum tamen aliquid . . . per spatia locorum,*
> something bodily . . . occupying physical space,

*sive infusum mundo sive etiam extra mundum per infinita diffusum*
whether spread into the world or, outside the world, spread
through infinite space.
(7.1.1)

He begins to see another way of imagining, but cannot hold
onto it:

*Per quales enim formas ire solent oculi mei,*
Through the kind of forms my eyes were used to go [over]

*per tales imagines ibat cor meum,*
my heart went through the images of those very things,

*nec videbam hanc eandem intentionem qua illas ipsas imagines*
*formabam non esse tale aliquid,*
but I did not see that this very activity, by which I formed
the images was not something of that kind [i.e., physical],

*quae tamen ipsas non formaret nisi esset magnum aliquid.*
an activity which however would not have formed [the
images] unless it was itself something big [and real].
(7.1.2)

That is, he did not recognize at the time that his own activity of
thinking and imagining is itself utterly real, and has power to
affect the world, even though it does not have the physical characteristics of shape or weight or mass.

This is still an issue for us. As I said above, in our world
there are powerful forces that want to say that the imaginings
or intentions in the mind are indeed physical, indeed that the
whole process of thought, including self-consciousness, is reducible to a physical cause and effect.

It might be helpful if you asked yourself what you think about this matter in our own world today. Are the intellectual and emotional movements that Augustine describes in fact reduceable to physical changes? How would you know? Does asking this help you see the difficulty in which Augustine finds himself?

In any event, he was still imagining God as having physical qualities and characteristics. One way he did this was to think of God as a physical substance like light or maybe a mist, that could permeate the whole world. But to think this way is to imagine that God will be more fully present say in an elephant than a sparrow, he said, and that was absurd. He wanted to think of God as being completely present everywhere, and could not give up his need for a physical way of imagining this.[3]

This focus on physicality in one sense comes from the Manichees, who believed that all reality was physical. Is it also possible that the focus on physicality was driven by fear, fear that if God were not a physical reality, he would not exist at all? Might it be that it is his desire to avoid the possibility of no God at all that drives his inability to imagine God as having no physical attributes or qualities?

## WHAT IS THE ORIGIN OF EVIL? (7.3.5–7.7.11)

Another great question haunts him, also grounded in what he learned from the Manichees, namely, the origin of evil. If God is good and created everything in the world, how does anything evil come to be? Why does he not eliminate it? If you say, as Christians often do, that evil is the result of our freedom of will—our capacity to choose the bad instead of the good—that simply moves the question up the ladder so to speak: *Unde igitur mihi male velle et bene nolle?*, "Why is it that I want evil and don't want good?" (7.3.5). He states and elaborates this question over several pages, but without any real progress. He says that he is accepting more and more the faith of the Catholic Church, though still imperfectly. In particular he needs an explanation of evil of a kind he does not yet have.

He then digresses to another topic, his rejection of astrology. This rejection is strongly confirmed by a story told by one Firminius about his own birth, which occurred on the same day, indeed at the same time, as the birth of a child to one of his father's slaves. The two babies had exactly the same horoscope, predicting exactly the same kind of life, but in fact, to us not surprisingly, they led totally different lives, Firminius as a wealthy slave owner, the other as his slave. This is enough for Augustine to reject astrology completely, as though it were finally disproved.

> *His itaque auditis et creditis (talis quippe narraverat)*
> When these things were heard and believed [by me], with such a man telling the story,
>
> *omnis illa reluctatio mea resoluta concidit*
> all my reluctance dissolved and fell to the ground
> (7.6.9)

When astrology seemed to work, as its proponents claimed, in fact this happened only by luck and coincidence:

> *inde certissime conlegi ea quae vera consideratis constellationibus*
> hence I concluded with certainty that those things which were truly said after examination of the constellations
>
> *dicerentur non arte dici sed sorte*
> were said not by skill but by chance
> (7.6.9)

What is most striking to me here is Augustine's use of the word *certissime*, which means "most certainly." Certainty is the state he has been desiring all along, yet how can he be certain of what he says about Firminius? The story is one he heard from Firminius himself, who got it from his father, either or both of whom could be mistaken or just lying. Augustine recognizes that possibility, but says that the story was confirmed in a general way by other reports of the horoscopes of twins, born perhaps minutes apart—including Jacob and Esau, who certainly led different lives.

At this interesting moment, Augustine is claiming the sort of certainty he has repeatedly desired but could not find; but we can see that this certainty is really not present, for Augustine is revealing, despite what he says, that he is resting his conclusion not on absolute certainty, as the adverb *certissime* claims, but upon something very different, his well-grounded belief. To be able to assert the validity and force of this kind of belief is perhaps a bigger step for him than he wants to acknowledge. It opens up a wonderful set of questions about what sorts of beliefs are credible and well-grounded and defines our responsibility to think these questions through.

Thus his false hope of perfect knowledge has at least for the moment collapsed, and that is real progress.

Augustine next thanks God for freeing him from the chains that had tied him to the false science of astrology and its manifestation in horoscopes. Then he returns to his search for the origin of evil:

*et quaerebam unde malum, et non erat exitus.*
and I was seeking the cause or origin of evil, but there was no path [to that knowledge].
(6.7.11)

But then he says:

> *Sed me non sinebas ullis fluctibus cogitationis auferri ab ea fide*
> But you did not allow me by any fluctuations in my thinking
> to be drawn away from the faith
>
> *qua credebam et esse te et esse incommutabilem substantiam tuam*
> by which I believed you existed and that your substance
> could not be changed,
>
> *et esse de hominibus curam et iudicium tuum*
> and that both your care for human beings and your power of
> judgment [truly] existed
>
> *et in Christo, filio tuo, Domino nostro, atque scripturis sanctis*
> *quas ecclesiae tuae catholicae commendaret auctoritas,*
> and that in Christ, your son, our Lord, and in the holy
> Scriptures which the authority of your catholic church
> commends,
>
> *viam te posuisse salutis humanae ad eam vitam quae post hanc*
> *mortem futura est.*
> you set up the way of salvation and to that life which will
> exist after this death.
> (6.7.11)

* * *

Let us put on our translator's hat for a minute. Can you make
sense of the Latin enough to compare it with the English translation? Are they saying the same things? Or are there significant
differences between them? How would you define those differences? How would you translate the Latin?

* * *

Here Augustine is making a confident statement of core beliefs he shares with orthodox Christians. It is incomplete, but nonetheless marks an important moment of progress. He can assert these commitments without embarrassment or shame that he cannot complete the list. This is another way in which he has already given up his need for intellectual certainty. What lies beneath these beliefs is not a process of purely intellectual persuasion but the full range of his experiences, from his entanglement with the Manichees to the allure of astrology, and certainly including as well: his experience of Monnica's beliefs (and her excessive involvement in his inner life); his inconclusive conversations with his friends in Milan; and his exposure to Ambrose, who did not fuss over him (as Monnica did) but taught him how to read the text of the Old Testament—not literally but as a source of continuing theological revelation—and, perhaps even more important, who greeted him with warmth and acceptance.

What seems to be the system of beliefs he is acquiring is in fact not so much a system, in a logical sense, as a set of occasions and moments, a set of stimulants to reflection and to life, grounded in his experience of feeling and thought, perception and imagination. What he gives us as readers is also a set of experiences, not a set of arguments or proofs. In this sense he offers us not just intellectual coherence but, as he should, everything at once. He is teaching us, by showing us, and by calling upon us to engage with him, what it means to be wholly alive, in all parts of the mind and heart at once.[4]

## ORIGIN OF EVIL REVISITED (7.7.11–7.9.14)

Now he returns to the topic of evil. The task of thought and understanding will now take place not so much in his mind, as in some place deep in his soul. He says about himself when he began to face the issue of evil, burning with desire,

> *Quae illa tormenta parturientis cordis mei, qui gemitus,*
> *Deus meus!*
> What were the torments of my heart, when it began birth-
> labor, how great my groans, oh my God!
> (7.7.11)

Why is the issue of evil so important to him? I think in part because the Manichees had a straightforward way of explaining the presence of evil, as Christianity really did not. If he cannot resolve this issue, that is, a part of him will feel that the Manichees were right after all.

One great help, he says, was his discovery of the work of the Neoplatonists, especially Plotinus and his student Porphyry, some of whose works had been translated from Greek into Latin. (He does not specify what works he has in mind, nor does he explain why he accepts them, insofar as he does.)

We know that these were not Christian writers but philosophers who saw themselves as following and explaining Plato. Yet when Augustine read them he was able to see, by a process he does not explain at all, several of the most basic elements of Christianity represented in their thinking and defended by elaborate argument, though as he says the words used are different.

Thus he saw them affirming:

> *quod in principio erat verbum et verbum erat apud Deum et*
> *Deus erat verbum. . . .*
> that in the beginning was the Word [that is, the Christ], and
> the Word was with God and the Word was God. . . .

*Omnia per ipsum facta sunt, et sine ipso factum est nihil.*
all things were made through him and without him nothing
was made.
(7.9.13)

The words I have quoted are the beginning of John's Gospel,
which goes on in much the same vein. Why Augustine thought
that the Neoplatonists said these things (though in different
words) I have no idea. But it is significant that his reading of
Plotinus is of a piece with his later reading of Scriptures; that
is, they are not to be read literally but as having meanings to be
discovered and stated by thoughtful and perceptive readers (like
him). This is another place where he is giving up an imagined
certainty for well-grounded judgment. Augustine finds some of
the passage from John reflected in the philosophers' writing but
not all of it:

> *sed quia verbum caro factum est et habitavit in nobis, non*
> *ibi legi*
> but that the Word was made flesh and dwelt among us, I did
> not read there.
> (7.9.14)

This is just a small piece of an extensive project in which Augustine reads the Neoplatonists in ways that support some but not
all standard Christian doctrine. We do not have the original
texts that he construes in this way, so we cannot trace out how he
reaches the conclusions he does. But I imagine that this mode of
reading involves a good deal of invention and imagination as his
readings of Scripture do too—and all to the good, as far as I am
concerned.

But these do not take him all the way home, as he elaborates: not only did the Neoplatonists lack the Incarnation, they lacked the Crucifixion, the Resurrection, the gentleness of Christ, and the character of eternal life:

> *etsi cognoscunt Deum, non sicut Deum glorificant aut gratias agunt,*
> even if they recognize God, they do not glorify him as God or give thanks,
>
> *sed evanescunt in cogitationibus suis et obscuratur insipiens cor eorum;*
> but they disappear among their intellectual processes and their foolish heart is obscured;
>
> *dicentes se esse sapientes stulti facti sunt.*
> saying they are wise, they are made stupid.
> (7.9.14)

In this work Augustine is getting strong but partial confirmation of his movement toward Christianity, which is from his point of view good. He rejects the philosophers partly for what they fail to see and to say as a matter of doctrine or proposition, but more deeply for their abstract intellectuality, which keeps them from praising God and from giving him thanks, that is, from having an actual relationship with him, shaped and reinforced by practices of prayer and worship. Their own assumptions about the role of the intellect lead them, of all things, into stupidity.

Augustine is here rejecting not only them, but stages in his own past, when he wanted to rely on his own intellectual superiority. That reliance is in the end a species of pride, and certainly not the life into which he wishes to move, the life exemplified in large part by his remote and somewhat silent mentor, Ambrose.

In the Neoplatonists he finds support for the movement he is making, but the support is incomplete.

## HIS VISION (7.10.16–7.21.17)

Then he strikes a wholly different note, well worth attention:

*Et inde admonitus redire ad memet ipsum,*
And advised by this [experience] to come back to my very self,

*intravi in intima mea duce te, et potui, quoniam factus es adiutor meus.*
led by you, I entered into my inmost parts, which I could do because you were my helper.

*Intravi et vidi qualicumque oculo animae meae*
I entered and saw with a certain eye of my soul,

*supra eundem oculum animae meae, supra mentem meam, lucem incommutabilem,*
above the actual eye of my soul, above my mind, an unchanging light,

*non hanc vulgarem et conspicuam omni carni, nec quasi ex eodem genere grandior erat,*
not the common light visible to all flesh nor was it a grander light of the same kind,

*tamquam si ista multo multoque clarius clarescat totumque occuparet magnitudine.*
as if this grew brighter and brighter so that it might occupy everything in its magnitude.

*Non hoc illa [lux] erat sed aliud, aliud valde ab istis omnibus. . . .*
Such was not this light, but different, different from all others. . . .

*Qui novit veritatem, novit eam, et qui novit eam, novit aeternitatem; caritas novit eam.*
Whoever knows truth knows this light, and whoever knows it knows eternity. Charity [Christian love] knows it.
(7.10.16)

This is the visionary or mystical side of Augustine, which we have not much seen, but which we will see again, especially in the vision he shares with Monnica in Ostia, just before her death[5] and the whole of Book 12. It is crucial, for it is an aspect of the self that cannot be reduced to intellectual skill or power, or to feelings, even feelings of love, but asserts the reality and value of another capacity entirely (7.10.16).

\* \* \*

The passage continues, until he hears a voice from on high saying:

*"cibus sum grandium: cresce et manducabis me.*
"I am food for adults: grow and you will consume me.

*Nec tu me in te mutabis sicut cibum carnis tuae, sed tu mutaberis in me."*
But you will not change me into you, as you do with the food of your flesh; rather you will be changed into me."[6]
(7.10.16)

At this point Augustine says something uncharacteristically unclear, at least to me:

*Et cognovi quoniam pro iniquitate erudisti hominem,*
And I saw that for his wickedness you have instructed man

*et tabescere fecisti sicut araneam animam meam,*
and you have made my soul waste away like a spider's web,

*et dixi, "Numquid nihil est veritas, quoniam neque per finita neque per infinita locorum spatia diffusa est?"*
and I said: "Is there no truth because it is not diffused either through finite or infinite spaces?"

*Et clamasti de longinquo, "Immo vero ego sum qui sum."*
And you called from a long way away, "No, in truth I am who I am."

*Et audivi, sicut auditur in corde, et non erat prorsus unde dubitarem*
And I heard, as one hears in the heart, and thereafter there was no ground upon which I might doubt
(7.10.16)

It is pretty clear that Augustine, perhaps like the Neoplatonists, is using the word "truth" to mean a whole set of connected things, related to the question whether God is immanent throughout the universe or not. The image of the spider web captures his own sense of lost power and capacity, probably of an intellectual kind, through his own failings and sins. I also think that the voice crying out, "I am who I am,"—as God does to Moses in Exodus 3:14—is experienced by Augustine as an irrefutable manifestation of God to him personally. He heard it as one hears in the heart. There is nothing more to doubt.

Why does this not bring his search to an end? What else does he want?

Part of the answer I think is that he is still caught up in the philosophical issues raised by the Neoplatonists, another part that he needs to go beyond the vision he reports. This is a vision of a real and important kind, no question, but he is using it to answer questions—about the diffusion of God through the world—that at the end he will leave behind.

In what follows next Augustine continues to engage with what I am a calling philosophical issues: Is everything that God created good? Does the fact that some things are perishable make them flawed? How about the fact that some things are more important than others? Should we think of the created world as containing God, or being contained by him? (A question, you will remember, that we saw raised early in Book 1.) In thinking about these things Augustine describes himself as moving up a ladder of a kind imagined by the Neoplatonists: from physical entities, to the soul perceiving things through the body, to the soul as a source of power, to reason itself. This gets him to the proposition that: *Tunc vero invisibilia tua per ea quae facta sunt intellecta conspexi*, "I saw that your invisible qualities are truly understood through the things you have created" (7.17.23).

Despite his immense efforts, he still cannot as it were get over to the God in whom he believes. What enables him to begin to do that is his recognition of Christ, *mediatorem Dei et hominum*, "the mediator between God and man" (7.18.24). He at first thought Christ to be merely a wise human being.

> *Quid autem sacramenti haberet verbum caro factum, ne suspiciari quidem poteram.*
> I was unable to get the faintest idea of the holy mystery of "the word made flesh."
> (7.19.25)

He thought Christ was completely human; by contrast, his friend
Alypius thought he was God through and through (7.19.25).

In outline at least, and thanks to reading Paul, he comes to
imagine Christ more fully as the church does. He can see now
that the books of the Neoplatonists simply fail:

> *Non habent illae paginae vultum pietatis huius, lacrimas*
> *confessionis,*
> These pages do not have the face of his piety, the tears of
> confession,
>
> *sacrificium tuum, spiritum contribulatum, cor contritum et*
> *humilatem,*
> your sacrifice, the disturbed spirit, the heart contrite and
> humble
>
> *populi salutem, sponsam civitatem, arram spiritus sancti,*
> *poculum pretii nostri.*
> the health and salvation of the people, the holy city your
> bride, the earnest money of the holy spirit, the cup that is
> our price [i.e., the price of our redemption].
> (7.21.27)

This is crucial. Augustine the pilgrim has been pursuing in an
earnest and energetic way a set of questions about the nature
of God, some of which he has resolved more or less to his satisfaction. But here we are told by Augustine the writer that he
has left out the most important things of all: the experience of
Christ himself, and the experience of those who give themselves
to him. Here, in what people actually do and suffer, in the relationship between the human being and God—particularly as
that is embodied in Christ—is the meaning and substance of the

truths about God he has been trying to work out. Here, in this life, is the church that is the presence of Christ among us. And a huge part of that "here" is found in the Augustine's own text, in his relation with God on the one hand and with us his readers on the other.

# 11

## THE CONVERSION IN THE GARDEN (BOOK 8)

IN A SENSE THE WHOLE of the *Confessions* is about Augustine's conversion, which is not simply a change of "belief" but a cluster of deep changes in his soul. As we have seen, the process of conversion has been immensely complex. That complexity will continue in the life not only of Augustine the pilgrim but also of Augustine the narrator, who is enacting his own conversion at second hand, as it were, while he tells the story of his earlier self.

That said, there are moments of great intensity, none greater than the famous scene in the garden, where he feels his conversion is not only decided but achieved.

Book 8 begins with a prayer by Augustine the writer giving thanks to God.

*Perfundantur ossa mea dilectione tua et dicant: "Domine, quis similis tibi?"*
May my bones be swamped with your love, and let them say, "Lord, who is like you?"

*Dirupisti vincula mea: sacrificem tibi sacrificium laudis[1].*
You have shattered my chains, let me make a sacrifice of praise to you.

*Quomodo dirupisti ea narrabo, et dicant omnes qui adorant te,*
*cum audiunt haec,*
I shall now say how you have broken the chains, and may all
people who have reverence for you say when they hear these
things,

*"Benedictus Dominus in caelo et in terra, magnum et mirabile*
*nomen eius."*
"Blessed is the Lord in heaven and on earth, great and
wonderful is his name."
(8.1.1)

This is a great moment in the life of Augustine the narrator.
What he says about the way he hopes those who hear these
things from him should respond—that is, with their own declaration of the greatness and blessedness of God—has immediate
significance for us, for that group of people certainly includes
us, the readers, who are soon to hear how the chains were broken. Augustine the narrator is thus making a call on us, a call to
behold what we are told will be the work of God and to respond
with appropriate feelings of awe and praise.

The fact that praise is specifically called for is also significant, for it recalls once more the first sentence in the *Confessions*:
*Magnus es, Domine, et laudabilis valde.* There is a circular motion
here that brings us back to the beginning, this time with us, the
readers, being asked to give praise to God. As I suggested earlier,
it would be possible to say that the main topic of the whole *Con-*
*fessions* is praise of God. It is how it begins, and the whole story
can be seen as offering the ground upon which that praise can
and should continue to the end—praise, as we have also seen,
that is meant to help us learn to love.

Augustine the narrator next tells us briefly that Augustine the pilgrim had come to certain theological conclusions

about the nature of God, in particular that he was eternal and imperishable.

But he quickly adds something in another key entirely:

*nec certior de te sed stabilior in te esse cupiebam.*
I was desiring not to be more certain about you, but to be more firmly in you.
(8.1.1)

He feels a need, that is, not for more or deeper intellectual understanding of the kind he has been pursuing in much of the *Confessions*, but for a different kind of relationship with God, a deeper sense that he is in God and God is in him. He first says God is within him in Book 1 (1.2.2) but repeats it again and again, until he reaches the climax in Book 10, to which I referred in chapter 1. Each time he says this he does so with greater understanding and intensity. In some sense, this is the main and evolving truth of the whole *Confessions*.

This is itself an immense step forward, without which I think the full conversion would never have taken place.

## SIMPLICIANUS (8.1.1–8.5.10)

*Et immisisti in mentem meam visumque bonum consepectu meo*
And you put it in my mind, and it seemed good in my sight,

*pergere ad Simplicianum, qui mihi bonus apparebat servus tuus et lucebat in eo gratia tua.*
to proceed to Simplicianus, who seemed to me to be a good servant of yours and your grace was shining in him.
(8.1.1)

Augustine the pilgrim here continues to focus his attention not on ideas, but on the way in which God can be present in him. He attributes to God himself the whole idea of seeking advice from Simplicianus. Accordingly, he thinks very differently about this meeting from the way he thought when he approached the Manichees or rhetoricians or the Neoplatonists or the astrologers. He he is not looking for intellectual confirmation (or disconfirmation) of a theory or generalization of any kind, or even wisdom of a sort that could be kept in the memory as a set of important truths.

Instead, he is looking for a person, a bit as he started to look for Ambrose, not for ideas but for the good effect that knowing such a person might have: *et lucebat in eo gratia tua*, "and your grace was shining in him" (8.1.1). He is looking, he says, for an experienced and thoughtful man of God to whom he can describe his difficulties, (*aestus meos*, my burnings, my passions, my anxieties), one who will *proferret . . . quis esset aptus modus sic affecto ut ego eram ad ambulandum in via tua*, "explain to me what would the best way for one situated as I was to become one who would walk in your way" (8.1.1). He is looking for a kind of father, to guide him and be with him. In presenting himself this way he is offering us an example to follow, this time himself acting as something of a father himself, one to whom we can turn.

His most practical problem is sexual, in the form both of his involvement with a woman he took up with after sending away the mother of his son Adeodatus, and in his relation, such as it is, to the rich young woman whom he is expected to marry and about whom he says: *cui deditus obstringebar*, "Having been given to her I was utterly fettered" (8.1.2).

I think it is clear that he had trouble dealing with his own sexual desires and habits, but I also think that sexuality was an image of more widespread difficulties, serving almost as a kind of allegory for the fallen state of humanity

Augustine defines his religious situation this way. He has pretty much given up the sort of ambitions for worldly success and honor that he once had. He had once been among those who could not distinguish the ultimate true good from things that merely seem good, but that is no longer true of him: he now sees God and his Word (that is, Christ) in the creation (8.1.2).

> *Inveneram te creatorem nostrum et verbum tuum apud te Deum*
> I had found you, our creator, and your Word [Christ], who is in your presence, God,
>
> *tecumque unum Deum, per quod creasti omnia.*
> and is with you one God through whom you created all things.
> (8.1.2)

Likewise: he had once been among those who know God but do not glorify him, but he had been rescued from that too.

> *Et inveneram iam bonam margaritam, et venditis omnibus quae haberem emenda erat, et dubitabam.*
> I had found the good pearl, which, after selling everything I have, I was to buy; yet I wavered.
> (8.1.2)

In other words he is almost there, but not quite.

His response, as I said above, was to go to Simplicianus, a much older man of fine reputation, who was to be the successor to Ambrose as Bishop of Milan. Ambrose truly loved

Simplicianus as a father, *vere ut patrem diligebat* (8.2.3). As O'Donnell says, the fact that Augustine turned to him is itself of great interest and importance.[2] Who else sought out people in such a way? Where did he even get the idea of it?

When Augustine described his situation, Simplicianus told him that he was wise to have read the Neoplatonist philosophers (in books translated from the Greek), for their beliefs were much closer to Christianity than those of other philosophers.

As a way of urging upon Augustine that he should imitate the humility of Christ, Simplicianus told him more about Victorinus, the translator of the philosophers, whose mentor he had been.

For them Victorinus was a man of great distinction as a philosopher and a teacher. A statue of him had been set up in the Forum in Rome, one of the greatest honors of the age. Think of him as an intellectual rock star or Nobel Prize winner. He had been a great defender of paganism, but quietly became a Christian, at least in his own mind. He often said in private to Sulpicianus: *"Noveris me iam esse christianum,"* "You know I am already a Christian" (8.2.4). Sulpicianus would reply that he would not accept that unless Victorinus appeared publicly in church, and Victorinus typically responded as a kind of joke: *Ille autem inridebat dicens, "ergo parietes faciunt christianos?",* "And he would laugh, saying, 'Therefore it is walls that make Christians?' " (8.2.4).

One reason for his hesitation was his very celebrity, which would lead the pagans to bring down anger on his head if he publicly converted. Another, perhaps related, is suggested by O'Donnell, that he wants to affirm the doctrines of Christianity without engaging in the collective and liturgical life which that doctrine calls for.[3] This is a desire shared by Augustine the

pilgrim, which makes the invocation of Victorinus by Suplicianus all the more appropriate.

I think Augustine the narrator includes this little interchange
partly as a way of presenting us with the special sort of relationship, kind and trusting, that existed between Victorinus and Sulpicianus: each admired the other deeply, and had great affection
for him, but they disagreed on the most important matter of all.
Yet on that very point each was able to allow himself and the
other to take whatever time was required to reach a decision in
the right way, that is, not forced but emergent.

When Victorinus thought it was time to join the church, he
simply said one afternoon, *"Eamus in ecclesiam: christianus volo
fieri,"* " 'Let's go to church; I want to be a Christian' " (8.2.4).
This he did, to huge effect. When it came time, as part of his
baptism, to say the Apostle's Creed (which contained the essential set of beliefs for a Christian of the time) officials said he
could say that privately if he wished. But Victorinus rejected
that option and declared his faith publicly at the usual place and
time. He is showing Augustine, and us, one way to deal with
the embarrassments involved in declaring belief, namely, to wait
until they are no longer embarrassing.

This story is told by Suplicianus to Augustine in connection with the issues of pride and humility. The point is that this
man, who was absolutely at the top of the prestige ladder, demonstrated an innate humility from which he benefited in many
ways—including the disappearance of his status anxiety and the
formation of a friendship with Sulpicianus of the rare kind he
has described. The conversion of Victorinus is thus offered by
Sulpicianus, and by Augustine the narrator, as a model of conversion. Not: this is how you must do it, but: this is a good way to
do it. He will shortly say:

*Sed ubi mihi homo tuus Simplicianus de Victorino ista narravit,*
*exarsi ad imitandum*
But when your man Simplicianus told me these things about
Victorinus I was burning to imitate him
(8.5.10)

## LOST COINS, LOST SHEEP, LOST SONS

Augustine next tells us that when Victorinus did make his profession of faith by reciting the Apostle's Creed, the large congregation (the Cathedral in Milan?) burst out with cries of rejoicing,
fed in part by the fame and standing of Victorinus himself.

This rejoicing leads Augustine to ask a significant question
about human behavior:

*Deus bone, quid agitur in homine*
Good God, what is going on with humankind

*ut plus gaudeat de salute desperate animae*
that it rejoices more at the salvation of a soul despaired of,

*et de maiore periculo liberate*
and one liberated from greater danger,

*quam si spes ei semper adfuisset aut periculum minus fuisset.*
than if hope has always been with him or the danger was less?
(8.3.6)

This is of course an issue in the Gospels too, where Jesus talks
about the shepherd who seeks for his lost sheep and rejoices
when he is found, about the woman who rejoices when her lost
coin is found, and most of all, when the father of the prodigal son
rejoices at his return. In all these cases finding what has been lost

is the occasion for rejoicing far greater than at the undisturbed presence of the sheep or coin or son who is not lost. Why?

Augustine says that this phenomenon is even wider: think of the joy of the general who wins a campaign he almost lost, the sailors who survive a storm, the man who recovers from an illness, the betrothed man who has to wait until marriage before having sex with his wife. Actually wider still: there is no real pleasure in eating and drinking unless there is hunger or thirst, both of which can be painful. Perhaps there is more joy over the rescued sinner because they experience deeper joy themselves, and that joy in a sense communicates itself to the congregation. Or perhaps it is because their notoriety will enable them to bring more people into the church.

Augustine has been spinning out this line of thought, but then he corrects himself:

*Absit enim ut in tabernaculo tuo prae pauperibus accipiantur personae divitum aut prae ignobilibus nobiles,*
Let it not happen that in your tabernacle persons of wealth should be received before the poor, or the well-known before the ordinary

*quando potius infirma mundi elegisti ut confunderes fortia,*
when you have rather chosen the weak of this world, so that you might confound the strong,

*et ignobilia huius mundi elegisti et contemptibilia,*
and you have chosen the unknown and despised of this world,

*et ea quae non sunt tamquam sint, ut quae sunt evacuares.*
and those who do not amount to anything as if they did matter so that you may empty out those who do [amount to something in the eyes of the world].
(8.4.9)

The importance of this passage is that in it Augustine starts off thinking as a good philosopher might think, considering possible rationales for the human behavior he is considering, and assembling them in an order that makes sense. But then he is reminded of the way Jesus has treated the poor and the rich, the weak and the strong, and this undoes his line of thinking entirely. He then goes on to give the example of Paul, who goes from being an important person in the Jewish world, a major figure in the persecution of Christians, to a person with really no status at all, and this is cast as a huge and positive event (8.4.9). Augustine thus shifts his orientation and corrects the whole way he is thinking, indeed the question he is pursuing. He closes the topic by saying that when a powerful person in the service of the devil is saved, it is greater defeat for the devil, who loses power that he had, and this makes it natural and appropriate that the people should rejoice more deeply. He thinks this is true in the case of Victorinus, which is what gave rise to his question.

## SEXUAL DESIRE (8.5.10–8.5.29)

He states explicitly that the major barrier to progress for him was his sexual desire.

*Ex voluntate perversa facta est libido,*
Out of perverse will desire was created

*et dum servitur libidini, facta est consuetudo, et dum consuetudine non resistitur, facta est necessitas. . . .*
and while I served that desire, habit was created, and while I did not resist habit, necessity was created. . . .

*Voluntas autem nova quae mihi esse coeperat,*
But a new will had begun to exist in me,

*ut te gratis colerem fruique te vellem, Deus, sola certa
iucunditas*
that I might freely worship you and that I might enjoy you,
God, the only certain joy
(8.5.10)

Augustine is thus consciously experiencing a clash of wills, one
against the other. This state is to be distinguished from other
states of mind we have seen, where he is experiencing a kind of
confusion. To use an image of human disease, instead of a vague
subcutaneous infection he cannot get at, Augustine has a boil
right on the surface, which he will have to puncture.

He now sets out to tell the story of his conversion as an event
taking place in real time (8.6.13). He knew he was in distress and
spent a lot of time in church (when he was not taken up by the
demands of his position as a rhetorician in the employ of the
emperor). One day a friend came to call and noticed that he had
a book by the Apostle Paul, of which as a Christian he entirely
approved. The friend then told the story of Antony of Egypt, a
Christian and a founder of a monastery.

At this point one Ponticianus, who was present, began to
tell a story about what once happened in the imperial city
of Trier, when one of his companions was exposed to a book
about St. Antony, which led to an immediate and complete
conversion. Ponticianus and his other friend were not themselves converted, but remained good friends with the man
who had been.

When Augustine hears these stories, this inflames his desire
to convert, but at the same time his resistance is increased.[4]
Finally he and Alypius find themselves in the garden attached
to their dwelling-place. Augustine's uncertainties have become
a war between two sides of himself, a war that seems to suggest
no possibility of a cease fire or treaty of repose. He experiences it

in one place as a war between the body and the mind, in another place as a total conflict between opposed wills.

> *Ideo mecum contendebam et dissipabar a me ipso,*
> I was struggling with myself and I was fragmented by myself,
>
> *et ipsa dissipatio me invito quidem fiebat,*
> and this fragmentation happened against my will,
>
> *nec tamen ostendebat naturam mentis alienae sed poenam meae.*
> nor did it reveal the nature of a strange or alien mind but the penalty [deserved by] my own mind.
> (8.10.22)

Here he is close enough to the Manichean position that there were two fundamental forces in the world, two souls in each person, one good, the other bad, that he takes time to explain that his situation was different: he had not two souls, but one soul that was divided against itself. He was tormented: now ready to accept his conversion, now resisting it with all his might. Quite unreachable by his silent friend Alypius, who was with him, he physically threw his body around in distress:

> *Ista controversia in corde meo non nisi de me ipso adversus me ipsum.*
> This quarrel within my heart was just me against myself.
>
> *At Alypius affixus lateri meo inusitati motus mei exitum tacitus opperiebatur.*
> And Alypius, fixed at my side, silently awaited the result of these wild movements[5].
> (8.11.27)

Here he discovers that the Manichean model fails on another ground, for it is possible for us to have a struggle between two sides of ourselves, both of which are good, or both of which are bad.

Augustine then moves to a different part of the garden, where he will be alone, and throws himself weeping on the ground.

> *Iactabam voces miserabiles: "Quamdiu, quamdiu, cras et cras?*
> *Quare non modo?*
> I shouted out my wretched words: "How long? How long? Tomorrow and tomorrow? Why not now?
>
> *Quare non hac hora finis turpitudinis meae?"*
> Why should this hour not be the end of my turpitude?"
>
> *Dicebam haec et flebam amarissima contritione cordis mei.*
> I was saying these things and weeping the most bitter regrets of my heart.
>
> *Et ecce audio vocem de vicina domo*
> And behold I hear a voice from the neighboring house,
>
> *cum cantu dicentis et crebro repetentis*
> with a song of someone speaking and repeating over and over,
>
> *quasi pueri an puellae, nescio: "Tolle lege, tolle lege."*
> perhaps a boy or girl I don't really know: "Pick up and read, pick up and read."
> (8.12.28–29)

So he returned to Alypius, and opened a book containing the letters of Paul, and read:

> *"Non in comessationibus et ebrietatibus, non in cubilibus et*
> *impudicitiis, non in contentione et aemulatione,*

"Not in carousing or drunkenness, not in love nests or lewdnesses, not in competition or envy,

*sed induite Dominum Iesum Christum et carnis providentiam*
*ne feceritis in concupiscentiis."*
but clothe yourself with our Lord Jesus Christ and do not make any provision for the desires of the flesh."
(8.12.29)

This was enough for Augustine. He had no wish or need to read further.

*Statim quippe cum fine huiusce sententiae quasi luce securitatis*
*infusa cordi meo omnes dubitationis tenebrae diffugerunt.*
Immediately with the end of this sentence, as if by a light of safety poured into my heart, all the shadows of my hesitation were scattered.
(8.12.29)

What is to me most remarkable here is the way Augustine in this context finds himself, really for the first time, able to trust what he cannot understand. An earlier Augustine would have doubted what he heard, or whether he heard it, or what kind of person was singing it, and felt that he did not have the certainty required to make a real commitment. Think how tempted he was by the practice of astrology and the horoscope.

Our Augustine does in fact wonder about the voices, but quickly concludes that this is a divine exhortation to open a book and discover a truth. And when the book speaks to him as this does, he is home free—home free because at last he is ready for it.

# 12

## WHAT IT MEANT (BOOK 9)

IN BOOK 9 WE LEARN ABOUT what Augustine did after his conversion in the garden: his movement toward baptism; his resignation as a teacher of rhetoric; his withdrawal with his friends, including Alypius and Nebridius, to a country estate called Cassiciacum, where they try to establish a perfected community; his movement with members of that group back to Africa; his relationship with his mother, particularly at the time of her death in Ostia—where they experience together a religious vision, modeled at least in part on the vision to which the Neoplatonists aspired, and where he begins to face life without her.

Augustine begins Book 9 thanking God for his conversion.

*O Domine, ego servus tuus, ego servus tuus*
Oh Lord, I am your servant, I am your servant

*et filius ancillae tuae:*
and the son of your handmaid:

*dirupisti vincula mea, tibi sacrificabo hostiam laudis.*
you have broken my chains, to you I shall make a sacrifice of praise.

*Laudet te cor meum et lingua mea,*
Let my heart praise you and my tongue likewise,

*et omnia ossa mea dicant, "Domine, qui similis tibi?"*
and let all my bones say, "Lord, who is like you?"

*Dicant, et responde mihi et dic animae meae, "Salus tua ego sum."*
Let them (the bones) speak, and may you answer me and say
to my soul, "I am your salvation."
(9.1.1)

Here Augustine returns to a central theme, established in the opening lines of Book 1: his desire to praise God. You will remember, from chapters 3 and 5, that as we thought about praise as an activity it became problematic, despite its seeming simplicity. Why does Augustine praise God? Does God need the praise? Why would he even want it? Yet praise is somehow basic to Augustine's sense of himself and his God. Why is this so?

As I suggested earlier, it might help to think about Augustine's praise of God not as something God wants or needs, but as something Augustine wants or needs. Why does he want so deeply to praise God? One possibility is that he is thankful to him, and that the praise is a way of expressing his gratitude. That makes sense psychologically, but still there is the question: If gratitude is the basis of praise, why is it not enough to give deep thanks?

Another possibility, which I suggested at the beginning of chapter 5, is that praise is really about love. For Augustine, praise of God is both an expression of love and a way of learning to love. Here however the emphasis seems different. When he concludes by asking God to say, "*Salus tua ego sum*" ("I am your salvation"), it sounds as though he is not trying to learn to love, or to express his love, but yearning to be loved, loved from on high.

* * *

He then goes on in a remarkable but not unfamiliar way:

> *Quis ego, et qualis ego? Quid non mali*
> Who am I? And what sort of person? What was not evil
>
> *aut facta mea aut, si non facta, dicta mea aut,*
> either in my deeds, or if not deeds, in my words,
>
> *si non dicta, voluntas mea fuit?*
> or if not in words, in my will?
>
> *Tu autem, Domine, bonus et misericors,*
> But you, Lord, are good and compassionate,
>
> *et dextera tua respiciens profunditatem mortis meae*
> and your right hand responded to the profundity of my death
>
> *et a fundo cordis mei exhauriens abyssum corruptionis.*
> and emptied out from the depth of my heart the abyss of corruption.
>
> *Et hoc erat totum, nolle quod volebam*
> And that was the whole thing: not to wish for what I had been wishing
>
> *et velle quod volebas.*
> but to wish for what you were wishing.
> (9.1.1)

This passage ends just where it should end, but how did this happen? In a sense Augustine chose it, but how and why? As he has just told us, it was God who saved him, reaching the death in his heart and then removing the abyss of corruption. What was his own role, if any?

He puts it this way:

> *Sed ubi erat tam annoso tempore et de quo imo altoque secreto*
> But where, after so many years, and from what deep and internal secret place,
>
> *evocatum est in momento liberum arbitrium meum,*
> was my free will called forth at just that moment,
>
> *quo subderem cervicem leni iugo tuo et umeros levi sarcinae tuae,*
> by which I could give my neck to your easy yoke and my shoulders to your light burden,
>
> *Christ Iesu, adiutor meus et redemptor meus?*
> Christ Jesus, my helper and redeemer?
> (9.1.1)

This passage is significant especially for two things: its evocation of Christ Jesus, his redeemer, and his claim of free will for himself. One of the tensions that runs through a lot of Augustine's theological writings is that between predestination and freedom of choice. In favor of predestination is the premise that God created all and knows all, including what free actors will choose to do. In favor of freedom of will are two things: our felt experience of freedom to choose and the moral sense that it would be wrong to punish anyone for what they could not help doing. In this passage Augustine is marveling that after so many years of bad choices of one kind or another he finally made the right choice, in the most important of matters, when he chose to be baptized.

He goes on to put freedom of will aside, and with it any claims of virtue that might be grounded on such a freedom, and says that it was really you—by whom he means Jesus, whom he just addressed? Or the Father to whom he has been speaking from the first line of the *Confessions*?—who threw away his love of triviality, his carnal desires, his ambitious wishes for wealth and for prestige:

> *Eiciebas enim eas a me, vera tu et summa suavitas,*
> You threw them away from me, you, the true and best
> sweetness,
>
> *eiciebas et intrabas pro eis omni voluptate dulcior,*
> you threw them away and you entered me, and in place of
> these desires you were yourself a desire sweeter than any
> voluptuousness
>
> *sed non carni et sanguini,*
> but not to flesh and blood[1],
>
> *omni luce clarior, sed omni secreto interior,*
> you were brighter than any light, but deeper within than any
> secret thing,
>
> *omni honore sublimior, sed non sublimibus in se.*
> you were more sublime than any honor (but not to those
> who lord it over others).
> (9.1.1)

Here Augustine is able to imagine God entering him, as he hoped would be the case when he "invoked" him early in Book 1. And he sees God as a source of immense pleasure.

What did this mean to him?

*Iam liber erat animus meus curis mordacibus ambiendi et*
*adquirendi*
My spirit was already free from biting cares of solicitation
and acquisition

*et volutandi atque scalpendi scabiem libidinum,*
and of luxuriation and scratching the scabies of lust,

*et garriebam tibi, claritati meae et divitiis meis*
and I began to talk comfortably to you, to my brightness,
and wealth,

*et saluti meae, Domino Deo meo.*
and my salvation, Oh Lord my God.
(9.1.1)


## MILAN AND BAPTISM (9.4.7–9.7.15)

One of Augustine's first concerns after his conversion was to
leave his job as a teacher of rhetoric, which he regarded as teaching falsity. He calls his position *cathedra mendacii*, the chair of
lies. He told his group of friends about his decision to leave, but
asked them to keep it a secret until after the festival of the grape
harvest, when he would make his decision public. The reason for
the delay, he says, was to avoid the appearance of self-impor-
tance in making himself news, so to speak; this would not be
such a problem during the festival, which was a period of vaca-
tion. Here he may be distinguishing himself from Victorinus,
who thought it was the right thing to make his baptism a public
event, even though this would bring anger upon him on the part
of the pagans. By contrast, Augustine seems to experience anxiety at the thought of making a clean and public break. It is not

irrelevant that he tells us here that he was experiencing physical distress in the form of a pain in the chest and difficulty breathing, both presumably signs of stress.

His friend Verecundus was concerned that he would lose his place in the group of friends Augustine had collected around him because he was not yet a Christian. Nonethless, and apparently out of a sense of commitment to the group, when he offered them the use of his country villa, Cassiciacum, the group leapt at the offer. Such a place was just what they needed to establish this community of thoughtful believers.

Augustine's friend Nebridius, a member of the group, was for the moment captured by the theory that Christ was fully divine and not really human at all, a view he was later to give up. Augustine's other great friend, Alypius, was by now a Christian and a member of the group. As the scene in the garden shows us he was especially important to Augustine.

When the time came for official release from his office, Augustine said to God:

*Eruisti linguam meam unde iam erueras cor meum,*
You rescued my tongue as you had rescued my heart

*et bendicebam tibi gaudens, profectus*
and I was blessing you, rejoicing, having at last come to

*in villam cum meis omnibus.*
the villa with all my friends.
(9.4.7)

\* \* \*

Notice now the structure of this short sentence, in Latin if possible, if not, in English. First Augustine speaks of rescue by God, rescue of his tongue—with which he speaks—and the rescue of his heart, the center of his being; then he remembers his rejoicing at this rescue, especially as it brought him to the villa with his beloved friends. This brief sentence tells the story of the core of his being, from rescue, to rejoicing, to a community of love.

\* \* \*

I do not quite know how to capture this, but for Augustine the transition he is making is a source of ineffable joy, joy of a pretty much unconflicted kind. He is buoyant and full of energy and excited by his future. For him his confessions are occasions of deep joy. In this sense, he really has been saved: his disorganized and conflicted self has become much more coherent and whole. He has attained a crucial kind of psychic integrity. The result is joy in his life and in his speech.

I think here of an experience of my own, in Italy. I was making my way from the altar toward the back of the church when the door flew open and a woman entered, looking over my shoulder with radiant joy in her smile and her face, glowing with life. I turned and saw that she was looking at the priest who was to be her confessor. Judging by what my Catholic friends in elementary school told me on the subject, her experience of confession was a far cry from theirs. But for me the woman's smile is a beautiful image that helps me think about the Augustine we come to know as he makes his confession in the *Confessions*. Confession can be joyous and free.

The next phase of Augustine's growth was his reading of the Psalms during the festival of the grape harvest. This was an intense experience since, like other readers of these extraordinary writings, he saw himself spoken to directly by the Psalms. (Perhaps they later became models for his own book of confessions.) The Manichees were still inhabiting his mind, and at one point he says he wishes they were present when he was reading Psalm 4 so that they could see and hear the effect it had on him.[2]

Here are three verses of Psalm 4 that clearly meant an enormous amount to him:

> *Cum invocarem, exaudivit me Deus iustitiae meae;*
> When I called upon him, the God of my justification heard me;
>
> *in tribulatione dilatasti mihi.*
> when I was in distress you enlarged me.
>
> *Miserere mei, Domine, et exaudi orationem meam.*
> Have compassion for me, Lord, and hear my prayer.
> (9.4.8)

The idea here is not that these are magical words producing a magical effect, but that Augustine was in a place where he could hear them in a new and deeper way, perhaps as though as if they had been written specifically to him, or perhaps as though he had written them himself. He brought them into his own soul.

His response to the Psalm is not unique. Something like it may happen especially in other aspects of religious life but not only there. A person may be completely gripped by a poem, or a passage in a play, or a short story, feeling it to be true and deeply revelatory in a new way, in some sense offering a new basis for life. At the same time, another equally sensitive and intelligent reader will appreciate the work's form and meaning, maybe with deep admiration, but without any sense of the ultimate truth that the first person experiences.

As we shall see in Part 3 of this book, Augustine's way of responding to Scripture was not to seek out its theoretical or theological propositions, that is, to translate it into conceptual discourse, but to engage with it imaginatively, to respond to it with his whole mind and heart.

Three other verses of Psalm 4 gripped him:

*"Quid diligitis vanitatem et quaeritis mendacium?"*
"Why do you love vanity and seek out a lie?"
(9.4.9)

*"Irascimini et nolite peccare,"*
"Be angry and no longer sin,"
(9.4.10)

*"obdormiam et somnum capiam!"*
"I shall sleep and take my rest."
(9.4.11)

I think the most useful way for us to think about what these three verses from the Psalm meant to Augustine is first to imagine that we ourselves are gripped by them and then to try to bring them within our own minds and imaginations, into the whole world of feelings. If we can imagine them expanding in this way, a bit like like Japanese paper flowers in water, we may be closer to understanding what they meant to Augustine than if we traced out what he says about them. This is a task each of us will have to perform on their own.

* * *

Can you imagine dwelling on these lines, in Latin or in English, in a kind of meditation that transforms them into something deeper, more permanent? Which would work better for you, the Latin or the English? Can you try first one, then the other? What do you conclude?

* * *

In any event it is clear that Augustine responded to this Psalm and many more with an extraordinary energy and warmth and imagination, making the verses part of his own mind and heart. Perhaps this experience, not only with Psalm 4 but with lots of others, led him to produce later in life his commentaries on all the Psalms, in which, as he does here, he finds and creates meanings of new kinds, with fresh intensity.[3]

At the end of the festival he formally resigned as a *venditor verborum*, "seller of words" (9.5.13). Looking toward his baptism, and showing the adequate sense of self regard that would make it possible, he wrote to Ambrose, asking what books of Scripture he should read. He was told to read Isaiah, which he tried, but without much success.

This is a remarkable and important fact. You may remember that earlier in his life he looked at the Scriptures but was unable to make anything of them.[4] But at the end of the *Confessions* he will engage in a brilliant and deep reading of the first verses of Genesis, and later in life will publish his commentaries on the Psalms, one of the great pieces of theological writing ever. But here he cannot respond in any productive way to Isaiah, one of the great books of the Old Testament. This is meant and I think is felt as a statement that he was still in a world in which Scripture meant little, a fact that is about to change enormously.

Augustine returned to Milan from Cassiciacum with Alypius to be baptized, bringing with him also his son Adeodatus, who was also one of the inner circle and a person for whom Augustine makes a point of expressing his love and admiration.

Though the process of baptism was lengthy and demanding,[5] Augustine reduces it to three words: *et baptizati sumus*, "and we were baptized" (9.7.15).

He then gives a brief account of the political and theological struggles that Ambrose and the cathedral church had had to face not long earlier, during which at one point the church and its congregation were besieged by armed forces organized by the emperor's wife. One result of this struggle, when it was over, was that the church adopted the practice of the Eastern Church of singing hymns and reading Psalms, a practice that enabled them to express more fully their joy at their survival as a church and community. This is another point at which joyfulness emerges as an essential part of the Christian life Augustine is joining.

Then, very briefly, he tells us that his group of friends had resolved to live together by a holy agreement, *placito sancto* (9.8.17), and to do so not in Italy but Africa, to which place they then set off.

## MONNICA (9.8.17–9.12.32)

Then, without much warning, we read this:

> *Et cum apud Ostia Tiberina essemus, mater defuncta est.*
> And while we were in Ostia[6] mother died.
> (9.8.17)

The rest of Book 9 consists of what amounts to a biography of Monnica, the most important person in his life. He explains what he will do this way:

> *Sed non praeteribo quidquid mihi anima parturit de illa famula tua,*
> But I will not pass over whatever my soul gives birth to about this servant of yours,

*quae me parturivit et carne, ut in hanc [lucem] temporalem,*
she who gave birth to me in the body, so that I might be
born into temporal light,

*et corde, ut in aeternam lucem nascerer.*
and in my heart, so that I might be born into eternal light.

*Non eius sed tua dicam dona in eam, neque enim se ipsa fecerat
aut educaverat se ipsam.*
I shall not speak of her gifts, but your gifts through her, for
she did not make herself nor did she educate herself.
(9.8.17)

His account begins with a stern but just servant who had raised
Monnica's father and then did much to raise her. This nurse prohibited the children from drinking water between meals, which
seems harsh indeed, especially for children living through the
North African summers. Perhaps as a result of this prohibition,
Monnica developed the habit of taking a little wine for herself
when she was asked by her parents to draw wine from a cask.
In time she took more and more until she was taking nearly a
whole cup each time.

This habit was broken by an accusation made by the maid-
servant who helped her in this task and called her a drunkard.
The servant was moved by malice, not Monnica's welfare, but
in this case, Augustine says to God, *de alterius animae insania
sanasti alteram,* "by the illness of one soul you healed another"
(9.8.18). I am reminded here of the earlier point when Augustine
insists that we should not forget that some sins have good results
(here thinking of his own captivation by the Neoplatonists, who
helped him break free from the Manichees).

When she was older (maybe 19) Monnica was given in marriage to one Patricius, Augustine's father, sometimes an angry
and difficult man, and not a Christian. She was patient, including

with respect to his infidelities, and managed to establish a good relationship with his mother—overcoming the hostility of some of the servant girls in order to do so.

As a general matter she had the gift of reducing rancor between opposing people. Augustine tells us that she used this ability to bring Patricius into the church before he died.

When Augustine and his friends were living together after baptism, he says she helped them in every way:

> *ante dormitionem eius in te iam consociati vivebamus*
> before she fell asleep,[7] while we were living together in you, Lord,

> *percepta gratia baptismi tui, ita curam gessit*
> with us having received the grace of your baptism, she showed such care for us

> *quasi omnes genuisset, ita servivit quasi ab omnibus genita fuisset.*
> as if she had given birth to us all, and she served us as if she were born of us all.
> (9.10.22)

Augustine now turns to the time of her death, when they were staying in a house in Ostia, with a garden. They were at the window, talking about eternal life, and feeling a kind of connectedness and wholeness which Augustine expresses as:

> *Sed inhiabamus ore cordis in superna fluenta fontis tui, fontis vitae, qui est apud te*
> but we opened the mouth of the heart to the celestial flowings of your fountain, the fountain of life, which is with you.
> (9.10.23)

From this they go on through several stages: thinking first about the goods of physical life; then rising to heaven, where the sun and the moon and the stars give light to the earth; then reaching wisdom itself. They return from this experience of silence to talking with each other. Then:

> *Sicut nunc extendimus nos et rapida cogitatione attingimus aeternam*
> Thus we now reached and with rapid thought touched eternal

> *sapientiam super omnia manentem.*
> wisdom, which remains always above all things.
> (9.10.25)

When they turned to each other again his mother said that now that she has seen him baptized she felt that she had nothing else to live for.

Soon after this she came down with a fever. She had wanted to be buried next to her husband, but now gives that hope up. All she asks is that *ut ad Domini altare memineritis mei, ubiubi fueritis*, "that you will remember me at the Lord's altar wherever you may be" (9.11.27).

When she died, Augustine grieved, but not as much as he expected, while Adeodatus wept copiously. His friend and colleague Evodius started to sing a psalm, which the whole group joined: *Misericordiam et iudicium cantabo tibi, Domine;* "I shall sing to you of your compassion and your judgment, Lord" (9.12.31).

As I said, Augustine himself grieved, but not as acutely as he thought he would or should; but then, why grieve deeply for the soul of someone who has gone on to eternal bliss? At different moments Augustine allowed himself a range of different responses. Toward the end:

> *et dimisi lacrimas quas continebam, ut effluerent quantum*
> *vellent,*
> and I shed my tears, which I had been holding back, so that
> they might flow as much as they want,

> *substernens eas cordi meo.*
> making them a support for my heart.

> *Et requievit in eis, quoniam ibi erant aures tuae,*
> And I rested in them because your [God's] ears were there,
> not the ears

> *non cuiusquam hominis superbe interpretantis ploratum meum.*
> of some person proudly interpreting my weeping.

> *Et nunc, Domine, confiteor tibi in litteris: legat qui volet, et*
> *interpretetur ut volet,*
> And now, Lord, I confess to you in writing; let them read
> who wish, so that they may interpret as they wish

> *et si peccatum invenerit, flevisse me matrem exigua parte horae,*
> and if they do find sin in my weeping for my mother such a
> brief part of an hour,

> *matrem oculis meis interim mortuam quae me multos annos*
> *fleverat ut oculis tuis viverem,*
> a mother to my eyes in the meanwhile dead, a mother who
> had wept for me many years so that I might live in your
> sight

> *non inrideat sed potius, si est grandi caritate,*
> let them not mock me; but rather if they have great charity

*pro peccatis meis fleat et ipse ad te, patrem omnium fratrum Christi tui.*

let them weep for my sins to you, father of all brothers in your Christ.

(9.12.33)

Here he is imagining almost for the first time another audience for the book he is writing and we are reading, not the ideal audience it seeks and defines in every sentence, but a real world audience, maybe hostile but certainly willing to express negative judgments.

What would it be like for him to imagine such an audience throughout his writing of the book? Until now he seems to write without any awareness that his audience could include people who are indifferent or hostile. Or has he throughout been strategic in relation to such readers in ways we have not recognized? These are questions we can take with us to Part 3, beginning immediately below.

Finally, his response to Monnica and her death seems to me to show a new capacity in Augustine, to see and understand and respond to another human being in depth and with accuracy. Not that he has been living a solipsistic life: his capacity to have friends is remarkable and a great strength. But in much of what he has said so far I have the sense that a large portion of his attention is on himself, on his own experience, on the character and quality of his conduct, all of which creates a kind of screen between him and others. His anxiety and uncertainty, his doubts and claims of belief, all have this effect. But in talking about Monnica in this book he seems to me to see her clearly and from a position of psychic balance and integrity. His attention is not diverted by his unresolved issues, for they are largely resolved. In this sense it is an enactment of what his conversion and baptism actually mean to him. We see something of the same shift in his relation to God, especially when he says that he has begun to "talk confidently" with God, as I earlier translated *garriebam*. This word has overtones that might be captured in such words as "chatter," "chat," "run on," or perhaps "say whatever was on my mind." Augustine's experiences have given his mind and soul new structures.

# PART III

# 13

# MEMORY, SIN, AND REDEMPTION
## (BOOK 10)

WITH BOOK 10 AUGUSTINE BEGINS what may seem to be a different kind of book. No longer is it the story of Augustine the pilgrim told by Augustine the narrator, speaking ostensibly to God. Rather it is composed by Augustine the narrator about his own past experiences and present thoughts and feelings. He sometimes seems to speak directly to his human audience.

The immense question Book 10 addresses is this: What does the complex and compelling story of Augustine's conversion which we read about in Book 9 actually mean for him, and why? What are his remaining problems or issues, and how does he address them?

## TRANSITION (10.1.1)

One might imagine a book about an author's conversion which goes on at great length about the internal and cultural experience that led up to their conversion and then simply stops. Or perhaps it goes on to tell us a little about the fulfilled life they enjoyed after the conversion.

Augustine does neither of these things, but brings himself and us into a new world, with its own difficulties and confusions, some of them serious. As he sees it, neither conversion nor baptism is the end of the story. These events do change the conditions on which his life is to be lived, but the life remains problematic. It is in fact one of his crucial points that even after baptism he does not achieve a perfected state or anything like it—a statement not only about his own life, but all human life. The question then will be, how to come to terms with this fact, how to live with this recognition.

The change I am talking about is marked for us by the fact that he is no longer talking in a past tense about past events, but in a present tense about present events.

In what follows we shall pay extended attention to the opening pages of Book 10, which are in important ways at once themselves transformative and necessary to what he achieves in the rest of it. Here he does much to define in new ways himself, his God, his human audience, and the relations he seeks among these persons. This work should prepare us for the extraordinary creativity we are then to witness.

Listen to the way he begins Book 10, speaking to God:

*Cognoscam te, cognitor meus, cognoscam sicut et cognitus sum.*
Let me know you, you who are my knower, let me know you as I am known (by you).[1]
(10.1.1)

A bold start, to put it mildly. What he asks is immense, apparently beyond the possible. How can a mortal and limited human being come to know the Creator of the universe and the Redeemer of humanity and the Spirit of God—the

Triune Christian God—in a way for which any claims of completeness or thoroughness or correctness could be made? Let alone how could one come to know them as completely as one is known?

It seems on the face of it impossible. Implicit in the subjunctive,[2] *cognoscam te*, is a request to God, namely, that he make it possible for Augustine to know him fully. But who is Augustine to make such a request of God? How is he imagining God when he addresses him this way?

We can read the opening sentence as defining a set of questions we can bring to the rest of Book 10: In what way does God know Augustine? (How do we know?) In what way does Augustine come to know God? (How do we know?) How do these things happen? (How do we know?)

How can he possibly know God as God knows him? What does he mean by that objective? Who is God to him, and who does he want to be to God?

He goes on immediately:

*Virtus animae meae, intra in eam et coapta tibi,*
You who are the strength and excellence of my soul,[3] enter it and fit it to you

*ut habeas et possideas sine macula et ruga.*
so that you may have it and possess it without spot or wrinkle.
(10.1.1)

This too is a lot to ask of the creator of the universe, that he enter your soul and perfect it. Who is Augustine to make such a plea as this? What can he mean by it? He tells us a bit more by way of explanation:

*Haec est mea spe: ideo loquor et in ea spe gaudeo, quando sanum gaudeo.*
This is my hope: for this reason I say it; and in that hope I rejoice, since I rejoice in salvation.[4]
(10.1.1)

Maybe we could read this as meaning something like this: "I know this is in a way an impossible request, but it is what in fact I am hoping for, and I feel justified in doing so because this is in part a hope for the salvation you offer." He goes on to say that other objects of human hope and aspiration are really valueless, perhaps implicitly saying that the very value of what he is hoping for justifies his hope he has. Then he talks a little about what he is doing in writing this part of his book, cast in terms of truth:

*Ecce enim veritatem dilexisti quoniam qui facit eam venit ad lucem.*
Behold, you have loved truth because the one who creates[5] truth comes to the light.[6]

*Volo eam facere in corde me coram te in confessione,*
I want to create truth in my heart before you in confession;

*in stilo autem meo coram multis testibus.*
[I want to do this] with my pen in the presence of many witnesses.
(10.1.1)

Augustine plans to confess and do so truly, itself an enormous demand on himself. How will he do this? With what success, how measured? How are we to know whether his confession meets the criterion of truth, especially if it implies "the whole truth."

In addition he is saying here that he wants the *Confessions* to have a wide readership in the world. This statement acknowledges that he is speaking not only to God, but to humanity—directly or indirectly—and has in fact been doing so from the beginning of the work.

This raises important questions: How does he imagine his human reader or readers? Why does he want to share his confession with them? How does he hope they will respond to what he has written? How does his writing encourage, or discourage, that response? What are the differences between Book 10 and those we have already read?

These are questions not only about his relation to his original audience, but about his relation with us, now, as his twenty-first-century readers. Who are we here? How does he seek to speak to us? Why is he telling us his confession?

It is significant that he speaks of this confession not as something he has been doing right along from the beginning of this work, but as something that he is planning to do now. Is there a sense in which this will be a different kind of confession from the confession—or confessions—to which we have already been exposed? And, as this question implies, should we see here not one confession, but a whole series of confessions—hence the title, *Confessiones*?

If so, we are invited to ask: What are the several confessions that make up this book? What distinguishes one from another? What unites them? Why are we offered, if we are, an array of confessions instead of just one?

## BEGINNINGS (10.2.2–10.5.7)

What is Augustine's own spiritual state as he begins this new confession? How is that state influenced by the great success of his conversion and baptism? He tells us this:

*Nunc autem quod gemitus meus testis est displicere me mihi,*
Now, however, because my groaning is a witness that I
displease myself,

*tu refulges et places et amaris et desideraris,*
while you shine and please and are loved and desired[7],

*ut erubescam de me et abiciam me*
so that I would blush for myself and fling myself away

*atque eligam te et nec tibi nec mihi placeam*
and would [simply] choose you; but [if I did I would] please
neither you nor myself.

*nisi de te.*[8]
unless [it came] from you.
(10.2.2)

That is, he is at a place of distress, and would like to throw
himself on the mercy of God, but hesitates because he recognizes that for him to do that would be pleasing to neither of
them—except to the extent that doing so was itself the work
of God.

He is telling us at the outset that conversion and baptism
have not solved the problem of living as a human being who is
always, like all people, burdened by sin and stupidity. What then
is the difference between his past and present state? Is it that he
is less confused? That he is clearer about where he goes wrong
and what to do about it?

Next he says this about confession:

*Et quo fructu tibi confitear, dixi,*[9]
And I have identified the fruits enabling me to confess to
you,

*neque id ago verbis carnis et vocibus,*
and I don't do it [i.e., confess] now with words and voices
of flesh

*sed verbis animae et clamore cogitationis,*
but with words of the soul and the clamor of thought
*quem novit auris tua*
which your ear knows [already]. . . .

*Confessio itaque mea, Deus meus, in conspecto tuo tibi*
My confession to you in your sight, my God,

*tacite fit et non tacite:*
is done silently and not silently:

*tacet enim strepitu, clamat affectu.*
it is silent with respect to noise, but loud in shouts of affection.[10]
(10.2.2)

He is now confessing, that is, in a new way, in the language of
his soul, not in what he calls a clamor—but with intensity nonetheless. This is in a way a promise both to his God and to us,
his audience, that what we will read or hear will be said in the
language of the soul.

How about us, the human beings he hopes to reach? He has a
different sense of us at different times, as the following will make
plain. He starts with a kind of complaint.

*Quid mihi ergo est cum hominibus, ut audiant confessiones meas,*
What is it for me that my fellow men should hear my
confessions

*quasi ipsi sanaturi sint omnes languores meos?*
as if they were about to heal all my failings?

*Curiosum genus ad cognoscendam vitam alienam,*
The race of men is eager to know the life of another person

*desidiosum ad corrigendam suam.*
but reluctant to engage in correcting their own.

*Quid a me quaerunt audire qui sim,*
Why do they want to hear from me who I say I am,

*qui nolunt a te audire qui sint?*
they who do not want to hear from you who they are?
(10.3.3)

He goes on to ask how they can possibly know whether he is telling the truth. All this defines an unpromising situation, with which Augustine deals in this interesting way:

*Sed quia caritas omnia credit,*
But because love[11] believes all things,

*inter eos utique quos conexos sibimet unum facit,*
among at least those whom, already connected,[12] it makes one with itself,[13]

*ego quoque, Domine, sic tibi confiteor ut audiant homines*
Lord, I confess to you in such a way that people can hear

*quibus demonstrare non possum an vera confitear.*
though I cannot demonstrate to them that I am confessing truly.

*Sed credunt mihi quorum mihi aures caritas aperit.*
But they will believe me, they whose ears love opens.
(10.3.3)

Here he is making explicit something he has already suggested, that in making his confession to the reader, he is doing so not so much in confidence that he will be heard and understood, but in the hope that what he says may be helpful to them. The center of this relationship is a kind of love. He cannot prove the truth of what he says, but knows that some of his readers will love him in ways that will lead to trust and belief, and that is what matters. For Augustine to write this way is itself an expression of love, an important move in a direction we have already seen him move, the direction of charity. His focus is not on himself but on those he might benefit.

But what value can his confession have? He sees that it might be valuable to them to read of his past sins and his repudiation of them, because this might give them hope of mercy themselves, if they were to do what he did. But what is the value of his confessing his *present* sins? Here he thinks:

*Volunt ergo audire confitente me quid ipse intus sim,*
They want to hear me confessing that I am in a place within,

*quo nec oculum nec aurem nec mentem possum intendere;*
where they are able to stretch neither eye nor ear;

*credituri tamen volunt, numquid cognituri?*
they wish to believe, but do they also wish to understand?

*Dicit enim eis caritas, qua boni sunt,*
Love [*i.e.*, charity], by which they are good people, says to them

*non mentiri me de me confitentem*
that I am not lying in making my confession,

*et ipsa in eis credit mihi.*
and this very love within them believes in me.
(10.3.4)

Once again, love, or *caritas*, is the key and remarkable term in this passage. *Dicit enim eis caritas*, "Caritas says to them," *non mentiri me de me confitentem*, "I am not lying in my confessing," *et ipsa in eis credit mihi*, "and this very love within them believes in me." A beautiful and brief expression of the relationship he imagines between himself and his readers: their capacity for love tells them that he is being sincere, as he is, and this knowledge leads them to belief. Trust and truth on both sides. What more could one want?

Thus he is imagining his readers—including you and me—as responding to his sincerity with love, love which then becomes the ground for belief. This is a way of asking us a series of questions. Will this be true of our experience as readers? Will we come to love him and believe in him? Is something like this in fact our experience of reading the *Confessions* so far? Have you ever been challenged by any writer in such a way as this?

Looking at the whole passage, he first doubts his audience, then comes to trust it, as he trusts in his own capacity to be honest, and in that way comes to trust his readers. He is both motivated by love and relying on love on the part of (some of) his readers. This is a remarkable foundation for what is coming.

How will this work? He calls on God to help his human audience respond well, that is, with the right kind of love:

*Amet in me fraternus animus quod amandam doces*,
Let the fraternal spirit[14] love in me what you teach to be loveable,

*et doleat in me quod dolendum doces. . . .*
and let it lament in me what you teach to be lamentable. . . .

*Respirent in bonis meis, suspirent in malis meis.*
Let them breathe refreshed at my good actions, breathe with sighs at my bad actions.
(10.4.5)

Then he sums up:

> *Hic est fructus confessionum mearum, non qualis fuerim sed*
> *qualis sim,*
> Here is the fruit of my confessions, not [expressing] the sort
> of person I was, but the sort of person I am,
>
> *ut hoc confitear non tantum coram te, secreta exultatione cum*
> *tremore*
> so that I may confess not only before you in secret
> exultation, with trembling
>
> *et secreto maerore cum spe,*
> and in secret grief, with hope,
>
> *sed etiam in auribus credentium filiorum hominum, sociorum*
> *gaudii mei*
> but also in the ears of believers who are the sons of men, of
> allies in my rejoicing,
>
> *et consortium mortalitatis meae, civium meorum et mecum*
> *perigrinorum,*
> and [the ears] of those who share my mortality, of my fellow
> citizens and fellow pilgrims,
>
> *praecedentium et consequentium, et comitum vitae meae.*
> going before and following and sharing my life.
> (10.4.6)

Here Augustine is telling us more about the kind of person he
is speaking to, and in this way defining his desired audience. Of
course those who do not respond as he hopes will not belong
in the ideal community he is establishing.[15] There may be those
who respond to his trusting love with hostility or scorn, but he

takes no steps to defend himself against them. We as readers know both that we are invited at every stage to join the group that he is addressing, and live on its terms, and that we are at the same time free to reject it.[16] Whatever we do, we are responsible for the choices we make.

It might be a good idea for you to stop now and ask yourself how Augustine here defines himself, his God, and his human audience. How is what you see or hear now different from what you saw and heard in the first nine books? Do you regard the change as progress, and if so, how defined? If not, why not?

In this context it is relevant that Augustine recognizes that every person has something within them that they do not know, that even their spirit does not know (10.5.7). God, however, knows it all, and is the ultimate judge. Certainly we cannot judge ourselves or each other properly. In what follows then, he says to God:

> *confitear ergo quid de me sciam, confitear et quid de me nesciam*
> let me confess what I know about myself and what I do not know
> (10.5.7)

This is the beginning of his new confession.

## WHAT DO I LOVE WHEN I LOVE YOU?
### (10.6.8–10.7.11)

As the question above suggests, the next topic of his inquiry is explicitly the nature of God. What does he love when he loves God?

He comes to this question this way:

*Non dubia sed certa conscientia, Domine, amo te:*
With internal certainty, not doubt, I love you, Lord:

*percussisti cor meum verbo tuo, et amavi te.*
you have pierced my heart with your word, and I have come
to love you.[17]
(10.6.8)

But:

*Quid autem amo, cum te amo?*
What do I love when I love you?
(10.6.8)

This crucial question is a way of asking who God is, where God
is, how God is; what can be known or believed about God; and
what it means to love him. As I suggested above, the answer has
to be problematic in the extreme. God is more or less by definition infinite in power, in understanding, and in virtue. How can
he be understood?

Augustine begins with a formulation that acknowledges the
limitations of human imagination: when I love you I do not love
beauty or light or song or flowers or perfume, he says, not manna
and honey:

*Non haec amo, cum amo Deum meum,*
It is not these things I love when I love you, my God,

*et tamen amo quandam lucem et quandam vocem et quendam
odorem et quendam cibum*

262 &#8455; MEMORY, SIN, AND REDEMPTION (BOOK 10)

yet I love a certain light and a certain voice and a certain
odor and certain food

*et quondam amplexum, cum amo Deum meum, lucem, vocem,*
*odorem, cibum,*
and a certain embrace, when I love my God—the light,
voice, odor, food,

*amplexum interioris hominis mei,*
and the embrace of my inner self,

*ubi fulget animae meae quod non capit locus,*
where there shines upon my soul a light no place has
captured,

*et ubi sonat quod non rapit tempus,*
and where there resounds what time does not snatch up,

*et ubi olet quod non sparget flatus,*
where there are odors that no breeze scatters,

*et ubi sapit quod non minuit edacitas*
and where there are tastes that no gluttony diminishes,

*et ubi haeret quod non divellit satietas.*
and where there is connection that no satiety tears apart.

*Hoc est quod amo, cum Deum meum amo.*
That is what I love when I love my God.
(10.6.8)

This is deeply poetic and mystical. How would you explain what
he is saying in this extraordinary passage? Why does he write
this way?

For Augustine God is not a concept or idea, nor in the usual
sense a person, like a human person, but a presence, made known

by the experience he offers one who is attuned to him. Augustine is facing in a real way the fact that both God and his experience of God are ineffable, except in the incomplete but intense way of a poem such as this. The heart of his relation with God is love—a key term that still needs to be defined, and will be defined largely by the way he uses it.

How does he define love in this passage?

What is this reality, this experience, that is, God? He goes on to say that on an imaginary journey he asked this question of the earth and the sea and the winds, the heavens, the sun and the moon and the stars, the whole physical world, all of whom say, "We are not the God you seek, but it is he who made us." The same is true of Augustine himself: he is not God but God made him. He knows that he should not look for God in the external world, but in his internal self and its experience. We are now in a deeply internal world, the world of the soul.

It is through his soul that he will soon ascend by stages to the God who created him, exposing him to a life that is wholly internal, and, as he will explain, deeply shaped by the faculty of memory (10.7.11). For memory is in a sense the central capacity of the human being, giving us our material of thought and imagination. It is what largely distinguishes us from other animals.


## OUTLINE

The rest of Book 10 is long, complex, challenging, full of life, and difficult to summarize.

Augustine begins by talking about memory, which he sees as the distinguishing capacity of the human being, essential to his or her life in every sense of the word. Everything we do takes place in the world of memory. It is in the world of memory that it will be possible for him to enact the kind of ascent to God I just referred to and which we saw described in the scene in Ostia between Augustine and Monnica. It is in the world of memory that we find the materials for hoping for a blessed life. Memory is an avenue to God. Augustine is engaged here in nothing less than a reimagination of what it means to be a human being.

To repeat what I said in chapter 1, in Augustine's view we start out with the inexplicable and incomprehensible gift of life. Thereafter we use memory constantly, not only when we write the story of our lives as he has been doing, but in leading our lives from day to day. Memory is the place we put whatever we have learned, whatever impressions we have formed in any aspect of our lives. Every person has a huge storehouse of memories, some of which are available, some of which she or he forgets permanently, others of which move into dark places in the soul from which they can be recalled. Memory is the embedded experience upon which we rely for everything, from the use of language to the formation of desires to the management of social relations. It is the heart of life.

But—as he makes us see in our own forgetfulness as readers of what he himself has told us—memory is profoundly unreliable. In a sense this book is the beginning of his real confession: the confession not of bad things he did as a boy, but of what he has come to know that he does not know, even about himself.

What we remember, he says, is not sense data, but sense data processed by thought and imagination. Memory is a way of locating ourselves in a process of which we know neither the beginning nor the end; a process that is in its essential nature internal, and in a deep way unverifiable. The "narrative" he has told us in the *Confessions* is really just the memory of memories, not a story of facts.[18]

As Augustine comes to realize that all he knows of the world depends upon his memory, which is mysterious and misleading and incomplete, he also comes to see what is for him the ultimate fact about his knowledge: that almost all he can be certain of is that God exists and is within him.[19] This is a long way from the bright young man proud of what he knew and could do with his knowledge. Everything except this new knowledge, everything from narrative to autobiography to philosophy to theology, is buried in the mystery of memory.

This is an amazingly rich and powerful image of human life, extending, as I said above, to the mystical ascent to God that he will describe.

Perhaps surprisingly, the passages about memory are followed instantly by something very different, a consideration of the ways in which human beings—notwithstanding their hope for a blessed life, a life in the eye of God—are drawn into sin, partly by their bodies, partly by their defective wills. As he develops this theme, using the issue of sexual continence as the paradigmatic example in his own life, Augustine sees that a life without sin is simply not possible. If we are to be reconciled to God and ourselves we need something else, in this case someone else, a mediator between God and humanity. In a sense he is saying that Christ is an almost logical necessity for a God of love whose created beings are in such need of redemption.

This outline does not begin to capture what is most impressive here, which is the way Augustine involves the reader directly in the experiences that he himself undergoes. He does not just tell us something he wants to say, that is, but—consistently with the passages we have already read—offers us as readers something like his own experience as a person engaged in a soul-deep struggle. The most I can do in this book is to examine a handful of passages from different places in this story which may demonstrate how he does this.

## MEMORY (10.8.12–10.17.26)

First, then, about memory. Augustine recognizes that all he brings with him on his ascent to God is what he remembers about himself and his experience. This discovery launches him on his long and excited essay on memory.

> *Transibo ergo et istam [vim] naturae meae,*
> Therefore I shall pass above even the force of my nature
>
> *gradibus ascendens ad eum qui fecit me,*
> rising by steps to him who made me,
>
> *et venio in campos et lata praetoria memoriae,*
> and come to the fields and princely estates of memory
>
> *ubi sunt thesauri innumerabilium imaginum*
> where there are treasuries of innumerable images
>
> *de cuiscemodi rebus sensis invectarum.*
> of all kinds of things brought in by my senses.
> (10.8.12)

After describing the way in which memories are organized, and what it is like to have access to such richness of his prior experience, he adds:

> *Intus haec ago, in aula ingenti memoriae meae.*
> I do these things within, in the immense hall of my memory,

*Ibi enim mihi caelum et terra et mare praesto sunt*
where the heavens and earth and ocean are present to me

*cum omnibus quae in eis sentire potui,*
with all the things which I have been able to perceive
through my senses

*praeter illa quae oblitus sum.*
beyond those things I have forgotten.

*Ibi mihi et ipse occurro meque recolo*
There too I meet myself, and remember myself,

*quid, quando et ubi egerim quoque modo,*
what, when, and where I did something in any way

*cum agerem, affectus fuerim.*
and when I did do so something, how it affected me.
(10.8.14)

In what follows, Augustine develops his rich and complex sense
of what memory is and how it works. Some of the items in our
memory are images of what we experience in the rest of life, like
a mountain view; for other things there are not images but the
things themselves—his example is a set of numbers, mine would
be a geometrical figure, like a triangle.

Memory also contains what he knows of literature and the
arts, and rhetoric too. Such things appear not as images, nor as the
things themselves, nor are they like a scent or food or touch. I think
what he is saying, without quite making it explicit, is that these are
activities he knows how to engage in. That is what memory brings
him. Philosophic questions work in much the same way.

Memory also contains feelings, *affectiones animi mei* (10.25.36),
but in a different way. To remember happiness is not to be happy, to

remember fear is not to be afraid. How about forgetfulness? How can it possibly be remembered? Perhaps we remember prior forgettings as a way of warning ourselves not to forget other things? Memory contains memories of false statements or false claims.

Our task as people of memory is to canvass what our memory holds in its mysterious and disorderly fashion, to select what we need or want, and put this material into a kind of composition: *ex quadam dispersione conligenda*, "out of such dispersion they must be tied together" (10.11.18).

Whatever it is, and however it works, memory cannot be "understood" in the usual sense of the term, that is in an intellectual and propositional way. It must be lived with. It is clear from what he says that Augustine knows how to live with memory. Yet his way is chaotic:

*per haec omnia discurro et volito hac illac,*
through all these things I run and fly, this way and that,

*penetro etiam quantum possum, et finis nusquam.*
I penetrate as far as I can, but there is no end.

*Tanta vis est memoriae, tanta vitae vis est in homine vivente mortaliter!*
So great a force is memory, so great a force of life in humanity living under the certainty of death!
(10.17.26)

## ASCENT (10.17.26–10.27.38)

At this point Augustine changes direction in an important way, seeing that the ascent not only depends upon memory—it transcends it.

*Quid igitur agam, tu vera mea vita, Deus meus?*
What therefore shall I do, you who are my true life, my God?

*Transibo et hanc vim meam quae memoria vocatur,*
I shall pass beyond this force of mine called memory;

*transibo eam ut pertendam ad te, dulce lumen.*
I shall pass beyond it to push on to you, sweet light.

*Quid dicis mihi? Ecce ego ascendens per animum meum ad te,*
What do you tell me? Look, I am ascending through my
spirit to you,

*qui desuper mihi manes, transibo et istam vim meam*
you who remain above me; I shall pass over that force of mine

*quae memoria vocatur,*
called memory,

*volens te attingere unde attingi potes,*
wishing to reach you any way you can be reached

*et inhaerere tibi unde inhaereri tibi potest.*
and to adhere to you any way you can be adhered to.
(10.17.26)

This is the beginning of his transcendence of memory, and with
it the rest of life, as he seeks a deeper and less troubled connection with God—the God he has been addressing ever since he
said: *Magnus es, Domine, et laudabilis valde* (1.1.1).

A bit later he asks:

*Quomodo ergo te quaero, Domine? Cum enim te, Deum
meum, quaero,*
How do I search for you, Lord? When I seek you, my God,

*vitam beatam quaero. Quaero te ut vivat anima mea.*
I seek a blessed life. I search for you that my soul may live.

*Vivit enim corpus meum de anima mea et vivit anima mea de te.*
My body lives from my soul and my soul lives from you.

*Quomodo ergo quaero vitam beatam?*
How therefore am I to search for a blessed life?
(10.20.29)

Am I to search my memory? But is the blessed life present in our memory? It certainly is not remembered as physical objects, or geometrical shapes, eloquence, or artistic elegance. Yet I do feel somehow that I know what blessedness is and I would not know that if it were not in my memory.

*Ubi ergo et quando expertus sum vitam meam beatam,*
Where, therefore, and when did I experience my own blessed life

*ut recorder eam et amen et desiderem?*
that I can remember it and love it and desire it?
(10.21.31)

Next a definition of the blessed life:

*Et ipsa est beata vita, gaudere ad te, de te, proper te:*
And this is the blessed life: to rejoice in you, about you, because of you;

*ipsa est et non est altera.*
that is what it is, and there is no other.
(10.22.32)

His search for God, throughout his memory and outside it too, culminated in his experience of truth:

> *Ubi enim inveni veritatem, ibi inveni Deum meum,*
> Where I found truth, there I found my God,

> *ipsam veritatem, quam ex quo didici sum non oblitus.*
> truth itself, which from the moment I learned it I did not forget.

> *Itaque ex quo te didici, manes in memoria mea,*
> From the time I learned of you, you remain in my memory,

> *et illic te invenio cum reminiscor tui, et delector in te.*
> there I find you when I recall you and I am delighted in you.
> (10.24.35)

This passage suggests a real and important question, which is what he means by "truth." We have seen this word before, where truth was, as here, a way of identifying the core of God's being as it is presented to us. But the term "truth" is an abstraction, not a person. What does he mean by it? Is he saying that God is revealed in any experience or statement or hope or relationship that is true?

In what follows he is talking about God not as an abstraction but as a person.

> *Ubi ergo te inveni, ut discerem te?*
> Where did I find you that I could learn about you?

> *Neque enim iam eras in memoria mea, priusquam te discerem.*
> You were not in memory before I learned about you.

*Ubi ergo te inveni ut discerem te, nisi in te supra me?*
Where did I find you that I might learn of you unless in you yourself, beyond me?

*Et nusquam locus, et recedimus et accedimus, et nusquam locus.*
And there was no place [where I could find you]. I went this way and that, but there was no place.
(10.26.37)

This is the point at which Augustine experiences his ascension to the presence of God, which he expresses in the following hymn or psalm. As you will see he has pretty well left behind him theological or conceptual language in favor of a language, and an experience, of personhood and love.

*Sero te amavi, pulchritudo tam antiqua et tam nova, sero te amavi!*
Too late I have loved you, beauty so old and so new, too late I have loved you!

*Et ecce intus eras et ego foris, et ibi te quaerebam,*
And behold, you were in me and I was outside, and that[20] is where I searched for you

*et in ista formosa quae fecisti deformis inruebam.*
and, myself deformed, I rushed into those beautiful things you have formed.

*Mecum eras, et tecum non eram.*
You were with me, but I was not with you.

*Ea me tenebant longe a te,*
Those things held me far from you,

*quae si in te non essent, non essent.*
those things which if they were not in you, did not exist
at all.

*Vocasti et clamasti et rupisti surditatem meam;*
You called and cried aloud and broke my deafness;

*coruscasti, splenduisti, et fugasti caecitatem meam;*
you shone and were bright and drove away my blindness;

*fragrasti, et duxi spiritum et anhelo tibi;*
you smelled sweet and I led my breath within and (now) I
gasp for you;

*gustavi et esurio et sitio;*
I have tasted you and I hunger and thirst [for more];

*tetigisti me, et exarsi in pacem tuam.*
you have touched me and I am afire for your peace.
(10.27.38)

As Augustine comes to realize that all he knows of the world
depends upon his memory, which is mysterious and misleading and incomplete, he also comes to see what is for him the
ultimate fact about his knowledge: that all he can be certain
of is that God exists and is within him.[21] This reverses the
usual direction (which begins with the self and its experience
and moves out, sometimes reaching God), for here Augustine
begins, once he gets there, with God as his foundation for
all else. This is a long way from the bright young man proud
of what he knew and what he could do with his knowledge.
Everything except this new knowledge, everything from narrative to autobiography to philosophy to theology, is buried in
the mystery of memory.

## INHERENT FAILINGS (10.28.39–10.43.70)

Next he turns quickly and radically from the image of perfect connection with God to the reality of his life:

> *Cum inhaesero tibi ex omni me,*
> When I have attached myself to you completely
>
> *nusquam erit mihi dolor et labor*
> there will be no sorrow or labor,
>
> *et viva erit vita mea tota plena te*[22]
> and my life, filled with you, will be [fully] alive.
>
> *Nunc autem . . . quoniam tui non plenus sum,*
> Now however . . . because I am not full of you
>
> *oneri mihi sum.*
> I am a burden to myself.
>
> *Contendunt laetitiae meae flendae*
> Joys that should be occasions for grief contend
>
> *cum laetandis maeroribus,*
> with griefs that should be occasions for rejoicing,
>
> *et ex qua parte stet victoria nescio.*
> and on which side lies victory I do not know.
> (10.28.39)

Thus begins the next long section of Book 10, which is a chronicle of his own sinfulness:

> *Ei mihi! Domine, miserere mihi! Ei mihi!*
> Woe is me! Lord, have compassion for me! Woe is me!

*Ecce vulnera mea non abscondo.*

Behold, I do not hide my wounds.

(10.28.39)

He will now tell us about the temptations to sin that he has failed to resist, or better, found impossible to resist fully. This is a long section, which I will summarize very briefly.

Prompted by God to resist the desires of the flesh, he goes through the senses, one by one, to show us how sinfulness is built into our experience of them. He is offering this material I think not as a unique account of failure, but as a representation of the human condition, in which every one of us is a wounded and fallen person.

He is still haunted by inappropriate sexual desires, which for him is the dominant form of the desires of the flesh. But eating and drinking are also pleasures that can take sinful form, as are the senses of scent and sound and sight. To offer one example, he talks about singing in church as a practice with obviously much to be said for it—but also against it, for sometimes the pleasure of the sound of music distracts him from the meaning of what is being sung. Not a major sin, but an instance of the way in which we can always lose our way. *Ita fluctuo inter periculum voluptatis et experimentum salubritatis*, "Thus I fluctuate between the danger of desire and the experience of health" (10.33.50).

The important thing here, and really throughout his self-examination, is that he cannot resolve the tension he describes. This is for him a failing, along with many others, that he cannot cure. He is permanently in the position of one who struggles with original sin.

In a kind of summary he says near the end:

*Lustravi mundum foris sensu quo potui,*

I examined the external world as well as I could by my senses

*et attendi vitam corporis mei de me sensusque ipsos meos.*
and I paid attention from my perspective to the life of my
body and my senses.

*Inde regressus sum in recessus memoriae meae,*
From there I went into the withdrawn places of my memory,

*multiplices amplitudines plenas miris modis*
those many places filled with wonderful variety

*copiarum innumerabilium, et consideravi et expavi,*
of innumerable things, I considered and was astounded by
them,

*et nihil eorum discernere potui sine te*
but I could perceive nothing of them without you

*et nihil eorum esse te inveni.*
and I could not find any of them to be you.
(10.40.65)

Despite all he said in the first half of Book 10, Augustine ends
up unable to be the person he should be. What is needed, absolutely needed, he says, is a mediator who can reconcile God and
humanity.

A true mediator has to partake both of humanity and divin-
ity. That is what you have given us in Jesus, the Christ. Thus he
concludes:

*Conterritus peccatis meis et mole miseriae meae*
Terrified by my sins and the mass of my misery

*agitaveram corde meditatusque fueram fugam in solitudinem*
I had been stirring my heart and thinking of fleeing to
solitude

*sed prohibuisti me et confirmasti me dicens,*
but you prohibited me and made me firm, saying

"*Ideo Christus pro omnibus mortuus est,*
"For this reason Christ died for us all

*ut qui vivant non sibi vivant,*
that those who live should not live for themselves

*sed ei qui pro ipsis mortuus est.*"
but for him who has died for them.

... *Et laudant Dominum qui requirunt eum.*
... And those who seek the Lord praise him.
(10.43.70)

# 14

## TIME (BOOK 11)

IN THE RETROSPECTIVE REVIEW of his own work, which he called the "Retractions," made near the end of his life, Augustine said that the first ten books of the *Confessions* were written about himself, *de me scripsi sunt*, the last three about the holy Scriptures, *de scripturis sanctis*. Book 10 does have the feeling of completion, as we have seen, and the last three books, as we shall see, are indeed about the Scriptures and how to read them.

In this work he does not argue for the genuineness or authority of the Scriptures, as we might expect someone to do today; likewise, he says nothing about their textual history. He takes them as given. The question he faces is how they should be read, and his answer lies in his performance. James J. O'Donnell says, "he leaves behind memory to live in the present,"[1] and, as we shall see, that "present" will be defined by Augustine as the razor thin moment in which we live, the moment that is itself the only reality: the past is unreal because it is gone, the future unreal because it has not happened yet. Augustine will be showing us how he reads the sacred texts, partly as a way of teaching us how to do so too—not that we should reach the same conclusions or imitate his style, but that we should assume responsibility for our responses and understandings and readings in something like the way he does his. As a reader of the holy texts he is not looking for precepts to be slavishly followed, or arguments that cannot be resisted, but for the unique kind of life he finds they can stimulate in the person who turns to them with heart and mind and imagination.[2]

## FROM GENESIS TO TIME (11.1.1–11.3.5)

Augustine begins Book 11 this way:

*Numquid, Domine, cum tua sit aeternitas, ignoras quae tibi dico,*
Since eternity is yours, can it be that you do not know what I am saying to you[3]?

*aut ad tempus vides quod fit in tempore?*
Or do you see in time what is done in time?

*Cur ergo tibi tot rerum narrationes digero?*
Why therefore am I telling you these stories of so many things?

*Non utique ut per me noveris ea,*
Plainly not so that you will come to know these things through me,

*sed affectum meum excito in te, et eorum qui haec legunt,*
but I will stir up my feelings about you, and the feelings of those who read these things

*ut dicamus omnes, "Magnus es, Domine, et laudabilis valde."*
so that we all may say, "Great are you, Lord, and most worthy of praise."[4]
(11.1.1)

Here he addresses a question we have had since we read the first words of the *Confessions*: Why does Augustine say all these things, write this whole great book really, to God who presumably knows them all already? Surely not to give him new information. Rather, it is written partly for Augustine's own benefit—as we have seen him put it elsewhere, to help him learn to love God; but here he adds also, "for the benefit of his readers" (as he has also said once or twice). But now he adds something new: he says these things so that he and his readers will be able to say together the sentence with which we began, *Magnus es, Domine, et laudabilis valde* (1.1.1), that is, that they will embody the church together. He closes this line of thought this way: *iam dixi et dicam, "Amore amoris tui facio istuc,"* "I have said it before and will continue to say it, 'I do this for love of your love' " (11.1.1).

What is this love that he has for God, that God has for him, that he has for us? Where do we see it defined or given content? Not in propositions, I think, but in our experience of reading him. Can we say more about what this experience is and how it works?

In an important sentence he asks:

> *Quando autem sufficio, lingua calami enuntiare*
> When will I be able, with my pen, my tongue, to declare
>
> *omnia hortamenta tua et omnes terrores tuos, et consolationes et gubernationes,*
> all your encouragements and terrors, consolations, and guides
>
> *quibus me perduxisti praedicare verbum*
> by which you led me to preach your word
>
> *et sacramentum tuum dispensasre populo tuo?*
> and dispense the sacrament to your people?
> (11.2.2)

Here Augustine for the first time defines himself as a priest, both in his preaching and in his administration of the Eucharist. This expresses I think a significant, but not elaborated, change in his relation both with God and with his reader. Why does he mention it here? A friend suggests it may be that he wants to mark a shift from focusing on himself and his own identity to the welfare of others, as a priest should do.

How does he respond to his own sense of inadequacy? How does he hope to grow into this new role? He tells us: *olim inardesco meditari in lege tua*, "for a long time I have been on fire to meditate on your law" (11.2.2), that is, to learn to read the Scriptures. *Sint castae deliciae meae scripturae tuae, nec fallar in eis nec fallam ex eis*, "Let your Scriptures be my chaste delights, let me not be deceived in them, nor myself deceive with them" (11.2.3).

A couple of pages later he begins his actual work with the Scriptures this way:

> *Audiam et intellegam quomodo in principio fecisti caelum et terram.*
> May I hear and understand how at the beginning you made heaven and earth.

> *Scripsit hoc Moyses, scripsit et abiit, transiit hinc a te ad te, neque nunc ante me est.*
> Moses[5] wrote this, he wrote and went away; he went from here, from you and to you, nor is he before me.
> (11.3.5)

A gentle beginning, but his consideration of the opening verses of Genesis will continue through all three of the remaining books. The mention of Moses I think is meant to preclude one way of reading a text, which is simply to ask the author what they meant. He would do that if he could, but Moses is gone. Augustine is imagining and making real a world in which texts can have a life of their own.

## THE CREATION (11.4.6–11.30.40)

He begins this way:

> *Ecce sunt caelum et terra! Clamant quod facta sint; mutantur enim atque variantur.*
> Behold! Heaven and earth exist! And they shout out that they have been created; they are changed and variable.
> (11.4.6)

His idea here is that since they are changeable they are not parts or aspects of God, who is, in his view, unchangeable and unchanging. If they are not part of God and they exist now they must have been created. Augustine has the heavens and earth say:

> *"Non ergo eramus antequam essemus, ut fieri possemus a nobis."*
> "Therefore we did not exist before we came to exist, as if we could be created by ourselves."
> (11.4.6)

Next a question:

> *Quomodo autem fecisti caelum et terram?*
> How did you create heaven and earth?
> (11.5.7)

Augustine says that you cannot have made them the way a craftsman makes something out of other objects or material, because there were no such things. So how did you do it?

*Ergo dixisti et facta sunt atque in verbo tuo fecisti ea.*
Therefore you spoke and they were made, and you made them by your word.
(11.5.7)

Here Augustine is using the words "speak" and "word" to capture his sense that the creation was made out of nothing. It was the sheer or pure act of God; and not just an action of his will, but the action of speaking. (Compare: "He said let there be light, and there was light.")

The act of speaking makes the creation all the more dramatic and impressive. For Christians it has another significance as well, which is that the "word" of creation here can be identified as the Word of creation identified in the opening passage of the Gospel of John, that is to say, Christ himself.

Next question: *quomodo dixisti?* "how did you speak?" (11.6.8). Here he draws on another occasion when God spoke, in order to differentiate them.

*Numquid illo modo quo facta est vox de nube dicens,*
Certainly not in the same way as was made the voice from the cloud, saying

*"Hic est filius meus dilectus"?*
"This is my son the beloved"?
(11.6.8)

Why not? Because the voice from the cloud *coepta et finita [est]*, that is, began and ended, because it took place in time, syllable by syllable. This means that there already was a world of creation living in time. But the very first creation took place before time. How then did you speak? Not through the usual modes of speech, which do have beginnings and endings, for they are in time, but through the Word:

> *Vocas itaque nos intellegendum verbum, Deus apud te Deum,*
> You call us to understand the Word, the Word that is God
> with you, God,
>
> *quod sempiterne dicitur et eo sempiterne dicuntur omnia. . . .*
> the Word who eternally is spoken and through whom
> eternally all things are spoken. . . .
>
> *Non ergo quicquam verbi tui cedit atque succedit,*
> Therefore nothing of your Word yields or changes
>
> *quoniam vere immortale atque aeternum est. . . .*
> because it is truly immortal and eternal. . . .
>
> *Nec aliter quam dicendo facis,*
> Not otherwise than by speaking do you act
>
> *nec tamen simul et sempiterna fiunt omnia quae dicendo facis.*
> nor however are all those things you make by speaking
> [themselves] synchronistic or eternal.
> (11.7.9)

It is important to see that in focusing on the idea of creation by speech Augustine is not stretching for some idiosyncratic reading of his own, but building directly on the Biblical text itself. For one striking aspect of the Bible story is the fact that, after the initial creation of heaven and earth, this God achieves his creation not simply through will power, or internal decision-making, but through speech, speech that is actually uttered. He is a God who acts with words.

What does this mean? In this passage Augustine is reading back from the explicit use of words to create light, the firmament, the waters, the animals and plants, and so forth to the first creation, that of the heavens and the earth, where the means of creation is not specified in the Bible. But it is true that this God of the Old Testament for the most part achieves his creation by speaking words (or to a Christian, by speaking through the Word). In this the Bible is presenting God as surprisingly like a human being, one who lives and acts through language. The whole of the Pentateuch is made the same way, by God working through language. Even in my writing this sentence, and in your reading it, we are cooperatively engaged in another stage of the life of the Word. This is the activity that produced the creation.

Augustine's question is: What happens at creation if it does not happen in what we know as time? Augustine tentatively says he does not know,

> *nisi quia omne quod esse incipit et esse desinit tunc esse incipit et tunc desinit,*
> unless all things that begin to be and cease to be, begin to be and cease to be

> *quando debuisse incipere vel desinere in aeterna rationae congnoscitur, ubi nec incipit aliud nec desinit.*
> when in eternal reason be it is recognized that they ought to begin to be or to cease to be—in eternal reason where nothing begins to be or to end.
> (11.8.10)

The world of God is a world without time, that is, until he creates time and with it a world in which things and creatures are constantly changing, coming into existence and departing from it. What he made in creating heaven and earth is a world of time and change and growth that is wonderful beyond our imagining.

Augustine says that this means among other things that the question, "What was God doing before he made heaven and earth?", misunderstands the whole situation (II.10.12). People asking that question do not understand yet: *non autem praeterire quicquam in aeterno, sed totum esse praesens*, "that nothing in the world of eternity passes by, but everything is present"; *nullum vero tempus totum esse praesens*, "whereas [in the world of time], no time is completely present" (II.11.13).

The reason time cannot be completely present is that it is constantly replacing what is past, and being replaced by what is to come. To the question, what God was doing "then," that is, before the creation, the answer is *non enim erat tunc, ubi non erat tempus*, "there was no 'then' when time did not exist" (II.13.15). Or as he puts it soon after,

> *Nullo ergo tempore non feceras aliquid, quia ipsum tempus tu feceras. . . .*
> There was no "time" in which you had not made anything, because you had not made time itself. . . .
>
> *Quid est ergo tempus? . . . Duo ergo illa tempora, praeteritum et futurum,*
> What therefore is time? . . . These two times, past and future,
>
> *quomodo sunt, quando et praeteritum non est et futurum nundum est?*
> how can they exist when the past no longer exists and the future is not yet?
> (II.1417)

He then pursues the questions, what should count as a long time, what a short time, and he concludes that actually the only real time, the only present time, is the tiny moment between the past that is gone and the future that is yet to be. When you utter a two-syllable word, the first is in the past before the second is uttered, and then it too is in the past.

*Quod autem nunc liquet et claret, nec futura sunt nec praeterita,*
It is now proven and clear that neither future things nor past things exist,

*nec proprie dicitur, "Tempora sunt tria, praeteritum, praesens, et futurum,"*
nor is it right to say, "There are three times, past, present, and future,"

*sed fortasse proprie diceretur, "Tempora sunt tria,*
but perhaps it is right to say that there are three times,

*praesens de praeteritis, praesens de praesentibus, praesens de futuris."*
the present about past things, the present about present things, and the present about future things.

*Sunt enim haec in anima tria quaedam et alibi ea non video,*
These three things are in the soul, and I do not see them elsewhere:

*praesens de praeteritis memoria,*
the present for things past is memory,

*praesens de praesentibus contuitus,*
the present for things present is intense attention,

*praesens de futuris expectatio.*
the present for future things is expectation.
(11.20.26)

Augustine then considers how time can possibly be measured; whether it can be produced or defined by the movement of objects through space; and whether celestial bodies define time and if so of what kind. In the course of this section he says:

> *Et confiteor tibi, Domine, ignorare me adhuc quid sit tempus,*
> And I confess to you, Lord, that I do not yet know what time is,

> *et rursus confiteor tibi, Domine, scire me in tempore ista dicere,*
> and again I confess to you, Lord, I know that I say these things in time

> *et diu me iam loqui de tempore, atque ipsum diu non esse diu nisi mora temporis.*
> and that I have spoken of time over a lengthy period and that this period exists only as the effect of time.

> *Quomodo igitur hoc scio, quando quid sit tempus nescio?*
> How do I know this when I don't know what time is?

> *An forte nescio quemadmodum dicam quod scio?*
> Or perhaps I do not know how I should say what I do know?

> *Ei mihi, qui nescio saltem quid nesciam!*
> Woe to me, for I do not know even what I do not know!

> *Ecce, Deus meus, coram te, quia non mentior!*
> Behold, my God, to you I do not lie.

> *Sicut loquor, ita est cor meum.*
> As my words are, so is my heart.

> *Tu inluminabis lucernam meam, Domine,*
> You will light my lantern, Lord,

*Deus meus, inluminabis tenebras meas.*
my God, you will bring light to my shadows.
(11.25.32)

What strikes me most about this passage is that Augustine sees
that he has come to the limit of what he knows, or can know.
This distresses him, but it does not disable him, or humiliate
him. The reason is that he has an audience, his God, to whom he
can speak from the heart. This movement away from a desire for
a comprehensive intellectual system or structure—which could
give the human who is able to grasp it mastery over some field of
thought or life—to a way of talking from his heart is one of the
deep movements of the whole of the *Confessions*. We will see it
again at the end of Book 11. But now he asks a question closer to
our experience.

*Sed quomodo minuitur aut consumitur futurum,*
But how is the future diminished or eaten up,

*quod nondum est, aut quomodo crescit praeteritum, quod iam
non est,*
since it does not yet exist, or how does the past grow, which
already has lost existence,

*nisi quia in animo qui illud agit tria sunt? . . .*
unless because in the soul facing the question there exist
three [times]? . . .

*Dicturus sum canticum quod novi.*
I am about to sing a hymn I know.

*Antequam incipiam, in totum expectatio mea tenditur,*
Before I begin, expectation extends to the whole
thing,

*cum autem coepero, quantum ex illa in praeteritum decerpsero*
but when I have begun, into the past goes whatever I pluck,

*tenditur et memoria mea, atque distenditur vita huius actionis meae*
and my memory attends to it; the life of this action of mine
is extended

*in memoriam propter quod dixi et in expectationem propter quod*
*dicturus sum.*
both into memory, because of what I said, and into
expectation because of what I am about to say.

*Praesens tamen adest attentio mea, per quam traicitur quod*
My attention is present, through which is carried what

*erat futurum ut fiat praeteritum. Quod quanto magis agitur et*
*agitur,*
what was future so that it is made past. The more this goes on,

*tanto breviata expectatione prolongatur memoria, donec tota*
with my expectation shortened, the more my memory is
expanded until soon

*expecatio consumatur, cum tota illa actio finita transierit in*
*memoriam.*
expectation is entirely consumed, when the whole action
goes into memory.
(11.28.37–38)

This is how it works he says, and the same way for the parts of
the hymn, in one direction, and a season's singing in another, and
in fact in a whole human life. Singing the hymn is thus an image
not only of time but all human life.

What interests me most here is that in recognizing that the
human mind or soul can look forward to what it hopes or fears,

and back to what pleases or displeases, Augustine is connecting his image of time, as the razor edge between past and future, to the image of human life developed in Book 10, grounded in memory. He is imagining the human being and human life in a way that was new, and is new, at least for me.

Time and memory as he imagines them limit the human person in mind and heart but also endow them with powers, powers that come from the abandonment of false ways of thinking and imagining. Our memories are all we really have, and they are not deeply reliable; in our actions in time we are constantly moving from a world, the past, that is not present to us, to another world, the future, that is also not present to us. Under these conditions one cannot have great confidence in the working of one's own mind. Pride in our intellect, or our will, or our knowledge, in our capacity to persuade others and to manipulate or manage the institutions and practices of our world, pride in all of these things is deeply misplaced. A tough message for a towering intellect like that of Augustine, but tough as well for lawyers and professors, and specialists of all kinds in our own world of today. But there is a positive message here as well: if we could accept what Augustine is saying about us, we might free ourselves, at least to some degree, from the various forms of pride that tend to dominate our own souls and hearts, and live with greater confidence in the capacities we have in fact been given.

Augustine's own response to all this uncertainty is to say to God, *Et stabo atque solidabor in te, in forma mea, veritate tua* "And I shall stand and be firm in you, in my own form, in your truth" (11.30.40).

# 15

## READING GENESIS
## THE CREATION STORY (BOOK 12)

AS I SAID EARLIER, the last three books of the *Confessions* are very different from the earlier books, which tell the story of Augustine's life from the beginning to his baptism. If the narrative books tell us how Augustine (at last) achieved conversion, the last three show us something of what it is like for him to live on these new terms. The relation between writer and reader is accordingly different, one in which the speaking Augustine shares with us, as well as God, the questions that beset him and seeks to answer them. As I said earlier, in a sense these three books are all in the present tense, while the others are in the past tense.

One of his goals throughout these final chapters is to show us how Augustine comes to connect with the Scriptures, which he regards as the words of God himself. Why the Scriptures? What he has said in the last two books points clearly in that direction. His vision that a human life works largely through a rich and inventive memory, which can always fail, seems to erase many of the props and stays we normally rely on as we shape our lives and interpret the lives of others. Upon what can we rely in such a world, if not the Scriptures?

We have seen that his vision of memory is followed by an account of time that reduces our experience to the dimensionless moment between the past that is over and the future yet to come. This is hardly encouraging to the reader who wants to manage their experience by building on established ways of thinking and perceiving. How is one to feel at home in a world in which time is reduced in such a way? Again, for Augustine the Scriptures provide an answer. What makes life livable for him on these uncertain and mysterious terms is the radical movement he exemplifies: from trusting what we think we know about the way the world works, and the way people work, to trusting a God we cannot possibly understand or describe, but with whom we can have the most important of all our relationships.

A crucial part of that relationship lies in the Scriptures and the life they make possible for their reader. The Scriptures are relatively stable resources Augustine can turn to when he has need or desire, as he can also turn to the church that is largely based upon them. For Augustine, who has a self he cannot understand in a world he cannot understand, the Scriptures thus stand out as a possible source of meaning, one that is at once authoritative and available—though in fact what they mean, abstractly or in any particular human context to which they are brought, is always a question, both for the individual and for his or her community. In a literal sense these texts are always the same, for the words are the same, but in the person who takes them seriously, and wishes to bring them to bear upon his or her life, they call into being a new and deep kind of imagination.[1]

To live with the Scriptures is not to experience a kind of stasis, but a complex and dramatic and uncertain life, a life that makes its own serious demands upon us and calls for real and difficult judgments. We have seen in Book 11 how Augustine starts out to read the first two verses of Genesis, but quickly finds that this leads him into his disquisition on time—not as a way of wandering from the main point, but as a necessity, as he sees it, to making progress.

In Book 12 he returns to the Bible itself, especially the first two or three verses of Genesis. We will read these verses in Latin of course, but just to remind ourselves of what we may carry in our own memories, here is the familiar King James version of the first two verses:

> In the beginning God created the heaven and the earth.
> And the earth was without form, and void; and darkness was upon the face of the deep.

\* \* \*

Suppose that without any knowledge of Augustine and his project, each of us was asked to explain the meaning of these verses in English. How would we even begin? I doubt any of us would be capable either intellectually or psychologically of bringing to the task anything remotely like the attention and energy that Augustine gives it.

\* \* \*

Here is the Latin text as Augustine will quote it, phrase by phrase:

> *In principio fecit Deus caelum et terram.*
> *Terra autem erat invisibilia et incomposita, et tenebrae erant super abyssum* (12.13.16).

\* \* \*

In the end Augustine thinks that with respect to some matters some of what he understands and says really is "true," and that opposing views must themselves be opposed; but with respect to other matters he thinks that he should not only tolerate difference of opinion, he should embrace it as a source of truth, and the same goes for the church. For the church that he is imagining into existence consists in no small part of a continuing conversation based on mutual respect and charity, a conversation of the kind he has been establishing with us as readers of the *Confessions* from the beginning.

## THE HEAVEN OF HEAVENS (12.9.9–12.10.10)

The first thing he wants to talk about is not the creation described in the verses quoted but something that is in some sense prior to them, namely, the creation of the "heaven of heavens," the eternal spiritual home for God and his angels. This is not to be confused with the physical heavens that are created along with the earth. The "heaven of heavens" is God's place, a place of angels, not shared with humanity until the life after death. Although it was created by God, it shares eternity with him, and like him is unchanging. In this sense it is outside time. Augustine calls it a *creatura . . . intellectualis* (12.9.9), by which I think he means that it is not physical any more than God himself is physical.

As for the creation of what might be called ordinary heaven—the heaven we can see when we look up to the skies—and earth, they were made out of a shapeless, formless matter, incapable of change, and hence also outside time.

So far Augustine is not developing the reasons he thinks this way. What is said here functions rather as a set of flags or pointers to discussions that will take place later in the book. There he will take the opportunity of defining both those things which he thinks are "true," and not to be opposed, and those things on which difference in understanding and perspective are wholly valid.

But first: a poem, or psalm, addressed to "Truth," which as we have seen is his word for God:

*O veritas, lumen cordis mei: non tenebrae meae loquantur mihi!*
O Truth, the light of my heart: let not my shadows speak to me!

*Defluxi ad ista et obscuratus sum:*
I have fallen toward these things and am in darkness:

*sed hinc, etiam hinc, adamavi te.*
but from this place, even this place, I have loved you;

*Erravi: et recordatus sum tui.*
I have strayed, yet I remembered you.

*Audivi vocem tuam post me, ut redirem:*
I heard your voice behind me, saying that I should return;

*et vix audivi propter tumultus impacatorum.*
and barely did I hear it, because of the tumult of the warlike ones.

*Et nunc ecce redeo aestuans et anhelans ad fontem tuum,*
And now look! I come back, burning and longing for your fountain,

*nemo me prohibeat: hunc bibam et hinc vivam.*
let nobody prohibit me; may I drink this, and from it may I live.

*Non ego vita mea sim: male vixi ex me.*
Let me not be my own life; I have lived badly on my own.

*Mors mihi fui: in te revivesco.*
I was death to myself; in you I am given life.

*Tu me alloquere, tu mihi sermocinare:*
Talk with me, have words with me.

*credidi libris tuis: et verba eorum arcana valde.*
I have believed your books, and their words are mysterious
indeed.
(12.10.10)

This prayer has an important role, for in a sense it tells once
more, and beautifully, the core story of the *Confessions* as a whole,
concluding with the implicit question, how to think about reading the mysterious Scriptures.

## INNER TRUTH (12.11.11–12.13.16)

In the next section of Book 12 Augustine sets forth what might
be called his foundational or essential beliefs. But the implica-
tions of the word "believe" would not be right. These are for
him fundamental and immutable truths, based on his own
experience—the experience he has been sharing with us from
the beginning—not propositions, supported by the kind of reasoning that seeks to identify what is more probable than not.
    Immediately after the prayer quoted above, he says:

*Iam dixisti mihi, Domine, voce forti in aurem interiorem,*
You have already said to me, Lord, with a strong voice in my
interior ear

*quia tu aeternus es, solus habens immortalitatem,*
that you are eternal, alone having immortality,

*quoniam ex nulla specie motuve mutaris*
because by no beauty or movement are you changed

*nec temporibus variatur voluntas tua,*
nor may your will change with the times

*quia non est immortalis voluntas quae alia et alia est.*
because a will is not immortal if it goes first this way, then
that.
(12.11.11)

Here Augustine is not summarizing a set of arguments that he
thinks conclusively show that God is immortal and unchanging. He has spent lots of time thinking about these issues, and
related ones; but it is not his thinking he is sharing with us, but
his experience—and not just any experience, the experience of
hearing the strong voice of God in the ear within his soul—not
his physical ear on the side of his head, but the receptive capacity of his deepest nature. Once again I want to say that for him
religion is a matter not of "belief" but of knowledge, and it rests
not on reason but experience.

\* \* \*

Let me suggest that you read this passage aloud, insofar as possible meaning what you are saying, as perhaps an actor might
do. Does this give you a sense of what Augustine is feeling and
doing, a sense that does not come through the translation?

We ourselves may not think the way Augustine does here, not
very often or not ever; but we might bring from this material
a challenge of sorts to our own ways of reading and thinking.
What are we missing?

*Hoc in conspectu tuo claret mihi et magis magisque clarescat, oro te,*
In your sight this is clear to me, and, I pray, may it become
clearer and clearer,

*atque in eo manifestione persistam sobrius sub alis tuis*
and in its revelation may I modestly persist beneath your
wings.
(12.11.11)

That is, what seemed certain to him beyond any question, and
in a sense continues to do so, is revealed as less than perfectly
understood.

In what he says next he uses much the same formula, *dixisti . . . voce forti in aurem interiorem*, "you have spoken with a
strong voice to my interior ear," which is telling him *omnes natu-
ras atque substantias quae non sunt quod tu es et tamen sunt . . .
fecisti*, that is, "you have made all natures and substances which
are not you, but still exist" (12.11.11). The same formula is then
used for a third time, this time telling him that *nec illa creatura*[2]
*tibi coaeterna est*, "not even the heaven of heavens is coeternal
with you" (12.11.12).

In each of these cases he soon develops his position further,
but what seems to me most important is that in all of them he
is resting his sense of truth upon what he has heard from God
with his interior ear. This is one more way in which, over the
whole of the *Confessions*, he has moved from a sense of God
as a physical being or force to a God who is a spiritual reality, not only in the world, but, equally important, within him.
That is where his God is. Augustine is also telling us that this is
where our God is too, within us, offering a truth resting not on
authority or theory or conceptual argument, but experience—if
we can hear it. We might say, indeed, that one of Augustine's
aims in the *Confessions* as a whole is to offer us an experience of
mind and spirit which will lead us to a sense of the reality of the
God within. We might even imagine this book as having been
written by Augustine's "God within" to our "God within," with

the hope that once we have experienced that conversation we are ready for the next step.

Next Augustine pursues the question of timelessness and coeternity, saying that there are two things that exist which are not subject to time, but are not coeternal with God either. First, the heaven of heavens is unchanging, and in that sense outside time; second is the earth, as it was at the beginning, when *terra autem invisibilis erat et incomposita, et tenebrae super abyssum*, "the earth however was invisible and without any structure and the shadows [were] over the abyss" (12.12.15). This disorganized material was created, of course, but its shapelessness meant that it was not subject to change; so it too is outside time. It is from the heaven of heavens and from this unorganized mass, *unde fieret alterum caelum et terra visibilis atque composita et aqua speciosa*, "that are made another heaven and a visible and organized earth and beautiful water" (12.12.15)—and in fact all the rest of the creation described in Genesis.

He sums up what he has said, in a crucial way:

*Hoc interim sentio, Deus meus,*
For the moment at least, my God, this is what I think

*cum audio loquentem scripturam tuam:*
when I hear your Scripture speaking:

*"In principio fecit Deus caelum et terram. Terra autem erat invisibilis et incomposita, et tenebrae errant super abyssum."*
(12.13.16)

What strikes me most here is the first phrase, in which he recognizes that this whole apparatus of understanding is only what he thinks now, at this moment, with the implicit understanding that it may properly change.

## OPENNESS TO DIFFERENCE
### (12.15.19‒12.31.42)

Next he addresses those who disagree with him, his *contradicto-res* (12.15.19). These people fall into two groups, those who agree with him about the essential truths summarized above, but disagree about other lesser matters, and those who reject the essential truths. The latter group he rejects. They are not part of the conversation that in his view is the church.

Here is how he puts this:

*Cum his enim volo coram te aliquid conloqui, Deus meus,*
I wish to have a talk before you, my God, with those

*qui haec omnia, quae intus in mente mea non tacet veritas tua, vera esse concedunt.*
who concede that all the things that your truth is telling me in my inner mind are true.

*Nam qui haec negant, latrent quantum volunt et obstrepant sibi. . . .*
But those who deny these things, let them bark as much as they want and make a big noise for themselves. . . .

*Cum his autem qui cuncta illa quae vera sunt falsos esse non dicunt,*
But with those who do not claim all those things that are true to be false,

*honorantes et in culmine sequendae auctoritatis nobiscum constituentes*
honoring and placing with us in the highest form of authority that must be followed.

*illam per sanctam Moysen editam sanctam scriptura tuam, et tamen nobis aliud contradicunt, ita loquor.*

your holy Scripture given forth by Moses, even though on some matters these people contradict us, with them thus I do speak,

*Tu esto, Deus noster, arbiter inter confessiones meas et contradictions eorum.*
But you our God be the arbiter between my confessions and their contradictions.[3]
(12.16.23)

Augustine is recognizing here that other people maintain positions that are at the core consistent with his own deepest truths, summarized above, but in other respects differ from him and from each other. His position will be that while he wants to maintain his own views of the nonessential matters, and will engage in argument to defend them, he and his interlocutors are equally and rightly alive in the church, doing what they should be doing. With them he calls for an attitude of charity and love. The people who reject those of his positions that he labels essential truths he regards as outside the conversation entirely.

He gives examples of the ways in which people might take positions that are different from his own, and each other, but nonetheless consistent with the essential truths. Given the fact that his text is the beginning of Genesis, it is not surprising that the examples deal with creation as well.

Here is a sample of what he does. Take the key sentence, he says,

*"In principio fecit Deus caelum et terram,"*
"In the beginning God made heaven and earth."
(12.20.29)

That means:

> *in verbo suo sibi coaeterno fecit Deus intelligibilem atque*
> *sensibilem vel spiritalem corporalemque creaturam*
> In his Word, which is coeternal with him, God made an
> understandable and perceptible and spiritual and corporeal
> creation
> (12.20.29)

Someone else might take it to mean:

> *In verbo suo sibi coaeterno fecit Deus universam istam molem*
> *corporei mundi huius cum omnibus quas continet manifestis*
> *notisque naturis*
> In his coeternal Word God made that whole mass of the
> corporeal world, with all the manifest and well-known
> natural forms and beings within it
> (12.20.29)

Another might take it to mean:

> *In verbo suo sibi coaeterno fecit Deus informem materiam*
> *creaturaecorporalis, ubi confusum adhuc erat caelum et terra, quae*
> *nunc iam distincta atque formata in istius mundi mole sentimus*
> In his coeternal Word God made the unformed material of
> corporal creation, when heaven and earth were still mixed
> together, which now we perceive to be distinct and shaped
> into the mass of this created world[4]
> (12.20.29)

Augustine gives many other examples, but these I think capture
the flavor of what he is doing. At one level he is determinedly

trying to do two things: to find a way to state his essential positions; and to give content to his view that a wide range of subsidiary interpretations are not only part of the scene, but a legitimate and valuable part of it.

At the end of the book, he summarizes his position confirming the value of those who differ from him, so long as they speak the truth—that is, so long as they are honestly committed to the essential positions that were given Augustine in his inner self:

*omnes quos in eis verbis vera cernere ac dicere fateor,*
All whom I recognize as discerning and saying truth in these words

*diligamus nos invicem pariterque diligamus te, Deum nostrum,*
let us love one another and at the same time let us love you, our God,

*fontem veritatis, si non vana sed ipsam sitimus,*
the fountain of Truth, if we thirst for that, and not for emptiness,

*eundemque famulum tuum, scripturae huius dispensatorem,*
and that same servant of yours [i.e., Moses],[5] the dispenser of scripture

*spiritu tuo plenum, ita honoremus, ut hoc eum te revelante,*
full of your spirit, let us so honor him that what you revealed to him

*cum haec scriberet, attendisse credamus*
when he wrote it down, we believe that he intended to express

*quod in eis maxime et luce veritatis et fruge utilitatis excellit.*
what in them was most excellent both in the light of truth and in the fruit of usefulness.

(12.30.41)

Thus we ought not to argue about what Moses meant in writing the Scriptures, my meaning or yours:

> *religiosius me arbitror dicere, "Cur non utrumque potius,*
> I think it is more religious to ask why not both,
>
> *si utrumque verum est, et si quid tertium*
> if both are true—and if a third thing
>
> *et si quid quartum et si quid omnino aliud verum quispiam in his verbis videt,*
> or if a fourth, or if any number of things someone sees something true in these words
>
> *cur non illa omnia vidisse credatur,*
> why should he not be believed to have seen all these things
>
> *per quem Deus unus sacras litteras vera et diversa visuris multorum sensibus temperavit?*
> through whom [referring to Moses] the one God has adapted to the capacities of many people, who would be able to see true and differing things in the holy scriptures?
> (12.31.42)

It is not entirely clear to me what he means by "true" and "truth"; perhaps those terms are the equivalent of his essential propositions, which we saw above, perhaps not; but in any case it is clear that his disposition has become far more open and generous and accepting of what others say out of deep conviction and careful thought.

Of his own writing he says:

> *Ego certe, quod intrepidus de meo corde pronuntio,*
> Certainly, and I say this boldly from the heart,

*si ad culmen auctoritatis aliquid scriberem*
if I were to write to the pinnacle of authority,

*sic mallem scribere ut quod veri quisque de his rebus capere posset*
I would rather write in such a way that whatever truth each
reader was able to grasp

*mea verba resonarent,*
my words would resound

*quam ut unam veram sententiam ad hoc apertius ponerem,*
than try openly to propose a single true meaning

*ut excluderem ceteras quarum falsitas me non posset offendere.*
by which I would exclude other meanings, the falsity of
which would not trouble me.

(12.31.42)


He has come a long way in a single book. And perhaps we can
read this last passage as telling us how to read the *Confessions*
itself.

# 16

## "KNOCK AND IT SHALL BE OPENED UNTO YOU" (BOOK 13)

AS HE SPOKE IN BOOK 11 mainly of God the Father, and in Book 12 mainly of the Christ, so in Book 13 Augustine will focus his attention mainly on the Holy Spirit, the third person of the Trinity.[1]

But in Book 13 he also has a new task, that of bringing the whole book we have been reading to a close. This is an especially difficult matter, given the complex and various life to which we have been exposed in reading it. Augustine likes to pursue questions of many kinds, and to come to conclusions too, but, as we have seen, his conclusions are seldom offered as permanent. We should certainly not expect to see here the presentation of a systematic set of propositions stating the truths at which he believes he has arrived and specifying the relations among them. He is closer to a poet than that kind of theologian, often putting before us tensions he can only temporarily resolve. On the other hand, he does clearly change and grow, casting off old issues, maybe old selves. Our task is to honor both truths.

As I have frequently said, in my view the goal of the *Confessions* is not to produce a set of conclusions offered as the truth but to engage his reader in a certain kind of life—the life he himself exemplifies, in which conclusions are almost always tentative. This is not a failing of the book in my view, but the opposite, its wonderful virtue.

When, as readers of the *Confessions*, we come to the end of the book Augustine has given us, we will still have to make our own way through the rest of life, including the side of life we think of as theological or religious. In doing so I hope you and I will be able to build upon the experience Augustine's writing has offered us. And as we continue—together with him and with each other—to participate in the conversation he has begun, and helped us to join, we shall become in our own ways members of the church he has been creating in this book—I do not mean the Roman Catholic Church, or any particular denomination at all, or even Christianity as a whole, but the community he has established with us, and perhaps we have established with each other. As engaged readers of his book we in a sense become members of the church he creates in it, even if we do not "believe" in "God." For Augustine's book is not really about "believing" but about knowing and being and experiencing, and about the living relations we can establish on that basis with each other and with God. His gift to us, founded on his sense of truth, is life itself.

You may remember that on the first page of the *Confessions* Augustine says that the wellspring of life for him—the source of the energy that becomes this book—is what he calls *fides*, or "faith." He does not define that crucial term then, but perhaps we can see the whole rest of his book as showing us what faith is and can be, in him and in us.

Open as he is to further thought and life, he does not want to end without some kind of conclusion, and how will he do that? How will he bring the *Confessions* to a close—or won't he?

## CREATION AND MOVEMENT (13.1.1–13.9.10)

He begins Book 13 this way:

> *Invoco te, Deus meus, misericordia mea, qui fecisti me*
> I invoke you, my God, my compassion, you who made me
>
> *et oblatum tui non oblitus es.*
> and who, when I forgot you, did not forget.
>
> *Invoco te in animam meam, quam praeparas*
> I call you into my heart, which you are preparing
>
> *ad capiendum te ex desiderio quod inspirasti ei.*
> for receiving you, by the desire you have inspired in it.
>
> *Nunc invocantem te ne deseras.*
> Do not desert me as I call on you.
> (13.1.1)

This is a rich piece of writing in which lots of things happen: Augustine calls God into his heart, which has been prepared to receive him by the very desire God has stimulated in him. Even though Augustine has at times forgotten God, God did not forget him. This is an expression of the complex situation in which he finds himself at the beginning of this last book. Try reading this passage aloud in Latin, as something you can mean. Imagine yourself speaking for Augustine. What happens when you do that?

As you will recognize, there is something here of a return to the very beginning of the *Confessions*, when "invoking" was seen as a problem—for example, does it come before or after "knowing"? Before or after "praising"? Before or after "believing"? Now he is able to invoke God directly and simply, without worrying about these other language games. Equally important, he is able to accept the fact that he is calling upon God to enter him and that God is within him. He no longer thinks of God as a material being and no longer worries about whether he can be contained or always contains.

He goes on to praise and thank God (though he does not use either term), saying that God has erased through forgiveness all the bad things he has done, and has at the same time anticipated the good things he might deserve:

> *priusquam essem tu eras, nec eram cui praestares ut essem,*
> before I existed, you existed; nor did I exist so that you
> might bring me into existence
>
> *et tamen ecce sum ex bonitate tua, praeveniente totum hoc quod*
> *me fecisti et unde me fecisti.*
> yet nonetheless I do exist out of your goodness, which came
> before me, this whole thing you have made and from which
> you have made me.
> (13.1.1)

You had no need of me, or anything I could do for you. Rather you made me:

> *ut serviam tibi et colam te, ut de te mihi bene sit,*
> that I might serve you and worship you so that from you
> goodness might come to me,
>
> *a quo mihi est ut sim cui bene sit.*
> from the one who made it possible that I should be one to
> whom goodness comes.
> (13.1.1)

This is a lovely image: he was created to serve God, not in order to please him, but so that he might receive goodness, from the very one who made him able to receive it. More generally, Augustine is concerned here with an issue that may explain some of his interest in the Genesis creation story, namely the apparently impossible or at least inexplicable fact of his own creation. How can it be that he exists? Or you, or me? Surely each of us has asked that question of our own existence.

Augustine says that none of us deserves to have been created. It is a free and immeasurable gift that we exist at all.

In thinking about creation Augustine makes a basic distinction between physical creation—such as the earth itself and the plants and animals in it—and spiritual creation. We humans are representatives of both kinds of creation, for we have both kinds of reality.

\* \* \*

Here he finds himself thinking about the Trinity and the Holy Spirit in a new way, which sets the stage for the rest of his book.

> *Ecce apparet mihi in aenigmate trinitas quod es,*
> Behold, the Trinity appears to me in a mystery, that is you
>
> *Deus meus, quoniam tu, pater, in principio sapientiae nostrae,*
> my God, because you, father, in the beginning of our wisdom
>
> *quod est tua sapiential, de te nata, aequali tibi*
> which is your wisdom, born of you, equal to you
>
> *et coaeterna, id est in filio tuo, fecisti caelum et terram. . . .*
> and coeternal, that is by your Son, you created heaven and earth. . . .

*Et tenebam iam patrem in Dei nomine, qui fecit haec,*
I already held that "Father" was the name of the God who
created these things

*et filium in principii nomine, in quo fecit haec,*
and "Son" the name of the "Beginning," in whom they were
made

*et trinitatem credens Deum meum, sicut credebam,*
and believing that my God was a Trinity as I in fact believed

*quaerebam in eloquiis sanctis eius, et ecce spiritus tuus*
*superferebatur super aquas.*
I searched your holy writing and behold! Your Spirit was
borne over the surface of the waters.

*Ecce trinitas Deus meus, pater et filius et spiritus sanctus, creator*
*universae creaturae.*
Behold the Trinity, my God, Father and Son and Holy
Spirit, creator of everything that is.
(13.5.6)

That is, he has known that as a matter of doctrine he should
think of God as simultaneously one being and three beings, but
he was not able to see this in a way that made sense to him. But
now he sees that the Spirit making its way over the waters of
creation can be seen as the Holy Spirit. The Father is the creator, the Son is the one through whom the act of creation was
performed—and who will later come to earth as the Christ who
dies and is born again, as our savior—and the Spirit is borne
over the waters, an image that needs to be developed.

Augustine now asks a question only he would ask: Why is the
Spirit mentioned and named only after the earth and the heavens
have been created and named? Why does the Spirit come after

the Father and the Son—who is defined as the "Beginning," or *principium*, and also, based on John's Gospel, the eternal Word?

He suggests that the reason for the apparent delay is that the Spirit's essential role is to "move above" the waters, and above everything that the waters can be taken to mean, so the Spirit cannot be portrayed until the things he "moves over" have been created.

But why does he have to be represented as "moving over"? What does it mean that he is? Here Augustine in a lovely passage appeals to St. Paul, who says:

> *quia caritas tua diffusa est in cordibus nostris per spiritum sanctum,*
> that your love is poured over us, in our hearts, by the Holy Spirit

> *qui datus est nobis, et de spiritalibus docentem*
> who was given to us, teaching us about spiritual things

> *et demonstratem supereminentem viam caritatis et flectentem genua pro nobis ad te,*
> showing us the highest path of love, and bending his knee to you on our behalf

> *ut cognoscamus supereminentem scientiam caritatis Christi.*
> so that we may recognize the highest knowledge of the love of Christ.

> *Ideoque ab initio supereminens superferebatur super aquas.*
> And therefore from the beginning, being of the highest order himself, he was brought over the waters.

> *Cui dicam, quomodo dicam de pondere cupiditatis in abruptam abyssum*
> To whom can I speak, how can I express the weight of desire [that carries us] into the broken abyss

*et de sublevatione caritatis per spiritum tuum,*
and the raising up of love through the Holy Spirit,

*qui superferebatur super aquas?*
who was carried over the waters?

*Cui dicam? Quomodo dicam?*
To whom can I speak? How can I speak?

*Neque enim loca sunt quibus mergimur et emergimus.*
For these are not (physical) places into which we sink and
from which we emerge.

*Quid similius et quid dissimilius? Affectus sunt, amores sunt,*
What is more similar, more dissimilar? They are feelings,
loves,

*immunditia spiritus nostri defluens inferius amore curarum*
[both the] foulness of our spirit pouring us down by the love
of earthly cares

*et sanctitas tui attollens nos superius amore securitatis, ut sursum
cor habeamus ad te,*
and your holiness carrying us up, by the love of stability, so
that our hearts may rise to you,

*ubi spiritus tuus superfertur super aquas, et veniamus*
where your spirit is carried over the waters and we may come

*ad supereminentem requiem, cum transierit anima nostra*
to that highest order of rest when our soul has passed
through

*aquas quae sunt sine substantia.*
the waters, which are without substance.[2]
(13.7.8)

The work of the Spirit, then, is to move over us, as we sink or fall into the abyss, and through his natural lightness of being, to raise us up again. The Spirit passes over us and brings us up. The abyss is not a physical place but an emotional and spiritual condition, represented imaginatively in the physical image. Likewise the rising and falling is not physical either, but takes place within the self. It too is represented by the physical image.

Here it is clear that Augustine's way of reading Scripture is not literal, but what is usually called allegorical, but I would prefer to call it imagistic. (Sometimes allegories can be as narrow and rigid and unfriendly and literal as the meanings they are trying to escape.) For Augustine, reading the Scripture is a creative and imaginative activity that calls upon us as readers to be creative and imaginative too. This kind of reading produces truths that do not exclude other truths. The conversation that is the church is not monistic but diverse, not empty but full, not dead but alive.

In the next passage Augustine uses the image of gravitation, in which everything has its natural place toward which it always wants to move, and where, once there, it is at rest—gasses rise, solids sink, wood and oil float on water, balloons soar. What are the analogues to these things in spiritual life?

This is what he says:

*Pondus meum amor meus; eo feror, quocumque feror.*
My weight is my love; by it I am carried wherever I am carried.

*Dono tuo accendimur et sursum ferimur; incardescimus et imus.*
By your gift we are set on fire, and borne upward; we are kindled and we go:

*Ascendimus ascensiones in corde et cantamus canticum graduum.*
we climb the stairs in the heart and we sing the song of climbing.

> *Igne tuo, igne tuo bono inardescimus et imus, quoniam sursum*
> *imus ad pacem Hierusalem*
> By your fire, by your good fire, we are kindled and we go
> because we go up to the peace of Jerusalem
>
> *quoniam iucundatus sum in his qui dixerunt mihi, "In domum*
> *Domini ibimus."*
> because I rejoiced in those who said, "We go to the house of
> the Lord."
> (13.9.10)

All the images here—of weight and lightness, of fire and ascension, of Jerusalem and the House of the Lord—represent internal conditions or activities, events and conditions of a spiritual kind, not literal physical events.

## MORE ON THE TRINITY (13.11.12)

We have the Father, the Son, and the Holy Spirit, often called the three persons of God—the three who are also one. Three in one, and one in three.

How can this possibly be true? A frequent answer is to say simply that this is a mystery. Our task is not to understand it but to live with it. This is not enough for Augustine, who was later to write a whole treatise on the subject. Already in the *Confessions* he thinks we can make the Trinity more nearly intelligible.

> *Trinitatem omnipotentem quis intelleget?*
> Who will understand the omnipotent trinity?
>
> *Et quis non loquitur eam, si tamen eam?*
> Who does not speak of it—if it is indeed the Trinity he talks
> about?

*Rara anima quae, cum de illa loquitur, scit quod loquitur.*
It is a rare soul that when it speaks of the Trinity knows
what it is saying.

*Et contendunt et dimicant, et nemo sine pace videt istam
visionem.*
People contend and fight, yet no one sees the vision [of the
Trinity] without peace.

*Vellem ut haec tria cogitarent homines in se ipsis. . . .*
I wish that people would think about this set of three within
themselves. . . .

*dico autem haec tria: esse nosse, velle.*
I mean this set of three: to exist, to know, and to will.

*Sum enim et scio et volo. Sum sciens et volens, et scio esse me et
velle,*
I exist and I know and I exercise my will. I am knowing and
willing and I know that I exist and have a will.

*et volo esse et scire. In his igitur tribus quam sit inseparabilis vita*
and I have a will to exist and to know. That there is in these
three an inseparable life [of three]

*et una vita et una mens et una essentia,*
and one life and one mind and one being

*quam denique inseparabilis distinctio et tamen distinctio, videat
qui potest.*
and that there is an inseparable difference, yet a real
difference, let the person who can see behold.
(13.11.12)

Just to mark the obvious, Augustine sees parallels to the Trinity in our own internal lives. We exist, we know, we will—three

different ways of being and acting, but all in one person. Each implies the other. This image is meant, I think, as a way of making the Trinity less mysterious, maybe less weird.

## IMAGISTIC READING OF SCRIPTURE
## (13.12.13)

We can see from what we have already read that Augustine is embarking upon a special way of reading and thinking about the Scriptures, not literally but as I say, imagistically, a way of reading by which the events of Genesis are seen as representing events of a very different kind in a very different time.

One effort is to connect baptism and creation, seeing each set of events as mirroring the other. I think almost no one today would think about the Old Testament and New Testament interacting in such a way. But let us see what Augustine does with it.

> *Procede in confessione, fides mea; dic Domino tuo,*
> Proceed into your confession, my faith; say to your Lord,

> *"Sancte, sancte, sancte, Domine Deus meus, in nomine tuo baptizati sumus*
> "Holy, holy, holy Lord, my God, in your name we are baptized

> *pater et fili et spiritus sancte, in nomine tuo baptizamus,*
> Father and Son and Holy Spirit, in your name we baptize others,

> *pater et fili et spiritus sancta,"*
> Father and Son and Holy Spirit,"

*quia et apud nos in Christo suo fecit Deus caelum et terram,*
because in our presence and in his Christ God made heaven and earth,

*spirituales et carnales ecclesiae suae.*
that is, the spiritual and carnal ones of his church.

*Et terra nostra antiquam acciperet formam doctrinae*
And our earth [that is, our nature] before it received the form of teaching

*invisibilis erat et incomposita, et ignorantiae tenebris tegebamur,*
was invisible and chaotic and we were covered with the shadows of ignorance

*quoniam pro iniquitate erudisti hominem, et judicia tua sicut multa abyssus.*
because you taught humanity about wickedness, and your judgment was like a huge abyss.

*Sed quia spiritus tuus superferebatur super aquam,*
But because your spirit was borne over the water

*non reliquit miseriam nostrum misericordia tua, et dixisti,*
your compassion did not desert our misery, and you said

*"Fiat lux"; "Paenitentiam agite, appropinquavit enim regum caelorum."*
"Let there be light"; "Repent, for the kingdom of heaven draws near."
(13.12.13)

By invoking the cry of John the Baptist in the last line of the passage Augustine connects the waters of baptism to the waters over which the Spirit passes in the Genesis story. This time the passing is obviously redemptive, which suggests that the passing of the Spirit in Genesis was also redemptive. Likewise, our state of formlessness is mirrored in the formlessness of the earth before it was given shape and life; in our case the shape and form came from teaching, especially from the teaching that was a preliminary to the rite of baptism. This part of the creation story parallels baptism and vice versa.

This is a way of imagining each part of the sacred text as offering in principle unlimited connections with other parts of that text, no matter how far removed they may be. In such work there is no test of rightness or truth except the nature of the experience it offers its readers.

What strikes me about this passage of what is often called "allegorical" interpretation is how far it seems from what we typically think of as allegory, that is, a story involving one set of beings or events or ideas which are said to mirror another such set in a mechanical way. This kind of allegory can be in its own way authoritarian and systematic and ultimately propositional in nature. Augustine's comparisons and conceptions are not like that, but full of suggestions, and gaps, and hints of further meaning. This way of reading Scripture is profoundly resistant to any claim that we have actually and finally understood anything in it—that is, any claim of certainty.

Rather, it opens up fresh and new ways of thinking of the meaning of Scripture and its possible connections with us and with other parts of Scripture as well. This is a great gift to the reader, who will have to find ways of living after they have closed this book and are being told that the Scriptures offer an immense resource, not least because they can be read in such an imagistic way. Thus he brings both "Let there be light" and "Repent, for the kingdom of heaven is drawing near" into a new context: the first is of course a phrase of the Old Testament, which he uses to identify and explain the experience of people today, the second a quotation from the New Testament.[3]

But they belong together. Here both quotations are used to identify and explain what was happening in this account of the Creation which is also an act of baptism. This is a way of creating a truth that is not exclusive of other truths.


## WHAT IS OUR CONDITION? (13.12.13–13.14.15)

Augustine believes that he has been saved, by Christ and by baptism. But what does it mean to be saved? Certainly not that we understand everything, or even that we fully understand anything. Likewise it does not mean that we no longer sin, for sin is inherent in human life: *Et ecce fuimus aliquando tenebrae, nunc autem lux in Domino,* "Yet behold, once we were shadows of darkness, now we are light in the Lord" (13.12.13).

\* \* \*

So what is the life of those who have been converted and thus saved? What does it mean to live in the light? To Augustine it means we live by faith and hope, not by certainty, here represented as vision:

> *Et tamen adhuc per fidem, nondum per speciem: spe enim salvi facti sumus.*
> And so far this is through faith not yet by sight; by hope we have been saved.

> *Spes autem quae videtur non est spes.*
> Hope that is seen is not hope.
> (12.13.14)

Here Augustine is making a direct reference both to 2 Corinthians 5:7, where Paul says, in the King James translation: "We walk by faith, not by sight" and to Romans 8:24, where he says, "For we are saved by hope, but hope that is seen is not hope, for what a man seeth, why doth he yet hope for?" What this is telling us is that for Augustine as for Paul, our lives on earth are not completed, still uncertain, still based on hope, not observed facts, in some sense provisional. Our condition is one of yearning, incompleteness. *Adhuc abyssus abyssum invocat, sed iam in voce cataractarum tuarum,* "Already abyss calls to abyss, but does so in the voice of your cataracts" (12.13.14).

This is imagistic reading, which calls for a right interpretation, which I may not be able to give. But to me what this means is that person calls to person, from the center to the center, and does so not in ordinary human voices, but in the voice of the God within us. Such are the waters of which he speaks.

> *Adhuc et ille qui dicit, "Non potui vobis loqui quasi spiritalibus, sed quasi carnalibus,"*
> Even he who says "I could not speak to you as spiritual beings but [only as] physical beings,"[4]
>
> *etiam ipse nondum se arbitratur comprehendisse, et quae retro oblitus,*
> even he does not think he understands, and having forgotten what lies behind him,
>
> *in ea quae ante sunt extenditur et ingemescit gravatus,*
> he extends himself to what is ahead of him and weighed down he groans
>
> *et sitit anima eius ad Deum vivum, quemadmodum cervi*
> and his soul thirsts for the living God as the deer

*ad fontes aquarum, et dicit, "Quando veniam?"*
for the springs of water,[5] and he says: "When will I arrive?"
(12.13.14)

Augustine is telling us that even St. Paul, as perfect a follower of
Christ as exists in the world, lives out of hope, not certainty, a life
of yearning and desire. He goes on:

*Et ego dico, "Deus meus ubi es?" ecce ubi es.*
I too say, "My God where are you?" and behold you are
there.

*Respiro in te paululum, cum effundo super me animam meam*
I am refreshed in you a little, when I pour my soul over
myself

*in voce exultationis et confessionis, soni festivitatem celebrantis.*
in a voice of exultation and confession and in the sound of
one celebrating a festive occasion.

*Et adhuc tristis est, quia relabitur et fit abyssus,*
And yet my soul is sad because it will slip and become an
abyss

*vel potius sentit adhuc se esse abyssum.*
or rather feels it has become an abyss

*Dicit ei fides mea, quam accendisti in nocte ante pedes meos,*
and my faith says to it, my faith which you have kindled in
the night [as a light] before my feet,

*"Quare tristis, anima, et quare conturbas me? Spera in
Domino."* . . .
"Why are you sad, my soul, and why do you disturb me?—
Hope in the Lord." . . .

*Spera in Domino; mane astabo et contemplabor; semper confitebor illi.*
Hope in the Lord; in the morning I shall stand before him
and behold him; I shall confess to him always.
(13.14.15)

What we see here is that for Augustine the life of the Christian
person is not one of uninterrupted bliss, or certainty of salvation,
or sureness of mind or feeling. At every stage there are uncertainties, worries, failures of mind and character, unmet desires,
moments (or years) of alienation. Neither the Scriptures nor the
church can be reduced to a recipe for holy living. We are saved
by hope not in the sense that our hope triggers a response in
heaven, but in the sense that our hope can give us a way of living
under the difficult conditions which the *Confessions* has made
vivid from the beginning.

One other thing Augustine makes clear is that whenever we
return to God, as he imagines or knows him, he is present in our
life as an interlocutor, one with whom we can converse about
the inmost parts of ourselves, and the fears and hopes and failings that can be found there. This is crucial because his book is a
kind of interlocutor too, and it offers us, as its readers, some part
of what he feels God offers him—tentative claims of meaning,
performances of true feeling and imagination, uncertainties, and
maybe obfuscations, all governed by a sense of complete trust on
one side, trustworthiness on the other.

He has brought us into a different imaginative universe (perhaps a bit as Dante does in the *Commedia*). Here is one of his
accounts of our condition:

*mane astabo et videbo salutare vultus mei,*
in the morning I shall stand near and see the salvation of my
face,

*Deum meum, qui vivificabit et mortalia corpora nostra propter*
*spiritum,*
my God, who will give life to our mortal bodies through the
Spirit

*qui habitat in nobis, quia super interius nostrum tenebrosum et*
*fluvidum misericorditer superferebatur.*
who lives in us, because over our inner being, our shadowy
and flowing inner selves, he has been carried in compassion.

*Unde in hac peregrinatione pignus accepimus,*
Whence in this pilgrimage we have received a promise

*ut iam simus lux, dum adhoc spe salvi facti sumus et filii lucis et*
*filii diei,*
that we are already the light, while we are saved by hope, and
children of the light and of the day

*non filii noctis neque tenebrarum, quod tamen fuimus.*
not children of the night, and of darkness, as we once were.
(13.14.15)

What I have written here does not capture the strength of
Augustine's longing, the depth of his joy, the confidence with
which he knows what he is saying, and saying not with his mind
but with his soul.

## EXPANDING IMAGES (13.15.18–13.38.53)

Of course I cannot trace out all the manifestations of Augustine's imagistic imagination, but I can perhaps give you a couple of samples. The first is his identification of the "firmament"
created in Genesis with the Scriptures themselves. One way he

does this is to see the firmament as a kind of skin, stretched out tight, which is also an image of the parchment, itself a kind of skin, on which the Scriptures were preserved.

In a more extensive way he says something like this: "There are other waters above this firmament, above these Scriptures, which are hidden from earthly corruption. There the angels read your face, O God, and its unchanging meaning. They read you, not the Scriptures and grasp your meaning directly. For us, however, the Scriptures are stretched out over us. Now we see the Scriptures, then we shall see face to face" (13.15.18).

Then he prays:

> *Oriatur de terra veritas, et iustitia de caelo respiciat,*
> Let truth come up from the earth and justice look down
> from heaven
>
> *et fiant in firmamento luminaria.*
> and let lights be made in the firmament.
>
> *Frangamus esurienti panem nostrum*
> Let us break our bread for the hungry,
>
> *et egenum sine tecto inducamus in domum nostrum,*
> and the needy without a roof let us lead into our house,
>
> *nudum vestiamus et domesticos seminis nostri non*
> *despiciamus.*
> and the naked let us dress and let us not despise the people
> our own house, our own seed.
> (13.18.22)

See how his imagination works. The lights in the firmament, in the sky, in the Scripture becomes lights of a very different kind, in the charity and fidelity by which the full humanity of others is

respected and responded to in a real way. In a few lines he makes
this explicit:

> *appareamus sicut luminaria in mundo,*
> let us appear as lights in the world,
>
> *cohaerentes firmamento scripturae tuae.*
> clinging to the firmament of your Scripture.
> (13.18.22)

A bit later he says that the Spirit gives different people different gifts, from healing to prophesy, and *haec omnia tamquam
stellae,* "all of these are like stars" (13.18.23). In this way his inventive imagery becomes not only a way of imagining God and the
scripture but a way of calling his reader to a life of charity.

From this point on Augustine turns his attention away from
what happens in the first two verses to what follows a bit later in
Genesis, really the rest of the creation. Here he is concerned with
the meaning of the events, for example: What do the swarms of
water-creatures and birds mean allegorically? Why do human
beings have the role that they do?

He is puzzled in particular by the fact that God blesses the
creatures of the water and the birds, created in water, and commands them to increase and multiply, as he also blesses and commands humankind, but he does not bless cattle and wild beasts
and creeping things and trees nor does he command them to
increase and multiply. How can this be made coherent?

This troubles him because he thought it would make more
sense for God to bless humanity alone, which after all he created
in his own image. But that is not what Genesis says.

In all of this he is elaborating his imagistic reading of Genesis. The spirit in which he does this is consistent with what we

have read: with a bone-deep acknowledgment of the truth that lies behind the Scriptures, he amplifies their meaning by seeing much more in a phrase or image than a literalist would ever see. In doing this he expresses and maintains his attitude of charity toward others who accept what are for him basic truths but build on that knowledge differently. What is important here is not so much the issue that occupied Augustine, but the way he dealt with it. Here he is speaking of the puzzle about blessing and commanding to multiply:

> *Quid igitur dicam, lumen meum, veritas?*
> What shoud I say, O my light, Truth itself?

> *Quia vacat hoc, quia inaniter dictum est? nequaquam pater pietatis;*
> That this is empty, that it is said pointlessly? By no means, O father of piety;

> *absit ut hoc dicat servus verbi tui.*
> far be it from me that the servant of your word should say that.

> *Et si ego non intellego quid hoc eloquio significes,*
> And if I do not understand what you mean by this statement,

> *utantur eo melius meliores, id est intellegentiores quam ego sum, unicuique quantum sapere dedisti.*
> let better ones do better, that is those more intelligent than I am, in how much you have given each of us to know.

> *Placeat autem et confessio mea coram oculis tui,*
> Let my confession also be pleasing in your sight

*qua tibi confiteor credere me, Domine, non incassum te ita locutum,*
in which I confess, Lord, that I believe you did not say this
emptily,

*neque silebo quod mihi lectionis huius occasio suggerit.*
nor shall I be silent about what the moment of this reading
suggests to me.

*Verum est enim, nece video quid impediat ita me sentire dicta*
*figurata librorum tuorum.*
It is true, nor do I see what should keep me from perceiving
figurative utterances in your books.

*Novi enim multipliciter significari per corpus, quod uno modo*
*mente intellegitur,*
I know that many things can be signified in the body, which
are understood as one in the mind.

*et multipliciter mente intellegi, quod uno modo per corpus*
*significatur.*
what is signified by the body as one thing can be understood
as many by the mind.

*Ecce simplex dilectio Dei et proximi,*
Behold the simple "love God and neighbor,"

*quam multiplicibus sacramentis et innumerabilibus linguis*
which in many sacred rites and innumerable languages,

*Et in unaquaque lingua innumerabilibus locutionum modis*
*corporaliter enuntiatur!*
even in the same language, and in countless forms of speech,
it is propounded—all in physical images!

(13.24.36)

This is a difficult passage, but I think what it means is that whenever we speak about God in images or stories, or fables, or rules of behavior, we inherently create issues of interpretation that can go on forever. But sometimes behind our locutions is a truth, or perhaps Truth itself, which is inherently one and unchanging. This unchanging meaning cannot be stated in human language in a nonproblematic way, but it is there, at the center of the universe. This reading would fit both with Augustine's toleration of, even his welcoming, a wide range of possible readings of a text and with his insistence on the unchanging and utterly stable presence of God himself. For Augustine it is important that he cannot fully understand or describe the God he knows, cannot reduce him to language, and in that sense cannot know him. But, as he demonstrates so magnificently throughout the *Confessions*, he can speak to this God, he can converse with this God, and in that sense he shows that he does know him.

Toward the end, not only of Book 13 but the *Confessions* itself, he says:

> *Domine Deus, pacem da nobis (omnia enim praestitisti nobis),*
> Lord God, give us peace (for you have given us everything), the
>
> *pacem quietis, pacem sabbati, pacem sine vespera. . . .*
> peace of quiet, the peace of the sabbath, peace without evening.[6] . . .
>
> *Dies autem septimus sine vespera est nec habet occasum,*
> The seventh day has no evening, no setting of the sun
>
> *quia sanctificasti eum ad permansionem sempiternam.*
> because you have sanctified it to continue forever.
> (13.35.50–51)

Later:

> *Tu autem bonum nullo indigens bono semper quietus es,*
> You however are the good, needing no good, always at rest
>
> *quoniam tua quies tu ipse es.*
> because you are your own rest.
> (13.38.53)

Then:

> *Et hoc intellegere quis hominum dabit homini?*
> And who of human beings can give it to a human being to
> understand this?
>
> *Quis angelus angelo?*
> What angel can give it to an angel?
>
> *Quis angelus homini?*
> What angel can give it to a human being?
>
> *A te petatur,*
> From you it must be asked,
>
> *in te quaeratur,*
> in you it must be sought,
>
> *ad te pulsetur:*
> in you it must be "knocked":
>
> *sic, sic accipietur,*
> thus, thus it will be received,
>
> *sic invenietur,*
> thus it will be found,

*sic aperietur.*
thus it will be opened.
(13.38.53)

Why "opened"? The word is an allusion to a crucial passage we have seen Augustine invoke on another occasion: "Ask, and it shall be given you; seek, and ye shall find; knock, and it shall be opened unto you" (Matt. 7:7).

\* \* \*

To me the astonishing thing about this ending is that it marks not an ending but a beginning. After all that Augustine has done to discover himself and God, to explain what he can and to embody what he cannot explain, after all his struggles with his language and culture, with his own mistakes and failings, with the impossibility of what he is trying to do, what he says to his reader is: "Knock, and it shall be opened unto you."

That is: "I have done what I can do; now it is up to you."

# CODA

I WANT TO CLOSE WITH a set of questions for you, the reader. My hope, as my subtitle suggests, is that by now you have learned something about reading the *Confessions* of St. Augustine, and that you feel you can continue to do it, on your own, always learning how to do it better. It is important to stress that we have together read only a small portion of what Augustine wrote. This is truly an introduction, not a substitute for the real thing, but I hope a useful one for each of you.

More particularly: Do you have the sense that you have been in touch with the mind and soul of Augustine? Has the Latin helped you feel that way? Have you even learned a little Latin? I hope so. I know that some people can make progress in learning a language by reading it, though I recognize that may not be true for you.

Do you have a sense that Latin really is different from English? That to read the Latin opens up possibilities and meanings that a translation precludes?

Have you seen Augustine struggling with his language? Remaking it? Making something new and beautiful with it? How do you evaluate what you see him doing?

How about the genre of the *Confessions*: Does he mark this as a new genre in some way, or does he build on other genres? How do you know?

Who has Augustine become in the course of your reading and how has that happened? Here you might think of the three Augustines: the pilgrim; the narrator, whose voice we have heard throughout; and the composer of the whole book, for whom the other two are characters in the drama he is creating.

Think of the question in terms of the voice you have heard. Has Augustine's voice changed in moving from the beginning of the book to the end? In what ways, and to what end?

His book is addressed to God: Who has God become, and how has that happened? Who in fact *is* this God? Is he the life that is created in this text? What is his church? The community of those who share this life?

What relationship exists between Augustine and his God? How has that changed in the course of the book?

I hope you come away with some awareness of who Augustine is and how he works, with his language, with his God, and with his audience.

* * *

But perhaps I have been too quick. Has it been a problem for you that this is a profoundly religious text of a certain kind? Perhaps if you are a conservative Christian you will find both what I say and what Augustine says disturbing because it is so open-ended. Or if you are an atheist or agnostic, you may feel that all talk about religion is inherently meaningless. Or wherever else you may be, on that or another spectrum, you may find that religious talk just makes you uncomfortable. In any of these cases I hope you have come to see that what matters in this book, its meaning in fact, is what Augustine and the reader—that is, you—have together created in the experience he invites you to share and make your own, and in your response to that invitation—a response he invites you to shape in your own way. This experience, this meaning, is real and alive. Whether or not it should be called "God" is an entirely different question.

I hope that your experience includes the recognition that he is speaking to you and me now, in our dangerous world and time.

I hope also that you feel that your sense of these things is your own, not mine, and that you are comfortable expressing your distance from me. As I said in the Preface, you could regard your experience of the book you have in your hand as reading the *Confessions* with a friend with whom you engage in conversation, a part of which can always be disagreement. The important thing is the nature of your own experience.

Have we done justice to the *Confessions*? Of course not. As Augustine makes clear, that is up to you.

# NOTES

## PREFACE

1. This was before I knew of the fine translation by Carolyn J.-B. Hammond, *Augustine: Confessions*, 2 vols., Loeb Classical Library (Cambridge, MA: Harvard University Press, 2014–2016). But even that, good as it is, would have left me wanting something else.

2. As I was preparing this book for publication I read in the *New York Times* an obituary of Reginald Foster, the chief Latinist for the Vatican: " 'You cannot understand St. Augustine in English,' Father Foster told *The Telegraph*. . . . 'He thought in Latin. It is like listening to Mozart through a jukebox.' " See Margalit Fox, "Reginald Foster, Vatican Latinist Who Tweeted in the Language, Dies at 81," Obituaries, *New York Times*, December 28, 2020.

3. See Jose Ortega y Gassett, "Miseria y Esplendor de la Traduccion," in *Obras Completas*, 7th ed., volume 5, *1933–1941* (Madrid: Revista de Occidente, 1970), 433. I owe my introduction to Ortega and his work to my late friend and colleague, Alton Becker, of whom I will say more below.

4. If you do find yourself wanting to engage with the Latin in a real way, let me suggest some resources:

    1. S. A. Handford and Mary Herberg, *Langenscheidt's Pocket Latin Dictionary* (Berlin: Langenscheidt, 1966).
    2. Richard E. Prior and Joseph Wohlberg, *501 Latin Verbs* (Hauppauge, NY: Barron's Educational Services, 2007).

3. The summary of Latin grammar at the end of Clyde Pharr's edition of Vergil's *Aeneid* (Wauconda, IL: Bolchazy-Carducci, 2007), or an equivalent in a standard Latin grammar.

4. The Perseus Latin Word Study Tool, to be found on the Web (http://www.perseus.tufts.edu).

5. The wonderful Oxford edition of the *Confessions*, edited by James J. O'Donnell (Oxford: Clarendon Press, 1992).

6. The Quickstudy three-page plastic-covered "Latin Grammar" (Boca Raton, FL: BarCharts, 2002).

7. The fine translation of the *Confessions* by Carolyn J.-B. Hammond in the Loeb Classical Library edition (Cambridge, MA: Harvard University Press, 2014–2016).

5. For the result of this work, see my *Living Speech: Resisting the Empire of Force* (Princeton, NJ: Princeton University Press, 2012) at places marked in the index.

Here's another experience: as one raised as an Episcopalian, for me the Bible was a text of the early seventeenth century, composed in the glorious language of the time. In some sense I knew that its history went back at least 1,500 years more, but that fact was not real to me until I started to read the Gospel of Luke in Greek. It was like an experience of time travel: 1,500 years went by in a second, and there I was reading the words of the original writer. It was as though I was sitting across the table from him.

I am speaking here of the New Testament. Some years later I learned enough Hebrew to have some sense of the immense difference between the language in which the Hebrew Bible was composed from both English and Greek. In doing this work I felt privileged to hear the voices of the original writers, even with my poor Hebrew.

6. To help you with the Latin I will typically present the Latin texts line by line, alternating with them English translations that to the extent possible mirror the Latin lines.

My thought is that this may well be beneficial even if you know no Latin, enabling you to go back and forth between the two texts and in the process helping you get a sense of the way the Latin works and what Augustine is doing. I gave a handful of non-Latinate friends some pages done this way in another context, and they all liked it,

saying such things as: "I enjoyed the Latin, just for the feel of it. Somehow it also gives me a sense of the permanence of the thoughts"; it
"lends both beauty and authenticity"; it "urges me not to go on or skip
the Latin, but to dig right in, using English as a tool to understanding
it"; "I really appreciate having the original text there. Of course I can
only read a bit of it, but I sense its rhythm; it allows me to read the
English more slowly and thoughtfully." I hope that readers of this book
will feel this way too.

7. In Saint Augustine, *Essential Sermons*, Boniface Ramsey, ed., Edmund
Hill, trans. (Hyde Park, NY: New City, 2007), 25–44. For a reading of
this sermon, see my "The Creation of Authority in a Sermon by St.
Augustine," *Villanova Law Review* 55, no. 6 (2010): 1129–1142.

8. James Boyd White, *Keep Law Alive* (Durham, NC: Carolina Academic
Press, 2019).

## ACKNOWLEDGMENTS

1. James J. O'Donnell, *Augustine Confessions* (Oxford: Clarendon Press,
1994).

2. Another version of chapter 1 was published both in White, *Keep Law
Alive*, 138–141, and in *Journal of Law and Religion* 29 (2014): 330–335. It is
reproduced here with kind permission.

## AN OUTLINE OF AUGUSTINE'S LIFE UP TO THE COMPOSITION OF THE *CONFESSIONS*

1. For a rich account of his baptism, see Garry Wills, *The Fount of Life:
Ambrose, Augustine, and the Mystery of Baptism* (Oxford: Oxford University Press, 2012).

## I. THE SHAPE OF THE *CONFESSIONS*

1. See Brent D. Shaw, *Sacred Violence: African Christians and Sectarian
Hatred in the Age of Augustine* (Princeton: Princeton University Press,
2011).

2. *Et ecce intus eras et ego foris, et ibi te quaerabam. . . . Mecum eras, et tecum
non eram*"; "And behold, you were in me and I was outside, and that is

where I searched for you. . . . You were with me, but I was not with you"
(10.27.38, that is: Book 10, chapter 27, paragraph 38).

3. In this set of relations Augustine is re-creating the church and giving it
a new kind of life.

## 2. THE FIRST THREE SENTENCES (BOOK I)

1. These questions are at the heart of a more general way of reading elaborated in my *When Words Lose Their Meaning: Constitutions and Reconstitutions of Language, Character, and Community* (Chicago: University
of Chicago Press, 1984). In particular I develop in that book the fact
that language itself can be a forceful carrier of its culture in a way that
presents a writer with an important set of difficulties and opportunities
in their effort to create new meaning.

2. See p. 337, n. 4.

3. How can you do this if you do not know how to pronounce it? Fortu-
nately its alphabet is very much like ours (actually vice versa). The big-
gest differences are: the letters *C* and *G* are always "hard"; *E*, when long
would rhyme with "bay"; *I*, when long sounds like the I in "machine";
*O*, when long sounds like "home," when short like "obey"; *S* sounds like
"hiss," never like "his"; *T* always sounds like "tin," not like the second T
in "station"; *V* sounds like our *W*. Diphthongs: *AE* sounds like "I"; *OU*
sounds like "couch"; *EI* sounds like "eight"; *OE* sounds like "toil"; and
*UI* roughly as "we."

4. For other examples of the invention of genre, see the texts read in my
*When Words Lose Their Meaning*, each of which does create something
of a new genre: Homer's *Iliad*, Thucydides's *History of the Peloponnesian
War*, Plato's *Gorgias*, Jonathan Swift's *A Tale of a Tub*, Samuel Johnson's
*Rambler* essays, Jane Austen's *Emma*, Edmund Burke's *Letter on the
Revolution in France*, the Declaration of Independence, the Constitution of the United States, and the opinion of John Marshall in *McCull-
och v. Maryland*. It is in fact the invention of genre that provides a large
part of the answer to the question implied in the title, What are we to
do when words lose their meaning? Invent a new genre!

5. Latin does not capitalize *Dominus* or *Deus*, as we capitalize "Lord"
and "God." But for the sake of familiarity, in my translation I follow

the English practice. Likewise I do not follow the Latin practice that begins a sentence with a lowercase letter, but capitalize the first word of a sentence as we do in English.

6.  The practice derives from the Septuagint, the translation of the Hebrew Scriptures into Greek made in Alexandria by learned Jews during the third and second centuries BCE. This book was written to render the Hebrew Scriptures accessible to the large number of Hellenized Jews who had lost their command of Hebrew.

The Hebrew Scriptures speak about God in different ways, sometimes as *Elohim*, which means "God," sometimes by the name, *YHWH*. A Jew is never supposed to pronounce this name, so the practice grew up of saying *Adonai*, or "my lord," wherever *YHWH*'s name appeared in the text. In the Greek of the Septuagint the distinction between these terms is preserved: *Elohim* is translated as *Theos*, God; *Adonai* is translated as *Kurios*, which in Greek means "Lord"; in Latin *Theos* becomes *Deus*, and *Kurios* becomes *Dominus*.

This history helps explain where *Dominus* came from, and shows that in origin it is not really a name, but a substitute for a name.

In the New Testament the words *Kurios* and *Dominus* are both used of Jesus. The phrase "Jesus is Lord," against this background, has at least in shadow the meaning, quite threatening to traditional Judaism, "Jesus is *YHWH*." In the sentence quoted above, Augustine is quoting from a Psalm, where *Dominus* and its antecedent *Kurios* both mean *YHWH*.

7.  James J. O'Donnell, *Augustine: Confessions*, 3 vols. (Oxford: Clarendon Press, 1992), 1:11.

8.  See Psalm 48:1, "Great is the Lord, and greatly to be praised"; Psalm 96:4, "For the Lord is great, and greatly to be praised"; Psalm 145:3, "Great is the Lord, and greatly to be praised."

Translators will often identify other possible Scriptural antecedents for what Augustine writes, some more persuasive than others. It is important to recognize that even the passages quoted in this note, which are clear antecedents, are not specifically referred to in the text. They are background that some readers will recognize, others not.

9.  Notice that although this is in some way a theological book, at no point does Augustine in any exhaustive way purport to define God, or explain

what he does. I think he is making clear his sense that nothing he could say would describe God adequately, or even coherently. Instead of speaking about him he speaks to him. He is inviting us to do the same: not to theologize but to praise.

10. Of course other Psalms do address God directly, so in this respect they are perhaps an authority for what Augustine is doing, but it is still true that here he changes the language he quotes.

11. "Ask, and it shall be given you; seek, and ye shall find; knock, and it shall be opened unto you." Here is what Augustine says: *Tu autem bonum nullo indigens bono, semper quietus es quoniam tua quies tu ipse es. Hoc intellegere, quis hominum dabit homini? Quis angelus angelo? A te petatur, in te quaeretur, ad te pulsetur: sic, sic accipietur, sic invenietur, sic aperietur.* You being the good, needing no good, are always at peace because your peace is what you are. What human being can give it to another to understand this about you? What angel can give it to another? From you, God, it must be asked, in you it must be sought, it is your door upon which one must knock; thus it will be acquired, thus it will be found, thus it will be opened (13.38.53).

12. For an interesting account of the grammatical structure shared by most Indo-European languages, see Hermann Fränkel, "Three Talks on Grammar," *California Studies in Classical Antiquity* 7 (1974): 113–154.

For a fine effort to write an English that feels like Latin, see Richard Hooker, *The Laws of Ecclesiastical Polity* (1594), discussed in my *Acts of Hope: Creating Authority in Literature, Law, and Politics* (Chicago: University of Chicago, 1994), 82–124.

13. Thus *est*, the third person singular of the verb "to be," does not mean "is," exactly but "he, she, or it is."

14. Another possibility is that *sapientiae* is dative, in which case a literal translation might be: "there is no number to your wisdom." In the Latin text these two possibilities exist side by side, without resolution.

15. Actually there is no good translation of the simple word *homo*. At one time people would have felt comfortable using the word "man," but for us this is heavily marked for gender. What word will do? Can you improve on "person"?

16. In English we have what are called "articles" that commonly precede nouns, definite and indefinite in character, thus: "the house," or "a

house," "the door," or "a door." Latin has no such forms, which means that in translating we must add what is not there in the original.

17. *Circumferens* is neither a finite verb, like *vult*, nor an infinitive, like *laudare*, but a participle, which is usually best translated by an English participle, or "–ing" word, here "carrying around." The Latin participle is a hybrid, half noun and half verb, having gender and number like a noun, tense and aspect like a verb.

18. *Peccati* is genitive singular, hence the "of," and *sui* is in concord with it. Compare *mortalitatem suam*. Here it looks as though in this phrase "mortality" is being redefined as the "testimony" of his sin, an implicit reference to Adam's death-bringing sin.

19. You will notice that, as here, I sometimes translate a Latin word or phrase in a different way at different times. That is a conscious decision, meant to reflect the fact that there are many possible translations for any word or sentence from another language.

20. *Delectet* is in the subjunctive mood, which expresses not only the root meaning of the verb, but an emotion or wish of the speaker, like hope or fear, in this case a sense of moral obligation. And what should he "delight" to do? "To praise you," in Latin *laudare te*. In other words, the object of the verb "delight" is an infinitive "to praise."

21. For a somewhat similar shift in a famous place, think of Psalm 23, which begins talking about "The Lord" who is the speaker's shepherd in the third person, but then shifts to the first: "Yea, though I walk through the valley of the shadow of death, I will fear no evil, for *Thou* art with me."

22. In thinking about what Augustine means by "rest" and "restlessness," I find that a well-known poem by George Herbert comes repeatedly to mind. It may well have been influenced by this very sentence, since Herbert was a serious reader of Augustine. In fact he made a point of leaving "St. Augustine's works" to a Mr. Bostock in his will (F. E. Hutchinson, *The Works of George Herbert* [Oxford: Oxford University Press, 1941], 382).

Here is the poem:

"The Pulley"
　　When God at first made man,
Having a glass of blessings standing by,
"Let us," said he, "pour on him all we can.

Let the world's riches, which dispersèd lie,
    Contract into a span."

    So strength first made a way;
Then beauty flowed, then wisdom, honour, pleasure.
When almost all was out, God made a stay,
Perceiving that, alone of all his treasure,
    Rest in the bottom lay.

    "For if I should," said he,
"Bestow this jewel also on my creature,
He would adore my gifts instead of me,
And rest in Nature, not the God of Nature;
    So both should losers be.

    "Yet let him keep the rest,
But keep them with repining restlessness;
Let him be rich and weary, that at least,
If goodness lead him not, yet weariness
    May toss him to my breast."

23. If you are interested in finding books that might help you, let me perhaps surprisingly recommend, in addition to the books cited in the Preface, that you start with a set of books written to young children in Great Britain, meant to prepare them for the more demanding work that lies ahead. The books I have in mind are amusing and so far as I know accurate and it might in any event make it easier to take on the task to know that ten-year-old kids are doing this in the UK. See Theo Zinn, *So you Really Want to Learn Latin Prep?*, 3 vols. (Kent, UK: ISEB Publications, 2006).

    For a more grown-up course, see Glen M. Knudsvig, Gerda M. Seligson, and Ruth S. Craig, *Latin for Reading: A Beginner's Textbook with Exercises*, rev. ed. (Ann Arbor: University of Michigan Press, 1986), which is a wonderful experiment in language teaching.

24. Thus *anima*, meaning "soul," is feminine; *locus*, meaning roughly "place," is masculine; and *bellum*, meaning "war," is neuter.

25. Augustine *Confessions*, Michael Foley, ed., F. J. Sheed, trans. (Indianapolis/Cambridge: Hackett Publishing Company, 1942), 3.

26. See this excellent essay: John Crowe Ransom, *Poems and Essays* (New York: Vintage Books, 1955), 118–134.


## 3. MOVEMENT FROM ONE MODE OF THOUGHT AND EXPRESSION TO ANOTHER (BOOK I)

1. Ludwig Wittgenstein, *Philosophical Investigations*, 3rd ed. (New York: Macmillan, 1958).

2. Here we have a problem arising from the use of the subjunctive *sit* coupled with *prius*: Is he asking whether we *do* in fact invoke or praise first, or, as the subjunctive suggests, whether we *should* invoke or praise first. I hope that I capure something of this uncertainty when I cast the verb in our subjunctive, this way: "whether it be first."

3. Notice that the Latin structure rests on a participle, *nesciens*, which would be awkward in English, hence the relative clause, beginning "who does not. . . ." This is a respect in which the two languages work differently.

4. *Praedico* is a complex term, the most basic meaning of which is "say beforehand." It includes "prophesy" and "foretell." By Augustine's time it had also come to mean "preaching."

5. For interesting work about preaching in the late Empire, see Carol Harrison, *The Art of Listening in the Early Church* (Oxford: Oxford University Press, 2013), and Lisa Kaaren Bailey, *Christianity's Quiet Success: The Eusebius Gallicanus Sermon Collection and the Power of the Church in Late Antique Gaul* (South Bend, IN: University of Notre Dame Press, 2010).

6. See *Romans*.vi0:14–15. Here Augustine is functioning not only as a borrower but as an interpreter—the role he will have at the end of the *Confessions*. With respect to the famous sentence, "faith comes by hearing," see Romans 10:17.

7. "Faith" is of course an English word. The Latin term is *fides* which has a range of dictionary meanings, including trust, confidence, trustworthiness, sincerity, commercial reliability, promise, word of honor, belief, guardian care. Our task will be to try to get a sense of what Augustine means by the term from the way he uses it.

8. In this connection, see Charles T. Mathewes, "Book One: The Presumptuousness of Autobiography and the Paradoxes of Beginning," in

*A Reader's Companion to Augustine's* Confessions, ed. Kim Paffenroth and Robert P. Kennedy (Louisville and London: Westminster John Knox Press, 2003), 7–23.

9. See Brent Shaw, *Sacred Violence: African Christians and Sectarian Hatred in the Age of Augustine* (Cambridge: Cambridge University Press, 2011).

10. For elaborations of Becker's mode of analysis, of which I have given the merest sketch, see A. L. Becker, *Beyond Translation: Essays Toward a Modern Philology* (Ann Arbor: University of Michigan Press, 1995).

11. Here: *Et quomodo* is roughly "and how"; *invocabo*, "shall I invoke"; *Deum meum*, "my God"; *quoniam*, "because"; *utique in me ipsum eum vocabo*, "surely I shall call him [*eum*] into myself"; *cum invocabo eum*, "when I invoke him?"

12. Compare his commentary on Psalm 52, where the meaning of *invoco* comes up. Augustine says: *Quid enim est invocare, nisi vocare in se? In se ergo vocare, hoc dicitur invocare*, "What is it to 'invoke' except to call into oneself? 'To call into oneself' is what 'invoke' means" (Psalm 52).

13. *Veniat:* third person singular present subjunctive of *venio*, "I come."

14. Here I shall begin to indicate the place in the *Confessions* where passages I cite or reproduce can be found. Up to now it has not been necessary since we have simply been reading in order the first few pages of Book 1. The system of reference I am using is peculiar to the *Confessions*, which in its history has been divided up in three ways: into books, into chapters, and into paragraphs (the latter two starting over with each new book). The standard way to cite a passage is to list all three references, and this system of citation will be followed in the text below.

15. There is another important point here: as I have said, the culmination of the *Confessions* is Augustine's recognition that he knows that God exists and is within him. Here he seems to have part of that perception, but in a relatively thin and unproductive way, and in any case does not recognize the limits of his other kinds of knowledge, which he will later come to see. The adumbration here of the position he comes to at the end is in my view highly artful, at once connecting beginning and end and marking a difference between those two positions.

16. But his struggle with that language continues: *An quia non possunt te totum capere omnia, partem tui capiunt et eandem partem simul omnia capiunt? An singulas singula et maiores maiora, minores minora capiunt? Ergo est aliqua pars tua maior, aliqua minor? An ubique totus es et res nulla*

*te totum capit?*, "Or because all things are not able to contain you, do they contain a part of you, and do they all contain the same part? Or does each part contain different parts of you, the larger units larger parts, the smaller ones smaller? Is there a part of you that is greater, a part that is lesser? Or is the whole of you everywhere, and nothing holds you entirely?" (1.3.3).

17. "And it repented the Lord that he had made man on the earth, and it grieved him at his heart" (Gen. 6:6).

18. Literally, "are mute." Perhaps he is saying: don't give up on talking about God simply because most of those who do talk about him in effect say nothing.

19. Here is my own reading of this passage, published years ago. What do you think of it? "Augustine here locates his reader and himself in a world and relation in which language cannot do what we are likely to think of as its usual job: it cannot describe or name or work as an adequate set of communications, because what the speaking self confronts is not comprehensible by us or expressible in our language. He expresses this by breaking down both his own and his reader's confidence in language itself, creating directly in the reader a sense of dislocation that is rather like his own as he confronts his God. Augustine thus reduces himself to an essential human core, consisting of an impulse to praise, which he calls faith; an active sense of the inadequacy of his mind and language; and his capacity to speak not about but to another, whom he can address as 'thou.' " See James Boyd White, *"This Book of Starres": Learning to Read George Herbert* (Ann Arbor: University of Michigan Press, 1994), 32.

20. See Psalm 35:3.

21. See Genesis 18:27.

## 4. REMEMBERING EARLY CHILDHOOD AND LANGUAGE BREAKING DOWN (BOOK 1)

1. At birth he had been registered as a catechumen, that is, as one on the road to baptism. It is not clear to me whether the decision to cancel the baptism was his or his mother's.

2. The word translated "compassion" is a complex term, *misericordia*, the root meaning of which is the capacity to suffer in the heart for another.

It is often translated "mercy," but I think that term in English is too top-down, too discretionary, to do justice to *misericordia*.

There is a related problem in connection with the Old Testament, where the crucial word *chesed* has often been translated as "mercy" in English and in Latin as *misericordia*. Both of these translations seem to me just wrong: the basic meaning of *chesed* is faithfulness to a covenant. That, not mercy or compassion, is the quality so frequently invoked in the Psalms and elsewhere.

3. I owe these references to the translations in Henry Chadwick, trans., *Saint Augustine: Confessions* (Oxford: Oxford University Press, 1991) and Carolyn J.-B. Hammond, *Augustine: Confessions*, 2 vols., Loeb Classical Library (Cambridge, MA: Harvard University Press, 2014–2016).

4. It is important to note that Augustine does not cite these Scriptural passages explicitly. It is his readers and editors who have found them, and some of their findings are more persuasive than others. But a person with a memory like that of Augustine himself, who in his *Sermons* seems to have the whole of the sacred text at his instantaneous command, may well recall passages that few or none of his readers will think of. The big point is that there is in his mind, and in fact, a direct continuity between the *Confessions* and the Scriptures. To trace it out and explain how these shadow references work in the text itself is beyond my own capacity and the scope of this book.

5. It is thus an expression of what he has earlier called *fides*, usually translated as "faith."

6. In this connection, see John Cavadini, "Book Two: Augustine's Book of Shadows," in *A Reader's Companion to Augustine's* Confessions, ed. Kim Paffenroth and Robert P. Kennedy (Louisville and London: Westminster John Knox Press, 2003), 25–34.

7. *Ex quo* [from whom: masc., i.e., father] *et in qua* [in whom, fem., i.e., mother], a pair of moves that we cannot directly imitate in English.

8. This is a hard sentence: let me rearrange the words to fit English expectations: *bonum meum ex eis* [my good from them] *quod ex eis non sed per eas erat* [which was *from* them, not *through* them] *bonum erat eis* [was good for them too]. What happens if you try to trace out this structure in the Latin, then try to reproduce it in English?

9. *Salus* is a rich term, which can be used to mean simply "health," of mind or body or soul, or "salvation," in whatever particular sense that

term is meant. As Chadwick, *Confessions*, page 7, tells us, this phrase is foreshadowed in 2 Sam. 23:5.

10. *Implerentur* is subjunctive.

11. For a lovely book about the extent to which the New Testament is built on the testimony of reliable witnesses, see Richard Bauckham, *Jesus and the Eyewitnesses: The Gospels as Eyewitness Testimony* (Grand Rapids, MI: William Eerdmans, 2006).

12. In Latin this word has nothing to do with purity, but means not *nocens*, that is, not harmful.

13. In a similar vein, he will say over and over, especially toward the end, that he does not know something, or does not remember it, or that memory and knowledge do not reach as far as he and we would like. Those expressions have their roots right here in the opening book, but as the text proceeds they change and intensify their meaning.

14. *Nonne ab infantia huc pergens veni in puertiam? Vel potius ipsa in me venit et successit infantiae?*, "Did I go from infancy to boyhood? Or rather did it [*ipsa*, i.e., boyhood] come into me and take the place of infancy?" (1.8.13).

15. *Non enim docebant me maiores homines, praebentes mihi verba certo aliquo ordine doctrinae sicut paulo post litteras*, "It was not that older people were teaching me, offering me words in a certain structure of teaching, as they did a bit later with letters" (1.8.13).

16. More fully: *Cum ipsi appellabant rem aliquam et cum secundum eam vocem corpus ad aliquid movebant, videbam et tenebam hoc ab eis vocari rem illam quod sonabant cum eam vellent ostendere. hoc autem eos velle ex motu corporis aperiebatur tamquam verbis naturalibus omnium gentium, quae fiunt vultu et nutu oculorum ceterorumque membrorum actu et sonitu vocis indicante affectionem animi in petendis, habendis, reiciendis fugiendisve rebus. Ita verba in variis sententiis locis suis posita et crebro audita quarum rerum signa essent paulatim conligebam measque iam voluntates edomito in eis signis ore per haec enuntiabam.* Or: "When they (the grown-ups) named something, and when, after making the sound, they moved the body toward it, I saw and I remembered that this thing was called by them what they said when they wished to point it out. What they wished appeared from this motion of the body, as if by the natural means of expression of all peoples, which are made by the face and expression of the eyes and the actions of the other members and the sound of the

voice indicating the desires of the mind in seeking, having, rejecting, or fleeing from things. Thus when these words were put in their places in different sentences and frequently heard, I gradually acquired understanding of the things of which they were the signs, and as my mouth was trained to these signs I expressed my wishes through them" (1.8.13).

17. See especially Mathewes, "Presumptuousness of Autobiography," and Myles Burnyeat, "Wittgenstein and Augustine de Magistro," supplement, *Proceedings of The Aristotelian Society* 61 (1987): 1–24.

18. *Famulantibus* is a participle modifying *artibus*.

19. *Peccabam faciendo contra praecepta parentum et magistrorum illorum*, "I was sinning by acting against the directions of my parents and those teachers" (1.10.16).

20. For a lovely account of his baptism by Ambrose, see Garry Wills, *The Fount of Life: Ambrose, Augustine, and the Mystery of Baptism* (Oxford: Oxford University Press, 2012).

21. Augustine's *City of God* is a comprehensive defense of Christianity against the Roman culture into which he was educated.

22. Literally: "give birth to."

23. He makes a kind of apostrophe to God, in which he asks for the strength to endure what he calls God's "discipline" or *disciplina* (which means not so much punishment as teaching, teaching by experience) and to love God "most strongly" or *valdissime*.

24. This is an instance of a movement we see throughout the *Confessions*, from something bad to something good, a movement Augustine attributes to his God.

25. Subjunctive as a way of marking that it did not happen this way.

26. For a curriculum that seems at least from outside to be successful, see the Catachesis of the Good Shepherd. For a description of the method, see www.cgsusa.org.

27. He tells us that the insistence on compliance with rules of grammar and manners has gone so far that if a person says the word "human" (*homo*) in the old-fashioned way, without pronouncing the initial letter "h," he displeases men more *quam si contra tua praecepta hominem oderit*, "than if against your principles he hated someone" (1.18.28). This habit of mind has more serious consequences, he says, as we see in the one who accuses another in court, being vigilant in ensuring that he makes no error of grammar among men, *inter hominibus*, yet having no fear

that through the fury of his mind he may take away a man from men, *ex hominibus*, that is by securing his execution (1.18.29).

28. Can this mean, "even if you wished that I never grow up"?

29. See 1.6.10, quoted above, p. 93.

## 5. ADOLESCENCE, SEX, AND THE STOLEN PEARS (BOOK 2)

1. *Recordari*, "to remember" is passive in form but active in meaning; *amem* is first person singular subjunctive of *amo*, "I love."

2. Remember that the citation system—book, chapter, paragraph—begins over again in each book.

3. That is, God's.

4. A corrupt Roman patrician who led a conspiracy to overthrow the Roman Republic.

5. Here I think of George Herbert's poem that has as its title a phrase from Paul's Letter to the Ephesians. Here is the first stanza:

"Grieve not the Holy Spirit"

And art thou grieved, sweet and sacred Dove,
When I am sour
And crosse thy love?
Griev'd for me? The God of strength and power
Griev'd for a worm, which when I tread,
I pass away and leave it dead?

## 6. LOVE, PHILOSOPHY, AND MONNICA'S DREAM

1. Cicero was also known as Tullius, and "tullianae" are "Cicero's things," in this case his writings.

2. Here he is defending against the Manichees the righteousness of holy people in the Old Testament whose behavior is partly shaped by their customs and traditions. For something like this kind of pluralism, see the work of Richard Hooker, especially his *Preface to the Laws of Eccelsiastical Polity* (1594), where he argues that in matters of relative indifference one should obey the commands of worldly authority, but on

matters of first importance one should not yield. For more on Hooker, see my *Acts of Hope: Creating Authority in Literature, Law, and Politics* (Chicago: University of Chicago Press, 1994), 82–124.

3. James J. O'Donnell, *Augustine: Confessions*, 3 vols. (Oxford: Clarendon Press, 1992), 2:191, 195, says that *facinora* are serious sins deriving from wrath (*ira*), *flagitia* serious sins deriving from lust (*libido*).

## 7. FRIENDSHIP AND STRUGGLES WITH MANICHEISM (BOOK 4)

1. Another possibility is that the first person plural is just a formal way of speaking as an individual, a practice Augustine uses widely in his sermons, but I think not elsewhere in the *Confessions*.

2. The Latin word is *vani* the root meaning of which is "empty," but it also means, as the English cognate would suggest, "vain."

3. Henry Chadwick, trans., *Saint Augustine: Confessions* (Oxford: Oxford University Press, 1991), 52, tells us: "In Manichee texts, every meal of the Elect is a holy feeding on particles of light concealed in fruits and plants, helping to gain remission of sins for those Hearers who prepare it." Augustine was at this point one of the Hearers.

4. Or "glory."

5. Uncertainty on this matter is in keeping with his practice of drawing our attention away from the details of the narrative to something much more important, namely, the character and meaning of his own experience. Compare the fact that we never learn the name of the beloved friend who dies young, or really anything else about him.

6. A difficult sentence to translate smoothly. The fundamental idea is that true friendship requires a bond made possible by the Holy Spirit, who is himself a gift to us.

7. Compare George Herbert, *Affliction I*, "I took thy sweetened pill till I came where I could not go away or persevere."

8. For another take on the liberal arts return to the first sentence in this chapter.

9. Literally "freed from knots."

10. That is, return to you.

11. Chadwick, *Saint Augustine: Confessions*, 71, says that this prayer is "a mosaic of biblical allusions (Ps. 16:8; Ps. 35:8, Ps. 62:8; Exod. 19:4; Isa. 46:4)."

## 8. FROM THE MANICHEES TO AMBROSE (BOOK 5)

1. He is addressing God.

2. Here is a place where Latin words work very differently from English ones. In *sed ad fidem meam illius auctoritatem praeponerem*, *sed* means "but"; *praeponerem* is the verb, "I could put" (subjunctive); *illius auctoritatem*, his authority; *ad fidem meam*, to the support of my faith; *propter creditam sanctitatem*, because I believed in his sanctity [literally, his sanctity having been believed].

3. Similarly, he came to admire, and find congenial, Mani's love of literature (5.7.13).

4. In this book of all books, we must feel the seriousness of his condition when he contemplates with pleasure a life without confession itself.

## 9. CERTAINTY AND UNCERTAINTY (BOOK 6)

1. Here the word I have translated as "loved" is *diligebat*, which could mean something a little weaker, like "esteem" or "value." But we have just been told that she felt about him as she would an angel of God, which seems to call for the word "love."

2. At the end of his commentary on Psalm 48 Augustine addresses the statement in Genesis that God made humanity in his own image. He says this should not be read to reflect any physical similarity. Rather, it is our inner self that was made in God's image. *Vos autem, fratres, considerate vos homines factos ad imaginem et similtudinem Dei. Imago Deus intus est, non est in corpore: non est in auribus istis quas videtis, et oculis, et naribus, et palate, et manibus, et pedibus: sed est facta tamen: ubi est intellectus, ubi est meus, ubi ratio investigandae, ubi est fides, ubi est spes vestra, ubi caritas vestra, ibi habet Deus imaginem suam*, "Brothers, consider that you are men made in the image and likeness of God. The image of God is within, not in the body: not in those ears which you see, and eyes, and nostrils, and palate, and hands, and feet: but these things are created: where there is understanding, where my sense of self is, where the faculty of reason for the investigation of truth is, where faith is, where your hope is, where your Christian love is, there God has his image of himself" (Psalm 48.11).

3. The passage quoted here is found also at the very end of the *Confessions*, where it has a powerful force and resonance. See pp. 331–32.

4. That is, the erroneous beliefs and practices they had accepted.

5. See how he defines the kind of love he had for his friends, that it was *gratis*, that is freely given, without any sense that he might gain by it; and this is how he feels he is loved by them. This is a lovely definition of unselfinterested love, in his view the best possible kind.

## 10. IMAGINING GOD AND THE ORIGIN OF EVIL (BOOK 7)

1. For a good account of this process, see Garry Wills, *The Fount of Life: Ambrose, Augustine, and the Mystery of Baptism* (Oxford: Oxford University Press, 2012).

2. In using these terms he is not talking about what we would call the Roman Catholic Church today, but the Christian church of the empire as it existed in his time. The word "catholic" simply means "universal," and does not, as it would today, draw a line between Catholics and Protestants (who did not yet exist). He is concerned to defend the church against heresies, especially Donatism and Pelagianism. Donatism insisted that priests who buckled under to Diocletian in the great persecution of 305 should be regarded as having lost their status until they confess and are baptized anew. Pelagian believed that humans were created as essentially good and could achieve spiritual and moral perfection by their own efforts, without the action of grace, a view Augustine resisted.

3. For more on the physicality of God, from an older Augustine, see Chapter 9, n. 2, p. 353 for what he says in one of his commentaries on a Psalm about being made in God's image.

4. In this he is like Plato at his best. If you are interested in why I might say this, see my treatments of the *Gorgias*, the *Crito*, and the *Phaedrus*, respectively, in my *When Words Lose Their Meaning: Constitutions and Reconstitutions of Language, Character, and Community* (Chicago: University of Chicago Press, 1984); *Acts of Hope: Creating Authority in Literature, Law, and Politics* (Chicago: University of Chicago, 1994); and *The Edge of Meaning* (Chicago: Chicago University Press, 2001).

5. It may be of interest that her tomb was uncovered not long ago, by boys playing basketball. The fragments of this tomb constitute an actual physical remnant of the story we are learning.

6. He is speaking here of the Eucharist, in which the believer takes God into himself in order to be transformed.

## II. THE CONVERSION IN THE GARDEN (BOOK 8)

1. This is the genitive of *laus*, meaning "praise."
2. James J. O'Donnell, *Augustine: Confessions*, 3 vols. (Oxford: Clarendon Press, 1992), 3:6.
3. See O'Donnell, *Augustine: Confessions*, 3:22.
4. For the dramatic interior effects of Ponticianus's story on Augustine, see 8.7.16.
5. That is, movements of both the body and the soul.

## 12. WHAT IT MEANT (BOOK 9)

1. I think what he means here is both that flesh has natural delights, different from the delights of the spirit, and that it is not capable of participating in the higher delights of the soul.
2. This remark seems to express a kind of competitiveness with his old community, a wish that they could see how right he was to chose Christianity over Manicheism.
3. One of the great qualities of these commentaries (called the *Enarrationes*) is that for him the sacred texts of the Scripture are occasions for his own capacities of imagination and invention to do their work. He is not bound by literalist assumptions about the nature of meaning but sees that each person (or at least each preacher) should take responsibility for creating freshness and newness in reading the Psalms, and presumably other parts of Scripture as well.
4. For an account of baptism in Milan in those days, see Garry Wills, *The Fount of Life: Ambrose, Augustine, and the Mystery of Baptism* (Oxford: Oxford University Press, 2012).
5. At the mouth of the Tiber.
6. A standard way of talking about the death of early Christians, found frequently in Paul.

## 13. MEMORY, SIN, AND REDEMPTION (BOOK 10)

1. Look at the structure of this sentence, as it appears in Latin if possible, and notice how it consists of a chain of words all drawn from the same root: *cognoscam, cognitor, cognoscam, cognitus sum*, almost a dance. Does the effort to capture some of this with "know," "knower," "know," and "known" work the same way? Why? Why not?

2. This form is also that of the future indicative, but I think that would not work well in this context: "I will know you. . . ."

3. As we saw earlier, *virtus* in Latin means not only "virtue" but "strength" or "power," hence my translation.

4. Or "in health," or both at once.

5. Or "acts truly."

6. Light is here an image of the presence of God that we shall see elsewhere in this book.

7. That is, loved and desired by Augustine himself.

8. This is a hard phrase. I think it means "except for any good things in me that come from you—as all of them do."

9. I think this means something like: "I have already acknowledged the gifts from you that have enabled me to make a confession as I have done." But he is now going to confess more deeply and fully.

10. That is: my confession is made silently, without spoken speech, but intensely, driven by love; the internal sounds which cannot be heard are nonetheless loud indeed.

11. Love in the sense of *caritas*, or charity, generous and unselfinterested in nature. For "love believes all things," see 2 Corinthians 13:7.

12. Maybe: "Having connected them."

13. That is, among those whom it has already united.

14. The spirit, that is, of people in his audience who regard him with love, as a brother.

15. Once more I think of George Herbert, who writes at the beginning of the main section of his book of poems, this dedication (following the long and didactic poem with which he begins, "The Church Porch"):

> Thou, whom the former precepts have
> Sprinkled and taught, how to behave
> Thyself in church; approach and taste
> The church's mystical repast

> Avoid profanenesse, come not here:
> Nothing but holy, pure, and cleare,
> Or that which groneth to be so,
> May at his perill further go.

16. An additional note: at 10.4.6 he refers to those people whom God has ordered him to serve, meaning those who read his confessions.

17. *Amavi* is in the perfect tense, which usually means the events are in the past. "I loved you." But it can also include an element of the present tense: "I am in the present state of having loved you," or perhaps better as I translate it, "I have come to love you."

18. I think here of the opening paragraph of Ralph Waldo Emerson's essay on "Experience": "Where do we find ourselves? In a series of which we do not know the extremes, and believe that it has none. We wake and find ourselves on a stair; there are stairs below us, which we seem to have ascended, there are stairs above us, many a one, which go upward and out of sight."

19. See 10.27.38.

20. That is, outside the self.

21. See 10.27.38.

22. Notice how he returns here to the physical imagery of "fullness" of which he was so critical in book one. What are we to make of this?

## 14. TIME (BOOK II)

1. James J. O'Donnell, *Augustine: Confessions*, 3 vols. (Oxford: Clarendon Press, 1992), 3:250.

2. As I said in an earlier note, if you are interested in seeing instance after instance of his reading the Scriptures as he does here—really the way of reading he discovers in these last three books—Augustine's commentaries on the Psalms (*Enarrationes in psalmos*) offer wonderful examples.

3. Saying, that is, in the *Confessions* as a whole.

4. Quoting, of course, the very first sentence of the *Confessions*.

5. At the time of Augustine it was generally thought by Christians that Moses was the author of the first five books of the Hebrew Bible.

## 15. READING GENESIS: THE CREATION STORY
### (BOOK 12)

1. For wonderful examples, see Augustine's commentaries on the Psalms (*Enarrationes in psalmos*).
2. By which he means the Heaven of Heavens.
3. In calling here what he is producing his "confessions," he is distinguishing them from the arguments of those who disagree, rooting them not in his rational faculty but in the experience of the God within.
4. When, as in all of the examples, Augustine speaks of the "Word" through whom the creation takes place, he means to refer to the first chapter of the Gospel of John, where the Christ is spoken of as the Word, said to have been the essential agent of creation. In a similar way, in Book 13, Augustine will interpret the Spirit of God going over the waters as the third person of the Trinity, the Holy Spirit. As his sermons also make clear, he sees what we might call the Old Testament or Hebrew Bible as completely consistent with and expressive of Christian theology.
5. At the time Moses was thought to have been the author of the entire Pentateuch.

## 16. "KNOCK AND IT SHALL BE OPENED UNTO YOU"
### (BOOK 13)

1. O'Donnell tells us that Book 11 is at bottom about the eternity of God the Father versus the temporality of human beings; that Book 12 is about the unity and clarity of the Word, that is the Christ, versus the ambiguity and plurality of words expressing the Word; and that Book 13 is about the dynamic union of humanity and God in the form of the action of the Spirit in the world. James J. O'Donnell, *Augustine: Confessions*, 3 vols. (Oxford: Clarendon Press, 1992), 3:251. As you read and reread the three books you might ask how these comments help you understand them. Certainly it is true that in Book 13 we can hear Augustine talk about the Spirit in new and important ways.
2. Why without substance? I think because only the good has real substance in Augustine's world. Evil is a lack of substance, and the waters are what would hold us down.

3. Uttered by John the Baptist in Matthew 3:2, and by Jesus in Mark 1:15.

4. See I Corinthians 3:1.

5. Psalm 42 begins this way: "As the hart panteth after the water brooks, so panteth my soul after thee."

6. Drawing attention implicitly to the fact that other things are created during a day that has both morning and evening.

CPSIA information can be obtained
at www.ICGtesting.com
Printed in the USA
BVHW042123200623
666194BV00003B/26

9 780231 205016